涉外法治
人才培养
系列教材

总 主 编　石佑启
执行主编　韩永红

INTERNATIONAL
ECONOMIC LAW

国际经济法

王燕　编著
李燕　审校

法律出版社
LAW PRESS・CHINA
北京

图书在版编目(CIP)数据

国际经济法 : 英文 / 王燕编著 . -- 北京 : 法律出版社 , 2022
涉外法治人才培养系列教材 / 石佑启总主编
ISBN 978-7-5197-7211-6

Ⅰ . ①国… Ⅱ . ①王… Ⅲ . ①国际经济法—高等学校—教材—英文 Ⅳ . ① D996

中国版本图书馆 CIP 数据核字(2022)第 193502 号

国际经济法
GUOJI JINGJIFA

王　燕 编著
李　燕 审校

策划编辑 朱　峰
责任编辑 韩泓宇
装帧设计 贾丹丹

出版发行 法律出版社
编辑统筹 辞书·融出版编辑部　法律翻译与出版研发中心
责任校对 马秋婧
责任印制 吕亚莉
经　　销 新华书店

开本 710 毫米 ×1000 毫米　1/16
印张 20　**字数** 575 千
版本 2022 年 11 月第 1 版
印次 2022 年 11 月第 1 次印刷
印刷 北京虎彩文化传播有限公司

地址:北京市丰台区莲花池西里 7 号(100073)
网址:www.lawpress.com.cn
投稿邮箱:info@lawpress.com.cn
举报盗版邮箱:jbwq@lawpress.com.cn

销售电话:010-83938349
客服电话:010-83938350
咨询电话:010-63939796

书号: ISBN 978-7-5197-7211-6　　**定价:** 88.00 元

凡购买本社图书,如有印装错误,我社负责退换。电话:010-83938349

总　　序

面对世界百年未有之大变局，涉外法治人才培养已成为紧迫的国家战略。习近平总书记高度重视涉外法治建设和涉外法治人才培养工作。2019 年 2 月 25 日，习近平总书记在中央全面依法治国委员会第二次全体会议上的讲话中指出："要加快推进我国法域外适用的法律体系建设，加强涉外法治专业人才培养，积极发展涉外法律服务，强化企业合规意识，保障和服务高水平对外开放。"2020 年 11 月 16 日至 17 日，中央全面依法治国工作会议在北京召开，首次提出并确立了习近平法治思想并将其明确为全面依法治国的指导思想。习近平总书记用"十一个坚持"系统阐述了新时代推进全面依法治国的重要思想和战略部署。习近平总书记指出："要坚持统筹推进国内法治和涉外法治。""要坚持建设德才兼备的高素质法治工作队伍。"培养高素质涉外法治人才是坚持统筹推进国内法治和涉外法治的题中之义。习近平法治思想为加强涉外法治人才培养指明了前进方向，提供了根本遵循。我国亟需培养一大批具有国际视野，通晓国际法律规则，能够有效参与国际法律事务，且善于维护国家利益的高素质国际化人才。

"致天下之治者在人才，成天下之才者在教化，教化之所本者在学校。"高校是涉外法治人才培养的主阵地，而高质量的教材则是高校构建涉外法治人才培养体系的重要支柱，也是新时期高质量推进涉外法治人才培养工作的重要保障。但目前我国涉外法治人才培养中的教材建设仍是突出的短板。一方面，外文原版教材在体例与内容上大多呈现"西方中心主义"，较少关注我国的立法、执法、司法进展及实践需求，存在"水土不服"的弊端；另一方面，国内虽已出版一些英文、汉英双语法学教材和法律英语教材，但面向的读者群各有不同，且未形成体系。因此，自主编写一套满足新时期涉外法治人才培养需要的系列教材实乃必要与适时之举。

广东外语外贸大学法学学科在设立之初即将涉外法治人才培养作为特色，已基本形成"法学 + 外语"和"外语 + 法学"两种涉外法治人才培养模式。2002—2007 年，广东外语外贸大学曾陆续出版了"法律英语系列教材"（"十一五"国家规划教材）和"WTO 法系列教材"，在全国产生了较好的影响。自 2008 年起，又陆续出版了《国际商法》《国际贸易法》等多部英文、汉英双语法学教材，现已多次印刷、再版，被全国百余所高校选用。在此基础上，为积极回应新时期国家涉外法治人才培养的需求，我们与法律出版社合作启动了"涉外法治人才培养系列教材"项目，组织了一批具有涉外法治人才培养经验的一线教师，展开教材编写工作，旨在为我国涉外法治人才培养贡献“广外力量”，共同推进我国涉外法治人才培养事业的发展。

“涉外法治人才培养系列教材”包含法律英语类教材和英文法学类教材两个子系列。其中，法律英语类教材包含《法律英语》《法律翻译》《法律英语辩论》《法律英语听说》，英文法学类教材包含《国际经济法》《国际商法：理论与实务》《国际商事仲裁》。这是一个开放的项目，两个子系列下会有更多的相关教材编写并出版。“涉外法治人才培养系列教材”注重满足我国高校涉外法治人才培养教学的实际需要。在体例上，“涉外法治人才培养系列教材”的编写兼采国内外同类教材的优点，编者本着便利于使用者的原则进行章节和栏目安排。该系列教材设置了英汉对照术语表、类型丰富的练习题、拓展性阅读资料等栏目，供读者根据自身情况选用。在内容上，“涉外法治人才培养系列教材”的编写兼顾理论性与实用性、全球性与区域性。该系列教材既注重对法律规则的讲解，也注重对案例的剖析；既注重对重要国际条约、国际惯例的阐释，也注重对主要国家国内法的介绍，尤其关注中国相应的立法、执法和司法实践。在语言上，“涉外法治人才培养系列教材”的编者用英文写作。该系列教材以英语为直接媒介，致力于高效地提升使用者的法律英语应用能力、法律知识获取能力和法律问题解决能力。

“涉外法治人才培养系列教材”的持续出版需要良好的组织协调工作，需要专业的出版服务，更需要高素质的编者。该系列教材的编者要具有全球视野、家国情怀，还要具有丰富的一线教学经验，法律专业与英语水平“两强”，对涉外法治人才培养怀有极大热情，舍得投入大量时间和精力。在此谨对各位编者的辛勤付出和敬业精神致以崇高敬意！对法律出版社高水准的编辑出版工作表示衷心感谢！

“涉外法治人才培养系列教材”的编写是一项探索性、挑战性的工作。虽然编者已努力为之，但鉴于个体认知的局限，以及编写工作的复杂性、任务的艰巨性，难免会有诸多疏漏与不足之处。恳请读者不吝指正，以便教材编写工作不断改进、编写质量不断提升。

石佑启

2022 年 8 月

Foreword

Given the fact that the world today is in the midst of a once-in-a-century transformation, the training of legal professionals for foreign-related legal affairs has become an urgent national strategy. Xi Jinping, General Secretary of the Central Committee of the Communist Party of China (CPC), attaches great importance to the development of foreign-related rule of law and the training of legal professionals for foreign-related legal affairs. At the second plenary meeting of the Commission for Overall Law-based Governance of the CPC Central Committee held on February 25, 2019, Xi Jinping stressed the necessity to facilitate the development of a legal system on extraterritorial application of Chinese laws, to improve the training of legal professionals for foreign-related legal affairs, to promote the development of foreign-related legal services and to strengthen enterprises' compliance so as to maintain and support China's high-level opening up. The Central Conference on Work Related to Overall Law-based Governance was held from November 16 to November 17, 2020, which first put forward Xi Jinping Thought on the Rule of Law and made it the guideline of overall law-based governance. Xi Jinping proposed "eleven points that we must continue to implement" to formulate the ideas and strategic plans concerning overall law-based governance in the new era. He pointed out that "we must take a coordinated approach to the rule of law at home and in matters involving foreign parties" and that "we must develop a force of high-caliber legal personnel with moral integrity and professional competence". The training of high-quality legal professionals for foreign-related legal affairs is indeed the key to a coordinated approach to promoting the rule of law at home and in matters involving foreign parties. Xi Jinping Thought on the Rule of Law serves as both a beacon and a fundamental guideline for strengthening the training of legal professionals for foreign-related legal affairs. Now, China is in urgent need to foster a constellation of talents who are internationally-minded and have a good command of multiple countries' laws, being capable of effectively participating in international legal affairs and safeguarding China's interests.

"The key to good governance lies in talents; the key to fostering talents lies in education; the key to education lies in schools." Therefore, universities are at the forefront of training legal professionals for foreign-related legal affairs, and high-quality textbooks are the mainstay of establishing a system for training such professionals, as well as the guarantee for effective training of such professionals in the new era. However, the existing textbooks are far from being satisfactory with regard to the training of legal professionals for foreign-related legal affairs. On the one hand, the original foreign textbooks are mostly West-centered in their organization and content, and they rarely focus on China's legislation, law enforcement, and practical needs, which may even lead to problems of poor adaptability. On the other hand, although some law textbooks in English have been published at home, they target different groups of readers and are not systematically published. Thus, it is actually a necessary and timely move to compile a new series of textbooks to meet the needs of training legal professionals for foreign-related legal affairs in the new era.

Guangdong University of Foreign Studies has the tradition of training legal professionals for foreign-related legal affairs since its discipline of law was established. For now, two basic modes for training such professionals have been established — the "Law + Foreign Language" mode and the "Foreign Language + Law" mode. From 2002 to 2007, Guangdong University of Foreign Studies published the legal English textbook series (Eleventh Five-Year National Plan Textbooks) and WTO law textbook series, which had a good influence across the country. Since 2008, Guangdong University of Foreign Studies has published some English or bilingual legal textbooks such as *International Business Law* and *International Trade Law* which have been repeatedly printed, republished and used as textbooks by over a hundred colleges and universities across China. On such basis, in order to proactively respond to China's need of the training of legal professionals for foreign-related legal affairs in the new era, we cooperate with Law Press·China to launch the Project of Textbook Series of Legal Professional Training for Foreign-Related Legal Affairs (the Textbook Series). We have organized a constellation of teachers who have experience of training legal professionals for foreign-related legal affairs to write textbooks, aiming to contribute "Guangwai's power" to the training of such professionals in China.

The Textbook Series includes two subseries: legal English textbooks and legal textbooks (English version). Legal English textbooks include *Legal English*, *Legal Translation*, *Legal English Debate*, and *Legal English Listening and Speaking*. Legal textbooks (English version) contain *International Economic Law*, *International Business Law: Text, Cases and Readings*, and *International Commercial Arbitration*. Since the project is inclusive, more textbooks in the two subseries will be compiled and published. The Textbook Series places a high value on the practical needs of China's universities pertaining to the training and education of legal professionals for foreign-related legal affairs. For example, in terms of the organization of the textbooks, the Textbook Series draws on the advantages of similar textbooks at home and abroad with chapters and content being well arranged for readers' convenience. In addition to the main text, English-Chinese bilingual glossaries, a variety of exercises and supplementary reading materials are included for learners to use flexibly. In terms of content, the Textbook Series gives consideration to both theory and practice, as well as global application and local application. To be more specific, the textbooks not only focus on the explanation of rules of law, but also attach importance to the dissection of cases; they not only lay emphasis on the interpretation of international treaties and international conventions, but also place a high value on the introduction to major countries' domestic law, especially China's relevant legislation, law enforcement and judicial practice. In terms of language, the textbooks are written in English. In the course of direct English learning, such textbooks are aimed at efficiently improving learners' proficiency in legal English, to acquire legal knowledge and to solve legal problems.

The continuous publication of the Textbook Series requires good organization and coordination, as well as professional publishing service. More important, it needs high-quality authors who are internationally-minded, patriotic, rich in teaching experience, adept at legal studies and foreign languages, keen on the training of legal professionals for foreign-related legal affairs and willing to devote much time and energy to the training of such professionals. I hereby would like to show my highest respect for authors of their dedication and commitment, and express my heartfelt thanks to Law Press·China for its excellent editing and publishing service.

The publication of the Textbook Series is an exploratory and challenging task. Although authors have paid great effort to complete it, given the fact that personal cognition is limited and that the task is complex and arduous, it seems inevitable that omissions and deficiencies may exist in the Textbook Series. Please contact us if any mistake is found therein and we are glad to correct such mistake so as to improve the quality of the Textbook Series.

Shi Youqi

August 2022

Preface

Since the World War II, the Breton Woods institutions have become the engine keeping the global economic order and have liberalized the trade, financial and investment rules ever since. The World Trade Organization (WTO) and its predecessor General Agreement on Tariffs and Trade (GATT) have successfully hosted nine rounds of multilateral trade negotiations to reduce tariff and remove the non-tariff barriers. The International Monetary Fund and World Bank Group also ensured the stability of international monetary order and accelerated the economic recovery after the War. However, the multilateral trade, finance and investment rules develop slowly in 21st century, far lagging behind the needs of global economic governance. The Doha Round only received marginal success in signing the Trade Facilitation Agreement, reducing cotton subsidies among the Members. Meanwhile, the Group 20 (G20), established to cope with international financial crisis in 1997 and 2008, which provides a North-South cooperative mechanism has also lost its attractiveness due to the lack of formalism and disperse of power.

The legal environment of the global society became more unstable in the last a few years. The US required to include new subsidy rules and state-owned enterprises disciplines into the WTO covered agreements, and depressed the operation of Appellate Body Mechanism when it failed to do so. The deadlock faced by the multilateral institutions has diverted Members' attention into bilateral and regional agreement negotiation. The US and EU are taking lead to reach various complex and high-standard trade agreements such as USMCA, CETA, JEEPA to reshape the international economic rules, while China proposed the Belt and Road Initiative to construct a more inclusive world economy. The "Making America Great Again" policy proposed by the Trump administration has further divided the world. Especially, the US has made many discriminatory rules labeled as non-market economic rules to halt China's participation in its free trade agreement negotiation, blocking Chinese enterprises' transactions with companies from the US and other countries through the so-called the Entity lists and SDN lists.

No matter how the world economy will change, rule by law is always the theme of the global economic governance. In this background, China needs to equip itself with talents skilled in international economic law who can practice bilingually. Hence, it is significant for the universities and colleges to offer students the international economic law courses that are taught bilingually or even in English completely.

Against this backdrop, this textbook is written in English to provide the students with a comprehensive view of international economic law, covering multilateral, regional and bilateral rules on trade in goods, transboundary service, investment, finance, taxation, monetary issues and dispute settlement. The book helps the students understand the general economic rules that govern the economic issues among different countries, and further enrich their knowledge on enforcement of international economic law through case analysis. Beyond these, the book also touches some cutting-edge issues such as the conflicts and infusion of multilateral trade rules and regional trade agreements, the obstacles and deadlocks faced by the WTO and its possible reforms, the origin of non-market economic rules, the political and economic reasons hidden behind these rules, and the current debates on them.

As the book is written hastily, some inaccurate description or even errors might be unavoidable. The author is delighted to receive any comments and suggestions from the readers and users of this book via email swallow_wang79@163.com.

CONTENTS

Part I Basic Theories of International Economic Law

Study Guide

Part I helps the students understand the meaning of international economic law (IEL), the subjects of IEL, and sources, theories and principles of IEL. There are different academic views on IEL's subject matter and disciplines, which in turn, shape scholars' opinions on the definition of IEL. Most of Chinese IEL scholars uphold a broad definition of IEL which includes both public international law and private international law in the field of economic transactions. Based on this view, more and more scholars opine that transnational corporations and NGOs are also subjects of IEL. The sources of IEL mainly include treaties, customary international law, general principles of law. Not all resolutions made by the international organizations can be treated as the source of IEL, and precedents and legal scholarship are usually regarded as subsidiary means for the determination of rules of law. Regarding the theories and principles of IEL, Part I briefly introduces the realism, liberalism and constructivism in the realm of international relations, and the principles of sovereignty, state's permanent sovereignty over its natural resource, equity and mutual benefit, state's right to economic development, and international cooperation for development.

1 Definition of International Economic Law and Its Characteristics

International economic law (IEL), broadly speaking, refers to the international rules that directly concern transboundary economic transactions among nations, intergovernmental organizations.

The roots of international economic law can be traced back to ancient times. But the term became formally used in the mid-20th century and the meaning of it has always been contested ever since, especially on the issue whether international economic law only consists of public international law or it includes private international law as well. The classic theory considers that international economic law is a branch of public international law, and various western scholars have tried to define the term in their books. It is recognized by Ignaz Seidl-Hohenveldern that international economic law refers to those rules of public international law, which directly concern economic exchanges between the subjects of international law.① There are two aspects making Seidl-Hohenveldern's definition different from others. One is the definition that only relates IEL to public international law, the other is it includes those rules directly concerning economic exchanges. But Seidl-Hohenveldern does not explain how to distinguish between activities that directly affect economic exchange versus those that indirectly affect exchange.② John H. Jackson, also holds such view that IEL shall include only disciplines from public international law.

The above view, summarized by Professor Jinsong Yu, treats international economic law as international law of economy. From the perspective of methodology, the view emphasizes the traditional classification between public law and private law, between international law and domestic law. International economic law, according to the view, just refers to those international legal rules governing economic relations between states and between states and international organizations. The laws regulating economic relations between private persons from different countries are not within the domain of international economic law.③

David Bederman, on the opposite, believes that IEL shall include private international law as well. Authony Aust does not address the issue whether international economic law includes private international law or not in his book directly. But his opinion that international economic law covers mainly bilateral and multilateral treaties made since the World War II of trade, commerce and investment, suggesting he agrees that IEL includes both public international law and private international law.④

Steve Charnovitz prefers a pragmatic approach to decide the disciplines of IEL, and he thinks that the core of defining IEL is to distinguish its features from other disciplines. Apparently, IEL enjoys three distinct features. One is being international, that is, IEL is law applying to matters that cross borders. Secondly, IEL refers to economic matters. Production in an economy is a function of how efficiently the four factors of production—

① See Ignaz Seidl-Hohenveldern, *International Economic Law*, 3rd ed., Kluwer Law International, 1999, p. 1.

② See Steve Charnovitz, *What is International Economic Law?* 14 Journal of International Economic Law 3, 3–4 (2011).

③ See Yu Jinsong, *The Theories of International Economic Law in China*, 28 Legal Issues of Economic Integration 249, 251 (2001).

④ See Anthony Aust, *Handbook of International Law*, Cambridge University Press, 2005, p. 372.

land, labor, capital and management—are used. And thirdly, IEL belongs to the law disciplines. The law in IEL includes treaty and customary law, as well as soft law.①

What disciplines shall be included in international economic law becomes another debated issue among scholars.

David Bederman opines that IEL, at the minimum, includes (a) the background rules of private international commerce, (b) the architecture of the global trading and monetary systems, and (c) the principles for international development and investment.② Thus, United Nations Convention on Contract for the International Sale of Goods (CISG) is included in his textbook on IEL. Aust does not include rules on international monetary and banking as part of IEL, and disciplines set on International Monetary Fund (IMF), are intentionally omitted in his book.

Chinese scholars also express their different opinions on the definition and coverage of law discipline of IEL. Most of the Chinese scholars agree that a broad coverage of IEL disciplines shall be recognized. There are quite a few Chinese scholars who take a pragmatic view that IEL is the law which governs economic relations among nations, international organizations, and private persons who engage in transnational business transactions. It is the total range of norms concerning economic relations and economic organizations of international society, and an independent branch of law including rules of both international law and domestic law. International economic law is not international law of economy, but the law of international economy, thus, the rules governing transnational economic relations, no matter whether they are international law or domestic law, public law or private law, all belong to international economic law.③

According to Jinsong Yu, the coverage of IEL shall include five parts. The first part is international trade law, consisting of trade in goods, trade in technology and trade in services. International trade involves not only the transactions conducted between private persons but also those between the related nations and international organizations. Secondly, it includes international investment law, composed of foreign investment laws of capital-import countries, the overseas investment insurance systems of capital-export countries and bilateral and multilateral investment treaties. The third part is international

---

① See Steve Charnovitz, *What is International Economic Law?* 14 Journal of International Economic Law 3, 4–5 (2011).

② See David Bederman, *International Economic Law*, Foundation Press, 2001, p. 141.

③ See Yu Jinsong, *The Theories of International Economic Law in China*, 28 Legal Issues of Economic Integration 249, 251 (2001).

financial law, covering the law and rules drawn from both international law and domestic law, such as the International Monetary Fund Agreement, the legal regime of World Bank, banking law, securities law, and laws on the control of foreign exchange. The fourth part is international tax law, composed of international tax treaties and the foreign tax law of related countries, and the last component is international economic institutional law, that is, the international treaties or conventions concerning the constitution, policies, and functions of international economic institutions such as IMF, the World Bank, and the WTO.①

The scholars holding a broad definition of IEL disagree with the classical opinion that IEL covers only a part of the discipline of public international law that is directly concerned with economic exchanges, positing that such limitation to the coverage of IEL will fail to cope with the realities of present-day international life.② They include not only economic disciplines from public international law, but also treat *lex mercatoria* as a source of IEL. Private international law in the field of transboundary economy, evidenced by CISG, is nevertheless included in their books.

But there are also some scholars suggesting to constrain the coverage of IEL to public international law and certain domestic economic administrative laws and regulations. For example, Jianming Sheng opines that the IEL shall include public international law and domestic economic administrative rules only, and coverage of IEL shall be confined to regulations with respect to international trade, international investment, international taxation and other international affairs such as legal relationship regarding international organizations in relation to international environmental protection, international energy distribution, international economic development and assistance.③

It has to be admitted that the coverage of IEL is expanding, as people's concerns on the relationship and consequence of international economic exchange are no longer constrained to pure economic issues. And traditional conception of cross-border has become vague in the era of digital commerce. The definition and coverage of IEL have to keep evolving to cope with new challenges, and new domains might emerge in the realm of IEL and urge for regulatory cooperation among states. For example, when data becomes a new production factor in the world economy, new rules emerging in the field of digital

① See Yu Jinsong, *The Theories of International Economic Law in China*, 28 Legal Issues of Economic Integration 249, 254–256 (2001).
② 参见曾文革主编：《国际经济法》（双语版），对外经济贸易大学出版社 2012 年版，第 2–3 页。
③ 参见盛建明编著：《国际经济法》（英文版），对外经济贸易大学出版社 2017 年版，第 4–6 页。

trade will also become a component of IEL.

Therefore, this book takes a broad and functional approach in explaining the various disciplines in the domain of IEL. The book does not make an exclusive definition of IEL. Generally, the author supports a broad definition of IEL rather than a narrow definition that excludes private international law and domestic law in the domain of IEL. Moreover, it is necessary for this book to focus on economic disciplines in the field of public international law and Chinese economic administrative laws and regulations in the field of foreign investment.

2 Subjects and Actors of International Economic Law

Subjects refer to the actors that could enjoy the rights and bear the responsibilities that are stipulated by law on their names. Actors, while used in the disciplines of international relations, usually refer to the persons or institutions that participate in an international relationship. Traditionally, the scope of the actors in international relations is broader than that of the subjects in international law, as the former includes not only states and international governmental organizations, but also non-governmental organizations, transnational corporations, etc.

The paradoxical view is that the subjects of international law is sovereign states and intergovernmental organizations, and the sovereign states and intergovernmental organizations are subjects of IEL as well. The scholars opining that IEL only includes rules of public international law, usually adopt this view that the subjects of IEL should be limited to nations as well as to some international organizations.

Whether transnational corporations (TNCs) are a subject of IEL is an interesting question. The subjects delineated by Seidl-Hohenveldern nevertheless include TNCs, and this is also supported by more and more Chinese scholars such as Jinsong Yu and Jianming Sheng. However, Charnovitz opposes such opinion of inclusion of TNCs as a subject of IEL.

The literature in international affairs seldom uses the term of subject. Instead, they adopt another term—"actor" in their qualitative and quantitative studies. The actors do not need to possess rights empowered by public international law, or bear responsibilities stipulated by treaties independently. They include the sovereign states, intergovernmental organizations, nongovernmental organizations (NGOs), individuals, entities, TNCs. These actors, positively shape and influence the disciplines of IEL. The research on actors of IEL helps to depict the reasons and process of rule-making of IEL. By introduction of the term "actor", we will be able to understand how international economic law is formed and what kind of international economic relations are disciplined by the IEL.

Professor Jinsong Yu highly values the role that private persons play in international relations. Private persons play more and more important roles in transnational economic activities, especially the transnational corporations which have decisive roles in the modern international economy owing to their possession of abundant funds, advanced technologies, equipment and management skills. It would be divorced from reality if we disregard this fact and just limit the subjects of international economic relations to nations and international organizations. Therefore, international economic relations integrate as a unity, within which the economic relations between states, between states and international organizations, between states and individuals from other countries, and between private persons located in different countries, all closely link with each other.①

Hence, sovereign states and intergovernmental organizations are definitely subjects of IEL, while individuals, juridical persons, NGOs, and TNCs are nevertheless subjects of IEL as well.

3 Sources of International Economic Law

Since there is no supranational government and legislative bodies with authority to enact laws and regulations for all the countries, there can be significant difficulty in establishing the contents of international law. The classical view is the sources of IEL mainly include international treaties, customary international law, and other subsidiary sources stipulated in Article 38 of the Statute of International Court of Justice. But there are also some scholars pointing out that soft law and domestic regulations relating to the outward economic relationship can also be counted as sources of IEL.

Various sources contribute to the formation of international law. Treaties are the strongest and most binding type of the sources because they are consensual agreements

---

① See Yu Jinsong, *The Theories of International Economic Law in China*, 28 Legal Issues of Economic Integration 249, 254 (2001).

among the countries who sign them. Hence, treaties are considered to be the most authoritative source of international law. Treaties take different forms. Conventions, protocols, framework agreements that are formally signed by countries are all treaties.

At the same time, rules of international law can be found in customary state practice, general principles of law common to many countries, resolutions made by some international organizations, domestic economic regulations.

Thus, the legal source of IEL, in a broad sense, includes not only treaties, customary international law, general principles of international law, resolutions made by the international organizations as the international law source, but also domestic trade or investment regulations on external economic activities as the domestic law source. Some Chinese scholars such as Jianming Sheng and Wenge Zeng, in their textbooks, also argue that soft law shall be considered as a legal source of IEL.

3.1 International economic treaties

International economic treaties are the most important source of IEL. They are legally binding written agreements adopted by states or regions to determine their economic rights and obligations regarding certain economic matters. According to the number of contracting parties and whether the treaties are exclusive to non-participators, treaties are bilateral, regional or multilateral. Typical multilateral treaties include WTO covered agreements such as GATT, GATS, and TRIPS. They are non-exclusive treaties, with 164 members committed to them, and new members can accede to the WTO through the accession process.

Regional treaties are signed by a group of countries. They are usually exclusive to outsiders. In the domain of IEL, regional treaties are examplified by the Trans-Pacific Partnership (TPP), Regional Comprehensive Economic Partnership (RCEP), European Energy Charter, and US-Mexico-Canada Agreement.

Bilateral treaties are bilateral commitments between two countries, including the US-Australia Free Trade Agreement, Canada-EU Comprehensive Economic and Trade Agreement (CETA), and nearly 3000 bilateral investment treaties (BITs).

Apart from multilateral, regional and bilateral economic treaties, there are also plurilateral treaties in nature. Under the WTO, there are two plurilateral agreements in force, specifically, the Government Procurement Agreement and the Agreement on Trade in Civil Aircraft, which do not apply to all the members of the WTO, but are enforceable among the states that ratify them.[①]

The contents of economic treaties vary. Categorized by its coverage and contents, treaties may be divided into specialized treaties that concentrate on one issue, such as investment or intellectual property and comprehensive free trade agreements with broad coverage relating to trade in goods, transboundary service, investment, intellectual property, electronic commerce, government procurement, and other related issues. In the realm of foreign direct investment, it was once popular to negotiate specialized treaties in form of BITs, but today, more and more investment treaties are included in the comprehensive free trade agreements.

3.2 Customary international law

Customary international law (CIL) is more difficult to ascertain than the provisions of a written treaty, as it is created by the actual actions of states instead of written down rules. States believe that CIL must be obeyed by all the members of international community in international relations, acting otherwise would be illegal. Even if the rule of CIL is not written down, it still binds states, requiring them to follow it.

For example, in international relations, countries have given special diplomatic protection to ambassadors since ancient times. In ancient Greece and Rome, ambassadors from another country were not harmed while on their diplomatic missions, even if they represented a country at war with the country they were located in. In ancient China, there is also an old saying that ambassadors shall not be killed by the enemy country at war when they perform their diplomatic duties. Throughout history, most countries have publicly stated that they believe that ambassadors should be given this protection. The practice has been carried down and violation to it would be regarded as a breach of customary international law. Likewise, throughout modern history, states have acknowledged through their actions and their statements that intentionally killing civilians during wartime is illegal in international law.

Many CIL rules are found in the realm of public international law, and some are also apparent in the field of economic law. However, determining CIL is difficult, because,

---

① Some scholars opine that the Information Technology Agreement is also a plurilateral agreement. The author does not include it as a plurilateral agreement. Although the Agreement is negotiated on a selective basis, it is not exempted from the MFN treatment, which is different from the Government Procurement Agreement and the Agreement on Trade in Civil Aircraft.

unlike a treaty, it is not written down, and their extent of recognition is different. Some rules are so widely practiced and acknowledged by many states to be law, that there is little doubt that CIL exists regarding them; but other rules are not as universally recognized and disputes exists about whether they are truly CIL or not.

3.3 General principles of IEL

The third sources of IEL are the general principles of IEL, such as good faith and *pacta sunt servanda*. This is based on the theory of "natural law" , which argues that laws are a reflection of the instinctual belief that some acts are right while other acts are wrong. Certain legal beliefs and practices that are accepted by all developed legal systems reflect the general principles of law.

For instance, most legal systems value "good faith", that is, the concept that everyone intends to comply with agreements they make. Courts in many countries will examine whether the parties to a case acted in good faith, and take this issue into consideration when deciding a matter. The very fact that many different countries take good faith into consideration in their domestic judicial systems indicates that "good faith" may be considered as a standard of international law. In the realm of IEL, in case a dispute arises between two states, while there is no specified binding rules or the treaty terms are obscure, it is generally accepted that the treaty will be interpreted in good faith and the states are required to perform its duty in good faith.

The Latin formula *pacta sunt servanda* (agreements must be kept) is arguably the oldest principle of international law. Without such a rule, no international agreement would be binding or enforceable. In its most common sense, the principle refers to private contracts, stressing that contained clauses are law between the parties, and implies that non-fulfillment of respective obligations is a breach of the pact. *Pacta sunt servanda* is directly referred to in many international agreements governing treaties, including the Vienna Convention on the Law of Treaties. General principles such as pacta sunt servanda and good faith are most useful as sources of law when no treaty or CIL has conclusively addressed an issue.

3.4 Resolutions made by intergovernmental organizations

Not all resolutions made by intergovernmental organizations are regarded as legal sources of IEL. With respect to resolutions or decisions of the United Nations (UN) and other important international economic institutions, most Chinese scholars believe that they have certain binding force and can be used as subsidiary means for the determination of the rule of law.①

There were several influential resolutions made by the UN General Assembly in the 1960s and 1970s, which were even deemed as sources of general principles of IEL. For example, the 1962 Declaration on Permanent Sovereignty over Natural Resources is considered by many Chinese scholars that has produced a general principle named "states enjoy permanent sovereignty over its natural resource" in IEL. Similar resolutions and charter proposed by the UN General Assembly include the 1974 Declaration for Establishing a New International Economic Order and the UN Charter of Economic Rights and Duties of States.②

Even though many countries vote for these resolutions and declarations, expressing their view that these principles shall be accepted by the international community, it shall be noted that resolutions made by the UN General Assembly do not have binding force among its members, as they are only suggestive. Thereby, only those resolutions that are generally practiced by most countries in a continuous and consistent way and produce the effect of *opinio juris* will finally turn into the customary international law, or be codified by other treaties and become binding rules.

3.5 Precedents and legal scholarship

Recognized by the Statute of the International Court of Justice, there are two subsidiary means for the determination of rules of law, which are precedents and legal scholarship. While these sources are not by themselves international law, when coupled with evidence of international custom or general principles of law, they may help to prove the existence of a particular rule of international law.

Precedents of IEL include precedents of International Court of Justice (ICJ), panel or Appellate Body reports adopted by the dispute settlement body of the WTO, International Centre for Settlement of Investment Disputes (ICSID) arbitration awards and other judicial or quasi-judicial decisions made by similar multilateral or regional organizations. The ICJ, as the principal legal body of the UN, is considered as an authoritative expounder of law.

In accordance with Article 59 of the Statute of the International Court of Justice,

---

① 参见王铁崖主编：《国际法》，法律出版社 1981 年版，第 18–20 页；梁西主编：《国际法》（修订第 2 版），武汉大学出版社 2000 年版，第 49 页。

② 参见《国际经济法学》编写组编：《国际经济法学》（第 2 版），高等教育出版社 2019 年版，第 29 页。

rulings of the ICJ are only binding on parties to a dispute. However, rulings made in previous disputes have been referred by the Court in latter disputes. Thus, some scholars argue that the rulings made by the ICJ are precedents and produce influence on latter rulings, supporting their view that decisions of ICJ could be regarded as subsidiary source of IEL.①

The Appellate Body (AB) reports adopted by the dispute settlement body, even though named as reports, have long been regarded as precedents under the WTO. The treaty interpretation made by the AB in previous disputes has been frequently quoted by the AB in latter cases and is highly respected by the latter disputes. Therefore, many scholars believe that the AB reports are *de facto* precedents and AB's legal interpretation of WTO covered agreements definitely forms a part of the world trade law and influences the world trade relationship.

ICSID arbitration decisions and other institutional or ad hoc arbitration decisions concerning disputes between investors and host states are quite different. Those arbitration decisions only bind between the disputed parties. Unlike the AB reports, the arbitration decisions are frequently criticized to be inconsistent with each other and sometimes interpret the investment treaties far beyond its ordinary literal meaning. The latter arbitration panels seldom acknowledge the treaty interpretation made by the former panels as established rules on the same treaty terms. Such arbitration decisions are hardly precedents.②

Theories of the most authoritative scholars may be auxiliary means for determination of rules of law. The reason is that such theories exert great impacts on interpretation and application of law, and therefore are helpful in treaty interpretation. Thus, articles and books by distinguished law professors can be consulted to find out what international law is. An outstanding example is the theory elaborated by Mr. Calvo, the famous Argentine legal scholar and diplomat, which had impacted greatly on Latin American countries in handing disputes between these countries and foreign investors, hence had become an important auxiliary source of IEL. The Sutherland Report prepared by elites of trade exports in the WTO is another example showing the significance of legal scholarship in the rule-making of IEL.③

① 参见盛建明编著：《国际经济法》（英文版），对外经济贸易大学出版社 2017 年版，第 31-33 页。
② 参见盛建明编著：《国际经济法》（英文版），对外经济贸易大学出版社 2017 年版，第 31-32 页。
③ 参见盛建明编著：《国际经济法》（英文版），对外经济贸易大学出版社 2017 年版，第 34 页。

3.6 Domestic regulations on external economic activities

It is agreed by many Chinese scholars that domestic legislation for regulations and control of foreign-related economic relations are an important legal source of IEL. These domestic laws and regulations include constitutions, foreign-related economic laws, civil and commercial law that regulate the transboundary economic relations. In common law countries, these also include case law.①

Firstly, to reduce the discrepancies in treaty negotiation and maintain their flexibility in treaty enforcement, countries usually adopt general principles and obligations in dealing with overseas trade and investment in the treaties, and the specific execution of such treaties are further elaborated by the domestic laws and regulations. This is especially true for the regulation of foreign investment. The BITs ratified by capital exporting countries and capital importing countries only address several general issues such as the treatments to the investors, and host states' promise of expropriation of foreign investment only for public purpose against fair or full compensation, among other things. The market access of foreign investment and the screening process of foreign investments, in a large sense, are decided by domestic laws and regulations of host states.

Besides, there are also some areas that rule-making of international rules is lacking or lagged behind, which also suggests that domestic economic regulations in developed countries may finally become international economic disciplines. For example, apart from the global monetary governance by IMF, there are almost no treaties on monetary issue, and the rules governing currency and exchange rates mainly come from domestic regulations. This is because that most countries dare not give up too much sovereignty in the field of currency, as monetary law concerns with a country's macroeconomy polices and stability of its financial market. Even in the realm of world trade, the WTO covered agreements provide most detailed and comprehensive trade rules for its members, but there are still quite a lot of gaps to be filled by its members.

Secondly, the rules in many treaties, especially bilateral treaties, are led by the dominant country in negotiation. The contents of such treaties are actually part of domestic law of the dominant country. For example, the US has exerted continuous and concerted efforts to export its federal rules on appropriation, unfair trade remedies, and federal rules of civil proceedings such as affidavits and cross-examination of evidence to its free trade

① 参见《国际经济法学》编写组编：《国际经济法学》（第 2 版），高等教育出版社 2019 年版，第 29 页。

agreement (FTA) parties,[①] and required its parties to extend the copyright term according to the US Copyright Term Extension Act, making US free trade agreements (FTAs) a major vehicle of exporting US domestic laws and legal norms to the rest of the world.[②] The EU has taken the same path over the past decade, especially in proposing its intellectual property laws with "TRIPS plus" provisions in its FTAs.[③] The rules of negative listing and pre-establishment national treatment in investment regulation, anti-dumping and countervailing measures, terms of copyright protection, recognition and protection of geographical indications, competition neutrality principle of state-owned enterprises, transparency and full participation of stakeholders can all be found in the domestic laws of developed countries and regions like the US and EU.

4 Theories of International Relations and International Economic Law

As part of introduction to IEL, it is necessary to summarize the theories in disciplines of international relations and international economic law. However, international economic law theories, unlike international relation theories, are clearly established. In one article titled "The Theories of International Economic Law in China", Professor Yu discusses the concepts, coverage, actors and principles of IEL. They are definitely part of basic theories of IEL, but IEL theories shall also provide other important functions to IEL research. The theories may establish the general belief and analytical framework for the IEL research, and lay certain perquisite for IEL analysis. But these issues are either missing or failed to reach consensus in most textbooks or papers, so the following discussion will turn to international relation theories that also shed light on the study and research of IEL.

There are three major theories in international relations: realism, liberalism and constructivism. State interests, distribution of power, and anarchy are three keys that build realism.[④] Realism opines that power plays a major role in a world that states are major

---

① See Carlos G. Garcia, *All the Other Dirty Little Secrets: Investment Treaties, Latin America, and the Necessary Evil of Investor-State Arbitration*, 16 Florida Journal of International Law 301, 483 (2004).

② See Mark B. Baker, *No Country Left Behind: The Exporting of US Legal Norms under the Guise of Economic Integration*, 19 Emory International Law Review 1321, 1324 (2005).

③ See Ivo Krizic & Omar Serrano, *Exporting Intellectual Property Rights to Emerging Countries: EU and US Approaches*, 22 European Foreign Affairs Review 57, 58 (2017).

④ See Peter J. Katzenstein, Robert O. Keohane & Stephen D. Krasner, *International Organization and the Study of World Politics*, 52 International Organization 645, 655 (1998).

actors. States establish institutions based on their calculations of self-interest and relative gain, so institutions are not independent variables, but are decided by the power structure,① and shaped by powerful states to increase their share of world power. The openness or closure in foreign trade and investment will be inexplicable without understanding configurations of state interests and power. Treaty negotiation on economic issues is ultimately decided by states' material capability, and the major states set the terms of cooperation and institutions such as the WTO and IMF.

Liberal institutionalists fault realism that the theory belittles international cooperation among states.② On economic issues, states establish institutions to acquire absolute gain, which could function independently to constrain state's cheating and facilitate their interaction. Thus, states have incentives to cooperate with each other in the rule-making of IEL. Various economic treaties and international economic organizations not only work for the leading country's private purposes, but also act as collective goods that further regional economic integration, provide rules for governance, and guarantee states' expectation. In FTA negotiation, state's soft power together with its material power shapes the international order.

Constructivism is a new international relation theory which has just existed for less than 40 years. It is not a pure political theory, but the one absorbing nutrition from many other fields. This theory employs the concept analysis of philosophy-psychology and sociology to international relation theory, putting forwards a series of new concepts, such as culture, recognition, interaction and norm. At the same time, it applies these core concepts to analyze theoretically key issues of international relations between nations, benefits and conflicts, and raises a theory of international system and transformation system and that of communities peacefulness. The theory also has a practical meaning for understanding and solving international issues and how to form a new international order.

Realism, liberalism and constructivism all explain international relations and state's behavior from one or other perspectives. They all enrich our understanding about why IEL disciplines and rules are formed and how they function.

---

① See Stephen D. Krasner, *Global Communications and National Power: Life on the Pareto Frontier*, 43 World Politics 336, 346–356 (1991).

② See Robert O. Keohane, *After Hegemony: Cooperation and Discord in the World Political Economy*, Princeton University Press, 1984, p. 6–7.

5 Principles of International Economic Law

Most Chinese scholars refer to the Charter of Economic Rights and Duties of States (CERDS) when they discuss the principles of international economic law. CERDS was adopted by the UN General Assembly as part of its resolutions to establish the New International Economic Order in 1974. Although the Charter is not a binding treaty adopted by all the members of UN, it reiterates the principles that have been widely accepted by the international community.

Chapter 1 of the Charter outlines the fundamentals of international relations in the following terms, which can be seen as the principles of international economic relations among states.

Economic as well as political and other relations among states shall be governed, *inter alia*, by the following principles: (a) sovereignty, territorial integrity and political independence of States; (b) sovereign equality of all States; (c) non-aggression; (d) non-intervention; (e) mutual and equitable benefit; (f) peaceful coexistence; (g) equal rights and self-determination of peoples; (h) peaceful settlement of disputes; (i) remedying of injustices which have been brought about by force and which deprive a nation of the natural means necessary for its normal development; (j) fulfillment in good faith of international obligations; (k) respect for human rights and international obligations; (l) no attempt to seek hegemony and spheres of influence; (m) promotion of international social justice; (n) international cooperation for development; and (o) free access to and from the sea by land-locked countries within the framework of the above principles.

Many principles emphasized here are general principles of international law such as sovereignty, non-aggression, non-intervention and peaceful settlement of disputes. Other principles such as economic sovereignty, equality and mutual benefits, permanent sovereignty over natural resources, right to economic development are most relevant when discussing the principles of international economic law.

5.1 Economic sovereignty

Recognized by Article 1 of CERDS, every state has the sovereign and inalienable right to choose its economic system as well as its political, social and cultural systems in accordance with the will of its people, without outside interference, coercion or threat in any form whatsoever.

In terms of sovereignty, the state is usually understood as sovereign in the "Westphalian" sense— "inward and outward". Its external and internal sovereignty refers to the fact that it is the sole arbitrator for matters within its borders. It is necessary to define this precisely in order to avoid confusion, as "sovereignty" is a complex and ambiguous concept. The core of sovereignty is the right to legitimate arbitration. This right, in fact, originates from the social contract, in which citizens delegate the dispute settlement right to the government, which in turn allows the government to resolve disputes between citizens. In addition, through the act of social contract, citizens constitute the constitutional and legal order, which at the same time prevents the government's usurpation of the power it was given.

The meaning of the term "economic sovereignty" is not entirely clear and could be understood from four aspects. Firstly, it is the state's ownership over its resource. Secondly, economic sovereignty means state's self-sufficiency. That is, a state is economically sovereign if it is able to meet the needs of its population based on its own resources and its own reproduction. Thirdly, scholars believe that economic sovereignty includes lack of budget deficit and indebtedness to foreign creditors, meaning that a state has financial stability and regular servicing of the budget. Fourthly, economic sovereignty means the ability of the state to independently decide on the use of its own resources. Independent decision-making on own resources involves specific factors, such as currency control, credit channeling and interest rates, freedom of capital movement [import and selection of trade (economic) partners].①

5.2 Permanent sovereignty over natural resources

Article 2 of CERDS articulates the meaning of state's permanent sovereignty over natural resources:

"1. Every State has and shall freely exercise full permanent sovereignty, including possession, use and disposal, over all its wealth, natural resources and economic activities.

"2. Each State has the right: (a) to regulate and exercise authority over foreign investment within its national jurisdiction in accordance with its laws and regulations and in conformity with its national objectives and priorities. No State shall be compelled to grant preferential treatment to foreign investment; (b) to regulate and supervise the

① Excerpt from *Economic Sovereignty* written by Aleksandar Savanovic, published at IISES 12th International Academic Conference on 1 September 2014.

activities of transnational corporations within its national jurisdiction and take measures to ensure that such activities comply with its laws, rules and regulations and conform with its economic and social policies. Transnational corporations shall not intervene in the internal affairs of a host State. Every State should, with full regard for its sovereign rights, cooperate with other States in the exercise of the right set forth in this subparagraph; (c) to nationalize, expropriate or transfer ownership of foreign property, in which case appropriate compensation should be paid by the State adopting such measures, taking into account its relevant laws and regulations and all circumstances that the State considers pertinent. In any case where the question of compensation gives rise to a controversy, it shall be settled under the domestic law of the nationalizing State and by its tribunals unless it is freely and mutually agreed by all States concerned that other peaceful means be sought on the basis of the sovereign equality of States and in accordance with the principle of free choice of means."

State's right to utilize its natural resource is also given by the UN Convention on the Law of the Sea 1982. Article 193 of the Convention recognizes states' sovereign right to exploit their natural resources pursuant to their environmental policies.

But it does not mean that state's right over natural resource is not without limit. While providing the state with right to utilize the marine resource, the UN Convention on the Law of the Sea 1982 also requires that the state shall preserve and protect the marine environment.

In Stockholm Declaration of the United Nations Conference on the Human Environment of 1972, state's utilization of natural resources is required to comply with certain principles. For example, Principles 2 and 3 require that the natural resources of the earth must be safeguarded for the benefit of present and future generations through careful planning or management, as appropriate, and the capacity of the earth to produce vital renewable resources must be maintained and, wherever practicable, restored or improved.

Such requirements are also reflected in Article 30 of the CERDS, which states that the protection, preservation and enhancement of the environment for the present and future generations is the responsibility of all states. All states shall endeavor to establish their own environmental and developmental policies in conformity with such responsibility. The environmental policies of all states should enhance and not adversely affect the present and future development potential of developing countries. All states have the responsibility to ensure that activities within their jurisdiction or control do not cause damage to the environment of other states or of areas beyond the limits of national jurisdiction. All states should cooperate in evolving international norms and regulations in the field of the environment.

5.3 Equity and mutual benefit

The Declaration on Establishment of a New International Economic Order acknowledges that a new international economic order should be established on the basis of mutual equal treatment and that all members of the international society should conduct the most extensive cooperation on the principle of equity so as to eliminate economic gaps and achieve common prosperity. Article 10 of CERDS also explicates that "all States are judicially equal and, as equal members of the international community, have the right to participate fully and effectively in the international decision-making process in the solution of world economic, financial and monetary problems, *inter alia*, through the appropriate international organizations in accordance with their existing and evolving rules, and to share in the benefits resulting therefrom."

5.4 Right to economic development

States have right to develop their economies. This is also an embedded human right that every human has the right to participate in the economic activity and get rid of poverty. It is not only the state's right, but also its duty to make appropriate national development policies to improve the well-being of its citizens.

Article 4 of CERDS affirms state's right to engage in international trade and other forms of economic cooperation. Further, Article 5 stipulates state's right to associate in organizations of primary commodity producers in order to develop their national economies, to achieve stable financing for their development and, in pursuance of their aims, to assist in the promotion of sustained growth of the world economy, in particular accelerating the development of developing countries. These provisions are reflection of state's right to economic development.

5.5 International cooperation for development

The CERDS provides that international cooperation for development is the shared goal and common duty of all states. Every state should cooperate with the efforts of developing countries to accelerate their economic and social development by providing favorable external conditions and by extending active assistance to them, consistent with their development needs and objectives, with strict respect for the sovereign equality of states and free of any conditions derogating from their sovereignty.

International cooperation is an essential element of globalization. As states are more closely related with each other, no state is able to achieve its economic development without cooperation with other countries. The Declaration on Establishing a New International Economic Order points out that the interests of the developed countries and those of the developing countries can no longer be isolated from each other, that there is a close interrelationship between the prosperity of the developed countries and the growth and development of the developing countries, and that the prosperity of the international community as a whole depends upon the prosperity of its constituent parts.

The adoption of multilateral trade and finance treaties, proliferation of free trade agreements and BITs are just manifestation of intergovernmental cooperation.

International cooperation not only refers to the cooperation among states, but also calls upon cooperation from NGOs and civil society.

Chapter Review

1. What is the definition of IEL?
2. What are the different opinions about the nature and coverage of IEL?
3. Do you think United Nations Convention on Contract for the International Sale of Goods shall be included in the terrain of IEL?
4. What might be included in the domain of IEL when more rules in digital trade emerge?
5. What are the subjects of IEL? Do subjects need to enjoy rights and bear responsibilities on their own names in international law?
6. What are the different opinions on the subjects of IEL?
7. Do you agree that TNCs and NGOs are both subjects of IEL? Give your explanations.
8. Explain the theory of realism, liberalism and constructivism.
9. What are the differences between realism and liberalism?
10. Do you think states negotiate free trade agreements or bilateral investment treaties only for gaining power?
11. Can you name the sources of IEL?
12. What are bilateral, regional, multilateral, and plurilateral treaties? Can you give us some examples?
13. How does a custom develop as a source of IEL?
14. Can you name some general principles that can be treated as the source of IEL?

15. Are resolutions made by UN binding upon its members?
16. Do you agree that AB reports adopted by the DSB constitute precedents? Why? How about the ICSID arbitration decisions?
17. Do you think domestic regulations shall be considered as a source of IEL? Why?
18. State briefly the basic principles of IEL.
19. Explain the meaning of economic sovereignty.
20. Please name the conventions or declarations that state's permanent sovereignty over natural resources is declared.
21. In what documents are principle of equity and mutual benefit given?
22. Does the state have right to economic development? In which convention is this principle given?
23. What does international cooperation for development mean?

Key Terms

constructivism	建构主义
customary international law	国际习惯法
liberalism	自由主义
pacta sunt servanda	有约必守
permanent sovereignty over natural resources	国家对自然资源的永久主权
private international law	国际私法
public international law	国际公法
realism	现实主义

Further Readings

1. Trubek, David M. & M. Patrick Cottrell, *Robert Hudec and the Theory of International Economic Law: The Law of Global Space*, Social Science Electronic Publishing, 2008, available at https://ssrn.com/abstract=1144724 or http://dx.doi.org/10.2139/ssrn.1144724.

2. Yu Jinsong, *The Theories of International Economic Law in China*, Legal Issues of Economic Integration, Vol. 28: 249, 2001.

3. https://www.wto.org.

Part II World Trade Law

Chapter 1

Development of World Trade Organization and Its Institutional Structure

Study Guide

This Chapter explains the origin and development of World Trade Organization (WTO) and its institutional structure, decision-making procedures, and covered agreements for the students. The GATT came into force in 1947 after the development of its predecessor—the International Trade Organization failed. In 1995, the GATT 1947 was replaced by a permanent intergovernmental organization—the World Trade Organization, which has 70 bodies and more comprehensive agreements and disciplines on trade.

The institutional structure of the WTO includes the Ministerial Conference, the General Council, the Dispute Settlement Body (DSB) and the Trade Policy Review Body (TPRB), and specialized councils, committees and working parties. What's more, this structure includes quasi-judicial and other non-political bodies.

The decision-making process of WTO is complicate, and consensus, majority voting and reverse consensus could be used in deciding different matters.

After Uruguay Round of negotiation, the WTO covered agreements have been expanded to the realm of trade in service, investment, trade-related intellectual property, and the original disciplines on trade in goods have also been enriched.

The Chapter finally discusses the general principles of GATT, which are non-discrimination treatment, transparency, more favorable treatment to developing countries and free and fair trade. These principles, especially the non-discrimination treatment have become the cornerstone of the world trading system.

International trade has become an integrated part of our daily lives. Thanks to the multilateral trading system and rules established after the World War II, the foods we eat and the clothes we wear today are results of international trade. Today, the ideas of free trade and non-discrimination are deeply rooted in most of the states. But it is not always the case. Before the World War II, unilateral actions and in particular unilateral reactions or beggar-thy-neighbor policies were so popular among the western countries which caused disastrous consequence to world trade and economics during the interwar periods. The risk of an increase in the use, rectius abuse, of trade remedies is particularly high during periods of crisis when domestic producers pledge governments for protection from foreign competitors.① The end of World War II witnessed a significant change toward free trade ideology in the international community. It was believed that a highly economic dependent international society would reduce the risk of Wars at that time. Therefore, states and other entities worked together to find global solutions to global economic problems, and replaced the system primarily based on individualism, force and wars by a multilateral cooperative framework. Against such backdrop, the states in west-hemisphere, led by the US, created the so-called Bretton Woods institutions to achieve common ends of economic prosperity, and multilateral trade rules were developed for the first time to limit the possibility for states to discriminate and react unilaterally in dealing with trade affairs. The greatest achievement of the GATT and WTO is to replace the unilateral reactions by multilateral efforts and judicial processes, which enhance the legitimacy of globalization and provide an international economic order that is ruled by law.

1 Origin of the GATT

The multilateral framework of international trade originated from the end of the World War II. Against the painful historic lesson, the foremost aspiration in the minds of winner states after the War was to prevent destructive trade and currency protectionism. Therefore, when they met in Bretton Woods in 1944 secretly, they agreed to create the International Monetary Fund to stabilize the exchange rates of different currencies and to alleviate the balance of payment problems, to establish the World Bank to provide states with the necessary financial resources to restore their economies after years of War, and to adopt the General Agreement on Tariffs and Trade 1947 (GATT 1947) with multilateral trade rules to prevent states' excessive protective and unilateral measures such as the

① See Roberto Soprano, *WTO Trade Remedies in International Law: Their Role and Place in a Fragmented International Legal System*, Routledge, 2018, p. 1.

beggar-thy-neighbor policies.

Actually, the original cooperative package for the administration of world trade was far more ambitious and comprehensive than the GATT 1947. The diplomats from over 50 countries intended to establish the International Trade Organization (ITO) at first, which was a new specialized agency of the United Nations to govern the trade. The Charter of ITO provided not only world trade disciplines but also rules relating to employment, commodity agreements, restrictive business practices, international investment and services. It extended far beyond world trade disciplines. The aim was to create the ITO at a UN Conference on Trade and Employment in Havana, Cuba in 1947. Although the ITO Charter was finally agreed in March 1948, ratification in national legislatures was obstructed and finally proved impossible in some countries.

In 1950, the United States announced that it was not possible for it to acquire congressional ratification of the Havana Charter, meaning that the US gave up the idea of establishing the ITO. The US's withdrawal made the ITO Charter effectively dead. Fortunately, the international trade chapter of the ITO Charter was taken out and converted into GATT 1947 a year ago, which took effect among the 23 countries that ratified it in 1947. The GATT 1947 was designed to attain the substantial reduction of tariffs and other barriers to trade, and the elimination of discriminatory treatment in international commerce.

To reduce tariffs and remove various barriers to trade, nine rounds of multilateral trade negotiations have been held in total since the ratification of GATT 1947. Most of the negotiations were named after the city that major negotiations were done or the US president that led such multilateral negotiation. The nine rounds are called Geneva Round (1947), Annecy Round (1949), Torquay Round (1951), Geneva Round (1956), Dillon Round (1960–1961), Kennedy Round (1964–1967), Tokyo Round (1973–1979), Uruguay Round (1986–1994) and Doha Round (2001–).

The first round of negotiations resulted in a package of trade rules and 45,000 tariff concessions affecting USD 10 billion of trade, about one fifth of the world's total. The group had expanded to 23 by the time the deal was signed on 30 October 1947. The tariff concessions came into effect by 30 June 1948 through a protocol of provisional application. And so the new General Agreement on Tariffs and Trade was born, with 23 founding members (officially "contracting parties").

In the first six rounds, generous efforts were taken to reduce tariffs, and the Tokyo

Round was the first major attempt to tackle trade barriers that did not take the form of tariffs, and to improve the system. Major exercises were taken to strengthen disciplines on non-tariff measures, especially the voluntary export restrains (VER) and common market arrangements (CMA) adopted in exporting countries to avoid the trade remedies in strong importing states. A series of agreements on non-tariff barriers did emerge from the negotiations, in some cases interpreting existing GATT rules, in others breaking entirely new ground. In most cases, only a relatively small number of (mainly industrialized) GATT members subscribed to these agreements and arrangements. Because they were not accepted by the full GATT membership, they were often informally called "codes".

By the early 1980s the GATT was clearly no longer as relevant to the realities of world trade as it had been in the 1940s. For a start, world trade had become far more complex and important than 40 years before: the globalization of the world economy was underway, trade in services—not covered by GATT rules—was of major interest to more and more countries, and international investment had expanded. The expansion of services trade was also closely tied to further increases in world merchandise trade. In other respects, GATT had been found wanting. For instance, in agriculture, loopholes in the multilateral system were heavily exploited, and efforts at liberalizing agricultural trade met with little success. In the textiles and clothing sector, an exception to GATT's normal disciplines was negotiated in the 1960s and early 1970s, leading to the Multifiber Agreement. Even GATT's institutional structure and its dispute settlement system were causing concern.

The eighth, the Uruguay Round of 1986–1994, was the most extensive of all. It led to the WTO and a new set of agreements. In Uruguay Round, the coverage of world trade disciplines was significantly expanded to include rules on transboundary services, intellectual property rights and investment. In Doha Round, which is also called Development Round, further negotiations have been carried out on fields such as agriculture, environment protection, competition policy and so on.

In general, the GATT was a great success in removing tariff barriers and promoting trade. From 1948 to 1994, the GATT 1947 provided the rules for much of world trade and presided over periods that saw some of the highest growth rates in international commerce. With the reduction of tariffs and removal of non-tariff barriers, trade has become the engine of world economy since 1970s. Tariffs on industrial products have fallen steeply and now average less than 5% in most industrial countries. After its five decades of operation, world trade was 22 times the level it had been the time of the GATT's inception.① It seemed well-established, but throughout those 47 years, it was a provisional agreement and organization.

Table II-1 GATT Trade Rounds②

Year	Place/Name	Subjects Covered	Countries
1947	Geneva	Tariffs	23
1949	Annecy	Tariffs	13
1951	Torquay	Tariffs	38
1956	Geneva	Tariffs	26
1960–1961	Geneva Dillon Round	Tariffs	26
1964–1967	Geneva Kennedy Round	Tariffs and anti-dumping measures	62
1973–1979	Geneva Tokyo Round	Tariffs, non-tariff measures, framework agreements	102
1986–1994	Geneva Uruguay Round	Tariffs, non-tariff measures, rules, services, intellectual property, dispute settlement, textiles, agriculture, creation of WTO, etc	123

2 Replacement of the GATT by the WTO

The GATT 1947 provided only a few and general rules to regulate international economic relationships in the field of trade in goods, with no disciplines on transboundary

① See Sungjoon Cho, *The Social Foundations of World Trade: Norms, Community and Constitution*, Cambridge University Press, 2014, p. 15.

② Source: https://www.wto.org/english/thewto_e/whatis_e/tif_e/fact4_e.htm.

service, foreign direct investment, intellectual property protection and other issues closely attended by the developed states. Further, as a temporary agreement, it did not create an international organization and its authority over trade dispute settlement was also limited as the decisions made by the panel would not automatically become effective. Such defects have been attended by the United States, and it wished to replace such singular rules by a multifaceted organization that could provide robust regulations to service and intellectual property protection as well. Endeavors have been made in Uruguay Round. After eight years' negotiation, the deal of Uruguay Round was signed by ministers from most of the 125 participating governments at a meeting in Marrakesh, Morocco on 15 April 1994. And in that meeting, members agreed to establish WTO to replace the provisional GATT.

2.1 How WTO is different from the GATT

The World Trade Organization is far more than a simple extension of GATT. On the contrary, it completely replaces its predecessor and has very different features.

Firstly, the GATT was a set of rules, or a multilateral agreement, with no institutional foundation. There was only a small associated secretariat which had its origins in the attempt to establish the International Trade Organization in the 1940s. The WTO is a permanent institution with Ministerial Conference, General Council, working parties and committees, etc. Secondly, the GATT was applied on a provisional basis even if, after more than 40 years, it was said that the governments actually chose to treat it as a permanent commitment. The WTO commitments are full and permanent to its members except some provisions reserved by the members. Thirdly, the GATT rules only applied to trade in merchandise goods. GATT members did not make any commitments to trade in service and other issues. However, the WTO covers trade in services and trade-related aspects of intellectual property in addition to goods. Fourthly, while GATT was a multilateral instrument, by the 1980s, many new agreements had been added of a plurilateral, and therefore selective nature. The agreements which constitute the WTO are almost all multilateral and, thus, involve commitments for the entire membership.

When we talk about the GATT, we also need to know that GATT 1947 is different from GATT 1994. The GATT 1947 referred to the agreement entered into force in 1947, and it continued to exist until the end of 1995, thereby allowing all GATT member countries to accede to the WTO and replace the GATT 1947 by GATT 1994, which was far more comprehensive than GATT 1947.

2.2 Mandates and functions of the WTO

The mandates of the WTO are to make the world economy prosperous and to reduce poverty through free but regulated trade, which are clearly given by the preamble of The Agreement Establishing the World Trade Organization (Marrakesh Agreement):

"Recognizing that their relations in the field of trade and economic endeavour should be conducted with a view to raising standards of living, ensuring full employment and a large and steadily growing volume of real income and effective demand, and expanding the production of and trade in goods and services, while allowing for the optimal use of the world's resources in accordance with the objective of sustainable development, seeking both to protect and preserve the environment and to enhance the means for doing so in a manner consistent with their respective needs and concerns at different levels of economic development..."

The preamble of the WTO Agreement provides context to the treaty terms in the covered agreements. Thus, the mandate of the WTO does provide certain texture and colors in defining some ambiguous terms of the covered agreements. For example, in explaining whether the "exhaustible natural resource" in Article 20(g) of the GATT included living marine animals like sea turtles, the Appellate Body did refer to the preamble and took into account the mandate of the WTO that "allowing for the optimal use of the world's resources in accordance with the objective of sustainable development".

The functions of the WTO are set in Article 3 of the Marrakesh Agreement. The WTO shall facilitate the implementation, administration and operation, and further the objectives of the WTO agreements, provide a forum for negotiation of new trade or trade-related agreements, administer the Dispute Settlement System, conduct the Trade Policy Review Mechanism, and cooperate with other organizations to achieve greater coherence in global economic policy-making.

Among the various functions, the WTO plays an important role in settling trade disputes among its members, as there is either no or weak trade dispute settlement mechanism in regional trade agreements.

2.3 Membership of the WTO

By the end of 2019, the WTO has 164 members who represent 98% of world trade, and over 20 countries are seeking to join the WTO.

It shall be noted that the entrance of the WTO is open to separate customs territories possessing full autonomy in the conduct of their external commercial relations and in the other matters covered by the WTO Agreement. Hence, the WTO membership does not merely include states. Separate customs territories such as European Union and Hong Kong Special Administrative Region (SAR) of China are also WTO members.

There are two types of membership in the WTO. One is the original membership. It was given by the Article 11 of the Marrakesh Agreement that contracting parties to the GATT 1947 could join the WTO by accepting the terms of the Marrakesh Agreement and its multilateral trade agreements, and making concessions and commitments for both trade in goods and services. That is, the original members of the GATT 1947 do not need to go through an accession procedure to be a WTO member.

To other separate customs territories apart from its original members, if they wish to join the WTO, accession procedures shall be followed, and their economic and trade policies shall be brought in line with WTO rules. Governments of such separate customs territories shall negotiate its terms of entry with the WTO members.

Such accession procedure usually includes several steps. The joining country first discloses its trade and trade relevant polices to the relevant WTO committees and all the members of the WTO so as to let the members know about its domestic trade surroundings. Then, individual negotiations will be conducted between the joining country and its closely-trading nations, which are usually the major trading powers. The negotiation would continue until concessions are reached between them. Further, membership terms will be drafted and incorporated into the accession protocol and working party report. Finally, a decision that approves its accession will be made through consensus of Ministerial Conference or General Council or over 2/3 majority of membership.

3 Institutional Structure of the WTO

There is a total of 70 WTO bodies. Comparing to other intergovernmental organizations, the 70 bodies of the WTO have made for a heavy workload for the WTO diplomats. Among them, 34 are standing bodies, many of which meet on a regular basis, working efficiently and effectively in the past two decades.

The institutional structure of the WTO includes, at the highest level, the Ministerial Conference, at a second level, the General Council, the Dispute Settlement Body (DSB) and the Trade Policy Review Body (TPRB), and at lower levels, specialized councils, committees and working parties. What's more, this structure includes quasi-judicial and other non-political bodies, as well as the WTO Secretariat.

The Ministerial Conference is the supreme body of the WTO. It is composed of minister-level representatives from all its Members and has decision-making powers on all matters under any of the WTO covered agreements, such as adopting authoritative interpretations of the WTO agreements, granting waivers to Members, adopting amendments of the WTO agreements, making decisions on accession of new members, and appointing the Director-General and adopting staff regulations.

The General Council is composed of ambassador-level diplomats and normally meets once every two months. The General Council is responsible for the continuing, day to day management of the WTO and its many activities. In between sessions of the Ministerial Conference, the General Council exercises the full powers of the Ministerial Conference.

The General Council, the DSB and the TPRB are in fact the same body. When the General Council administers the WTO dispute settlement system and performs its duty of adopting the panel and Appellate Body (AB) reports, it convenes and acts as the DSB. When the General Council administers the WTO trade policy review mechanism, it convenes and acts as the TPRB.

There are three specialized councils under the leadership of the General Council: the Council for Trade in Goods, the Council for Trade in Services, and the Council for TRIPS. They carry out both the tasks which the General Council delegates to them and the tasks which the WTO Agreement, the GATS or the TRIPS explicitly confers on them. Furthermore, there are also dozens of committees and working parties established to assist the Ministerial Conference and the General Council in carrying out their functions. (see Figure II-1 below)

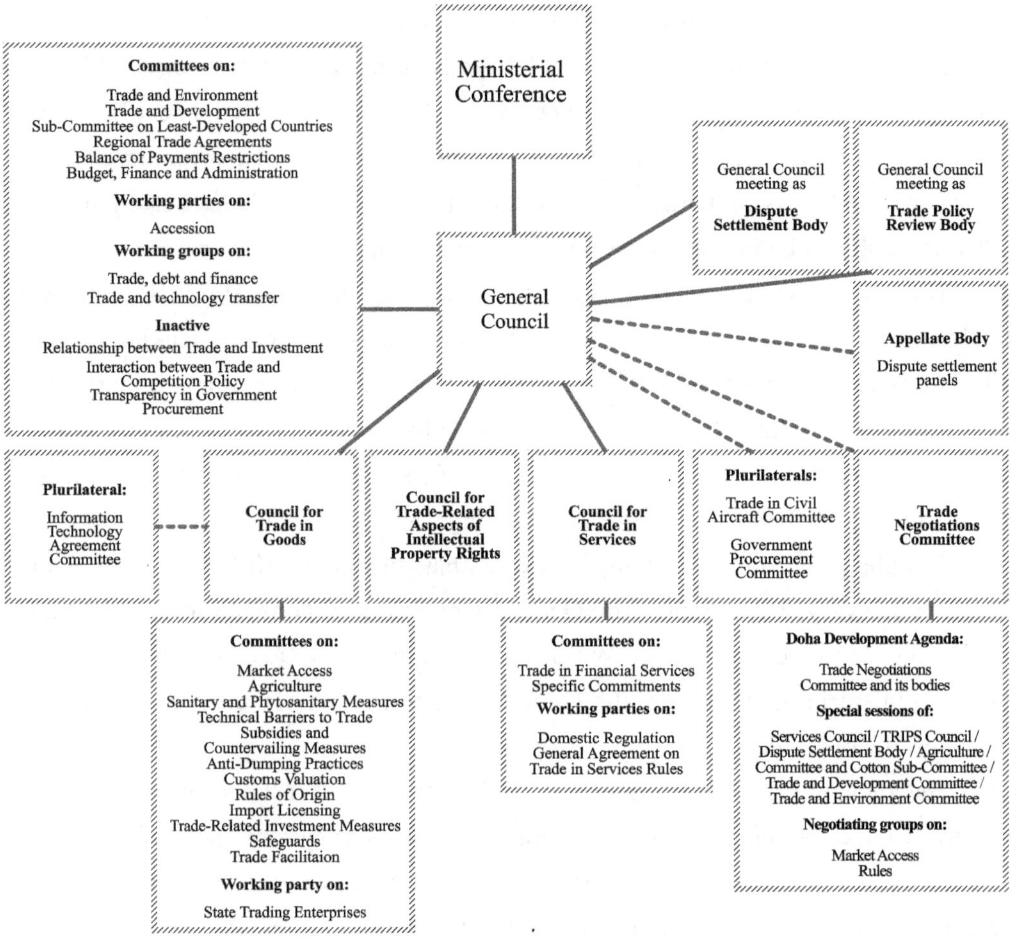

Figure II-1 Organization Chart of the WTO①

The WTO Secretariat, with offices in Geneva, has 630 regular staff and is headed by a Director-General. Its main duties are to supply technical and professional support for the various councils and committees, to provide technical assistance for developing countries, to monitor and analyze development in world trade, to provide information to the public and the media, and to organize the ministerial conferences. The Secretariat also provides some forms of legal assistance in the dispute settlement process and advises governments wishing to become members of the WTO. From 1995 to 2020, there had been six Directors-General: Peter Sutherland (1995), Renato Ruggiero (1995–1999), Mike Moore (1999–2002), Supachai Panitchpakdi (2002–2005), Pascal Lamy (2005–2013),

① Source: https://www.wto.org/english/thewto_e/whatis_e/tif_e/organigram_e.pdf.

and Roberto Azevêdo (2013–2020). Roberto Azevêdo is the sixth Director-General of the WTO. His appointment took effect on 1 September 2013 for a four-year term. In February 2017, WTO members agreed to appoint Mr Azevêdo for a second four-year term, starting on 1 September 2017. But he resigned from this position on 16 July, 2020. Ngozi Okonjo-Iweala is the seventh Director-General of the WTO. She took office on 1 March 2021, becoming the first woman and the first African to serve as Director-General.

4 Decision-Making of the WTO

The WTO adopts different decision-making procedures to decide different matters. Generally, Members first try to take decisions by consensus. This means unless a Member explicitly objects to the proposed decision, that decision is passed and taken. There is no voting taking place.

If consensus cannot be achieved, Article 11.1 of the WTO Agreement provides for voting on a one-country-one-vote basis. Decisions are then taken by a simple majority of the votes cast. It should be admitted that the consensus was once successful in attracting newly independent countries to join in the multilateral institution in the early days and allowing them to participate passively when the major trading powers had the capability of controlling the trade negotiations. But such decision-making procedure allows each Member to have the veto power to block the negotiation that could also dramatically cripple the law-making function of the WTO.

Apart from decision by consensus and simple majority voting, the WTO also adopts super majority voting in deciding vital issues. For example, the decisions on adopting authoritative interpretations require 3/4 majority approval of the Members, decisions on accessions are taken by a 2/3 majority of WTO members, decisions on waivers are taken by 3/4 majority of the Members, decisions on amendments require consensus of Ministerial Conference or General Council, or 2/3 majority of Members.

The most unique decision-making mechanism is adopted by DSB in approving dispute settlement reports. Such decision-making is called reverse consensus or negative consensus, developed from the positive consensus in GATT era. Originally, consensus of the DSB was required to approve the panel reports, meaning that the reports would be rejected if one Member objected to the result. After the WTO was established in 1994, stipulated by the Dispute Settlement Understanding, the panel and AB reports are approved as long as one Member approves it. Such reverse consensus approach has allowed the reports to be adopted by the Members nearly automatically, greatly enhancing the effectiveness and enforceability of the dispute settlement mechanism of the WTO.

5 The Covered Agreements of the WTO and the Attachments

The WTO lays a comprehensive set of disciplines on Members' measures relating to merchandized goods, transboundary service, intellectual property and investment. Most of the WTO's agreements were the outcome of the 1986–1994 Uruguay Round of trade negotiations. Some, including GATT 1994, were revisions of texts of its earlier agreements.

The family of WTO agreements consist of the following agreements, decisions and understandings.

5.1 Agreements on trade in goods

The disciplines on trade in goods are included in GATT 1994 and other agreements in the area of goods, which form the Appendix 1A of the Marrakesh Agreement.

GATT 1994 is developed from GATT 1947, consisting of: (a) GATT 1947, the original GATT with its amendments, as it stands up to December 31 of 1994; (b) decisions taken under GATT 1947 up to that date; (c) understandings reached in the Uruguay Round in areas of other duties and charges, state trading enterprises, balance-of-payment provisions, customs unions and free-trade areas, waivers of obligations, and tariff modification; (d) tariff schedules and the manner of implementation for these schedules as agreed to in the Uruguay Round.

Apart from GATT 1994, there are also 12 agreements specializing in agriculture, sanitary and phytosanitary measures, textiles and clothing, technical barriers to trade, trade-related investment measures, anti-dumping, customs valuations, preshipment inspections, rules of origin, import licensing, and subsidies and safeguard. Most of these agreements are concluded in Uruguay Round.

5.2 Agreements on trade in service

Attachment 1B of the Marrakesh Agreement consists of disciplines on trade in service, which are much more concise comparing to the disciplines on trade in goods, including the General Agreement on Trade in Services (GATS) and two protocols relating to the financial service, one protocol on free movement of natural persons, and one protocol on basic telecommunication.①

GATS includes two types of obligations and commitments, which are general obligations and specific commitments. Members' general obligation includes most-favored-nation (MFN) treatment, even though it is permissible to have initial exemptions from the MFN treatment. The general obligation means that members shall provide unconditional MFN treatment to other members on each department and sector of trade in service, unless certain areas or measures are exempted and recorded in the schedule.

Specific commitments are related to specific sectors. The sectoral commitments are applicable to specific sectors to which they relate. These are included in the respective schedules of the Members which form an integral part of the GATS. Members will take specific commitments in three sectors, market access, national treatment, and other commitments. That is, it is decided by the members to what extent it would allow the market access of trade in service and on what conditions it would provide national treatment to others. This is because trade in service was included in Uruguay Round about 1991, and the US was eager to conclude the negotiation. Thus, a specific commitment on the issue of market access, national treatment and other duties would reduce discrepancy among members.

5.3 Agreement on Trade-Related Aspects of Intellectual Property

Intellectual property right is a brand new issue negotiated in the Uruguay Round. A large number of countries participating in the negotiations had initially objected to the inclusion of intellectual property rights in GATT on the grounds that the subject had already been covered by World Intellectual Property Organization and GATT had jurisdiction only in the field of trade. As a compromise, the subject of the negotiations was termed trade-related intellectual property rights. But actually, its link with trade is vague and diminished, yet the original name remains.

The Members agreed to adopt the Agreement on Trade-Related Aspects of Intellectual Property Rights (TRIPS) as the Annex 1C of the Marrakesh Agreement in 1994. The Agreement includes seven types of intellectual property. They are patents, copyrights,

---

① The second protocol and the fourth protocol of GATS are relating to financial services. The third protocol is relating to the free movement of natural persons and the fourth protocol is about basic telecommunication.

trademarks, geographical indications, industrial designs, layout designs of integrated circuits and undisclosed information. Unlike the other covered agreements, TRIPS does not require absolute conformity with members' domestic regulations and measures on intellectual property protection. Instead, it specifies that it only prescribes the minimum standard for members. That is, members can maintain higher standard intellectual property protection rules without breaching TRIPS requirements.

5.4 Understanding on Rules and Procedures Governing the Settlement of Disputes (DSU)

The Understanding on Rules and Procedures Governing the Settlement of Disputes is recorded in the Annex 2 to the Marrakesh Agreement. The rules and procedures of the Understanding shall apply to disputes brought pursuant to the consultation and dispute settlement provisions of the agreements listed in Annex 1 thereof. There are 27 provisions and 4 appendixes in the DSU. The DSU includes principles and rules of dispute settlement between WTO members arising from the breach of WTO covered agreements or deprivation of trade benefits by the WTO covered agreements, which include a panel process and appellant process that are frequently used by Members.

5.5 Trade Policy Review Mechanism (TPRM)

The Trade Policy Review Mechanism is included in Annex 3 of the Marrakesh Agreement. This mechanism is intended to increase the transparency of national trade policies and to improve adherence to the rules of covered agreements of the WTO. According to the TPRM, the trade policies of all WTO members need to be reviewed by the WTO, and the frequency of each country's review varies according to its share of world trade. The Annex mandates that the trade policies of four Members with the largest shares of world trade (currently the United States, China, the European Union, and Japan) shall be reviewed every two years, the trade policies of next 16 trading powers shall be reviewed every four years, and others be reviewed every six years. A longer period may be adopted for the review of trade policies of the least-developed economies. The objectives of the TPRM, as expressed in Annex 3 of the Marrakesh Agreement, include facilitating the smooth function of the multilateral trading system by enhancing the transparency of Members' trade policies. Reviews are conducted by the TPRB on the basis of a policy statement by the Member under review and a report prepared by economists in the Secretariat's Trade Policy Review Division.

5.6 Plurilateral agreements in sectors of civil aircraft and government procurement

Most WTO covered agreements are multilateral as they are signed and obeyed by all WTO members. There were once several agreements under the WTO signed by a smaller number of members, which were called plurilateral agreements. Plurilateral agreements were popular in the Tokyo Round multilateral trade negotiation, but were criticized for its lack of collaboration, running counter to the spirit of the multilateralism. So in the Uruguay Round, the plurilateralism was successfully suppressed by the single-taking requirement, which was regarded as a victory of multilateralism. Today, two Agreements remain plurilateral in nature. They are the Agreement on Trade in Civil Aircraft and the Agreement on Government Procurement (GPA). The Agreement on Trade in Civil Aircraft eliminates import duties on all aircraft, other than military aircraft, as well as all other products covered by the Agreement such as civil aircraft engines and their parts and components, all components and sub-assemblies of civil aircraft, and flight simulators and their parts and components.[①]

The GPA is another plurilateral agreement within the framework of the WTO. By the end of 2020, the membership of this Agreement comprised 48 WTO members, and another 35 WTO members participated in the GPA Committee as observers. Out of these, 12 members are in the process of acceding to the Agreement at present. The fundamental aim of the GPA is to mutually open government procurement markets among its parties. The GPA is composed mainly of two parts: the text of the Agreement and parties' market access schedules of commitments on government procurement.

The text of the Agreement establishes rules requiring that open, fair and transparent conditions of competition be ensured in government procurement. However, these rules do not automatically apply to all procurement activities of each party. Rather, the coverage schedules play a critical role in determining whether a procurement activity is covered by the Agreement or not. Only those procurement activities that are carried out by covered entities purchasing listed goods and services, or construction services of a value exceeding specified threshold values are covered by the Agreement.

5.7 Other agreements concluded in Doha Round

The Annex 1, Annex 2 and Annex 3 Agreements of WTO were all concluded in

---

① This plurilateral agreement entered into force on 1 January 1980. There are 33 signatories to this Agreement.

Uruguay Round. After that, there were little progress in new treaty negotiation under the WTO. In Doha Round, there were only one new agreement titled Trade Facilitation Agreement (TFA) adopted by the Members. It entered into force in February 2017, following acceptance by over 2/3 of WTO members. The Trade Facilitation Agreement reduces red tape, cuts costs and makes it easier for businesses to enter overseas markets. Under the TFA, Members must comply with international best practice to publish relevant procedures and forms for importing goods online to streamline access to customs procedures, to allow exporters to submit import documentation before physical goods arrive, to clear goods before final duties and charges are calculated, to obtain precise and binding information on the tariff classification of their goods before arrival, and to mandate the quick release of perishable goods, which will reduce waiting times for clearance of agricultural exports in foreign ports.

The Organisation for Economic Co-operation Development (OECD) estimates the Agreement could reduce the costs of trading cross borders by more than 10% for developed economies, and globally by between 12.5% and 17.5%.

6 General Principles of the WTO

The general principles of WTO covered agreements include most-favored-nation treatment, national treatment, transparency, free and fair trade and preferential treatment to developing countries. The most fundamental principle of GATT is that international trade should be conducted without discrimination. The principle is given concrete forms in the most-favored nation (MFN) and national treatment rules. These two principles establish the cornerstone of the multilateral world trading system, that is, the non-discriminatory treatment.

6.1 Most-favored-nation treatment and its exceptions

The nondiscrimination rules prohibit trade discrimination among foreign members of the WTO, between imported products and like-domestic products. And the most-favored nation (MFN) requires a level playing field among imported products.

The principle is enshrined in Article 1.1 of the GATT, stating that: "[a]ny benefit in connection with exporting or importing given to a product of a most favored nation (whether a Member or not) has to be given to the like product of all Members without discrimination". The provision means that any advantage, favor, privilege or immunity ("benefits") granted by any member to any product originating in or destined for (import from or export to) any other country shall be accorded immediately and unconditionally to the like product originating in or destined for the territories of all other members.

The MFN standard includes a three-step analysis. Firstly, when challenging a measure that violates MFN treatment, the exporting state needs to prove that a benefit is enjoyed by other exporting states. The benefit can be entrusted in different forms. For example, it can be an advantage in form of reduction of tariff, a favor such as permission to export a scarce commodity, a privilege like tax remission and an immunity such as an exemption from a health hazard test.

Secondly, the essence of MFN treatment is the analysis of like products. Different treatment or discrimination would be established if a benefit is given to one state on one particular product, but not given to others on the same kind of product, with respect to customs duties and charges of any kind, or the method of levying such duties and charges, and all rules and formalities. But to circumvent MFN treatment, members usually classify products into several kinds and allege that different treatment given to different products would not violate MFN treatment. Thus, the concept of like product is significant. The like products analysis is not only relevant in Article 1.1, but also fundamental in Articles 2.2(a), 3.2, 3.4 and 6.1(a) of the GATT, etc, which has been formularized by the border tax adjustment standard by taking into account four elements: physical features, end use, consumer habits and tariff code (HS code), and is shown in the following example.

In *Spain–Coffee*, Spain had divided unroasted coffee into five tariff classification: Colombian mild, other mild, unwashed Arabic, Robusta and other. The first two were duty-free and the other three were subject to a 7% duty. Brazil claimed that all these were like products and different rates of duty were inconsistent with Article 1 of the GATT. The Panel noted that the classification was based on geographical factors, cultivation methods, or the processing of the beans. The Panel did not consider such grounds as sufficient for differentiation and no other member made such classification. Furthermore, the Panel found that unroasted coffee was mainly sold in the form of blends, combining various types of coffee, and that coffee in its end-use was universally regarded as a well-defined and single product intended for drinking. Besides, the Panel found that certain types of coffee were produced by the same kind of coffee beans. Thus, the Panel concluded that the five tariff classifications of unroasted coffee were to afford more preferential treatment to certain degree.

Thirdly, the MFN treatment has to be extended to members immediately and unconditionally. If a Member formulates an improved set of rules on the trade of goods within the framework of GATT 1994, it cannot limit the application of these rules to only those Members that fulfill some conditions. For example, on 7 November 1952, Norwegian and Danish representatives submitted an objection regarding the application of Belgian law levying a charge on foreign goods purchased by public bodies when those goods originated in a country whose system of family allowance and income tax law did not meet specific requirements as prescribed by Belgium's government. The government of Belgium at that time had a system of granting exemption from a levy to products purchased by public bodies only from countries which had a system of family allowance and income tax system similar to that of Belgium. Thereby, products originating in Luxemburg, the Netherlands, France, Italy, Sweden and the United Kingdom were provided such exemption, while a 7.5% levy was imposed on products originated from Denmark and Norway. The Panel on Belgian Family Allowances set up to examine this issue held this practice to be inconsistent with the principle of MFN treatment as, apart from other problems, it introduced an element of conditionality in the application of an advantage. The Panel concluded that since the Belgian government had granted exemptions from the levy to products originating in Luxemburg and the Netherlands, among other countries, it is clear that such exemption would have to be granted unconditionally to all other contracting parties, including Denmark and Norway.[①]

The MFN rule on service has different implications to the Members. Each Member shall accord immediately and unconditionally to services and service suppliers of any other Member treatment no less favorable than that it accords to like service and service suppliers of any other country. That is, no less favorable treatment is not only to be given to like service, but also given to the like service suppliers. For example, if a Member allows a foreign bank to operate within its territory, this benefit must be granted immediately and unconditionally to the service suppliers from other WTO members. However, the MFN rule on service is not a binding requirement that must be uniformly observed like the MFN treatment on goods, due to the MFN exemption provisions in the multilateral trade negotiation on service.

① Excerpt from GATT Dispute Settlement Report, Belgium–Family Allowances (Allocations Familiales), BISD 1S/59, adopted on 7 November 1952.

Although it is a general principle, the MFN treatment is not absolute. There are several exceptions that allow Members to deviate from this principle to provide more favorable treatment to others, without extending the treatment to all WTO members. The most widely used exceptions are evidenced in Articles 16, 20, 21 and 24 of the GATT.

To be more specific, the GATT allows the Members to promote international trade through regional economic integration. Hence, Article 24 of the GATT allows Members to create customs unions and free trade areas (FTA) and afford more favorable treatment among the parties in such customs unions and free trade areas.

The FTA refers to an economic group that a few states have reduced or eliminated tariffs among themselves, but maintain their own individual tariffs in dealing with other states, while customs union means that a group of states not only have reduced or eliminated tariffs among themselves, but also have established a common external tariff.

It is under this exemption that several regional economic groups such as the European Economic Community, the North American Free Trade Agreement, Comprehensive Progressive Trans-Pacific Partnership (CPTPP) and Regional Comprehensive Economic Partnership (RCEP), have been formed, and have maintained more favorable treatment with respect to tariff and non-tariff measures inside the groups.

Sometimes, countries need to restrict trade to protect their social value, so restrictions against imports from specific sources that protect public health, safety, welfare of humans and animals and national security are allowed by Article 20 and Article 21 of the GATT, even though the restrictions cause discrimination against products originating from different nations. This is also a manifestation of MFN exemption.

Further, pursuant to Article 16 hereof, an importing state can adopt measures to counter dumping and subsidization. Such measures are usually taken in form of anti-dumping duties or countervailing duties, which are importing duties targeting at specific products sold by specific exporters.

Preferential treatments afforded to the developing states according to the Generalized System of Preference (GSP system) is also exempted by the MFN treatment. The GSP system, also named the enabling clause or differential and more favorable treatment, reciprocity and fuller participation of developing countries, is contained in the Decision of the Contracting Parties of 28 November 1979. It allows members to accord differential and more favorable treatment to developing countries without affording such treatment to other members.

The other exceptions to MFN treatment include advantages accorded by a member to adjacent countries in order to facilitate frontier traffic permitted by Article 24.3 of GATT 1994 or benefits given by the plurilateral agreements such as Government Procurement Agreement, which is only applicable to its signatories.

6.2 National treatment and its exceptions

National treatment principle prescribes the obligation that an imported product, after entering the country of import, should be treated as a national product. The obligation is contained in Article 3 of GATT 1994, which requires that the imported product must not be subject to internal taxes or other internal charges in excess of those applied to like domestic products. And it must not be accorded treatment less favorable with respect to laws, regulations and requirements affecting their sale, purchase, transportation, distribution or use. Furthermore, a member cannot have any quantitative regulation requiring compulsory utilization of a product from a domestic source in preference to using a like imported product, or it cannot apply internal taxes or other internal charges or internal quantitative regulations in a manner so as to afford protection to domestic production.

In realm of trade in goods, the national treatment is stipulated by Article 3 of the GATT, which consists of three paragraphs. Paragraph 1 of Article 3 articulates a general principle that internal measures should not be applied so as to afford protection to domestic production. This principle is elaborated on in Article 3.2 with regard to internal taxation, and in Article 3.4 with regard to internal regulation.

Article 3.2 is further elaborated by two sentences, which are applied in slightly different situations. The first sentence reads that the products of the territory of any Contracting Party imported into the territory of any other Contracting Party shall not be subject, directly or indirectly, to internal taxes or other internal charges of any kind in excess of those applied, directly or indirectly, to like domestic products.

Judged from the paragraph, a Member challenging the first sentence of Article 3.2 shall establish two elements: (a) the imported and domestic products are like products; and (b) the imported products are taxed in excess of the domestic products.

For example, in *Japan–Alcoholic Beverages II*, the internal tax imposed on domestic shochu was the same as that imposed on imported shochu in Japan. The higher tax imposed on imported vodka was also imposed on domestic vodka. It appeared that identical products were thus taxed identically. However, the question was whether shochu and vodka should be considered to be like products. The Appellate Body found that shochu and vodka were like products, hence Japan breached Article 3.2.

The second sentence of Article 3.2 of the GATT, which requires no Member shall otherwise apply internal taxes or other internal charges to imported or domestic products in a manner contrary to the principles set forth in Paragraph 1, that is, to afford protection to domestic production has not been frequently challenged by Members as the first sentence. Interpreted by the Appellate Body, this sentence lays different requirements on Members. Firstly, the imported products and the domestic products are "directly competitive or substitutable products", the scope of which is broader than like products. Secondly, the directly competitive or substitutable imported and domestic products are "not similarly taxed". Thirdly, the dissimilar taxation of the directly competitive or substitutable imported and domestic products is "applied … so as to afford protection to domestic production". Each of these three elements must be established in identifying a measure that breaches the second sentence of Article 3.2.

Apart from different taxes, different treatment shall not be imposed among imported products and domestic products with respect to the laws, regulations and requirements affecting their internal sale, offering for sale, purchase, transportation, distribution or use, as required by Article 3.4.

Like MFN treatment, national treatment also has exceptions. The WTO covered agreements leave the Members some space for their differential or more favorable treatment to the domestic products. These exemptions are given on procurement of goods by government agencies for governmental purposes only, payment of special subsidies to domestic producers permitted by the Agreement on Subsidies and Countervailing Measures (SCM) or grandfathering clause in accession to the WTO, or screening of domestically produced cinematographic films.

6.3 Transparency

Transparency is also a principle cherished by the WTO. Article 10 of GATT 1994 prescribes the need for the publication of official materials in such a manner as to enable governments and traders to become acquainted with them. This principle implies two obligations to members. One is publication obligation, that is, the Members shall make open and accessible to the public and other governments on its laws, regulations, judicial decisions and administrative rulings of general application, agreements affecting international trade policy, and all relevant measures of general application. The other one is notification obligation, which is further elaborated in the separate agreements of the WTO. For example, Members shall notify its anti-dumping investigations and anti-dumping measures to the WTO every six months.

6.4 Free and fair trade

There is no doubt that the WTO is established on the principle of free trade, even though it has been harassed with various trade protective measures since 2018. The free trade principle requires a Member not to prohibit or restrict the import into or export from its territory. Although customs duty on an imported product is permissible, efforts are to be made in reduction of tariff and cap of tariff.

It is somehow controversial whether fair trade could be deemed as a general principle of the WTO. There are some illustrations of fair trade regulations embedded in the WTO. For example, the anti-dumping measures and countervailing measures, termed as unfair trade remedies, are also claimed to reflect fair trade principle, although it is also argued that these measures tend to be abused.

6.5 More favorable treatment to developing countries

It is argued by many developing countries, that more favorable treatment to developing countries shall be treated as a general principle of the WTO, which is also called the Generalized System of Preference (GSP system) or enabling clause, recorded in the Decision on Differential and More Favorable Treatment, Reciprocity and Fuller Participation of Developing Countries.

The GSP system came into existence under a ten year waiver on GATT Article 1.1 MFN clause in 1971, and it was made permanent in 1979 through the GATT enabling clause that authorized all GSP programs to operate under its provisions as interpreted by the WTO Appellate Body, and also to comply with WTO obligations including the decision on International Labour Organization core labor standards adopted under Paragraphs 4 and 8 of the WTO Singapore and Doha Ministerial Declaration.

The GSP program provides non-reciprocal, duty-free tariff treatment to certain products imported from designated beneficiary developing countries. There is also a graduation mechanism for the GSP programs. When developing countries receiving such non-reciprocal benefits get more advanced, they shall graduate from the GSP system.

Case II-1

EC–Asbestos[①]

Asbestos is a "fibrous mineral of hydrated silicates" which can be divided into two groups: amphiboles and serpentine. There are five varieties of asbestos within the amphibole group: anthophyllite, amosite (or brown asbestos), crocidolite (or blue asbestos), actinolite, and tremolite.

The serpentine group comprises only chrysotile (or white asbestos). These varieties of asbestos have different physical and chemical properties.

They are mainly amosite, crocidolite and chrysolite which are exploited for industrial and commercial purposes. The special qualities of asbestos fibers (for example, resistance to very high temperatures and to different types of chemical attack) due to their particular physical and chemical properties have meant that they have been put to many uses, for example, for the manufacture of industrial and consumer products and in the building industry.

On 24 December 1996, the French Government adopted and issued Decree No. 96-1133 banning asbestos, which provides that "for the purpose of protecting workers, [...] the manufacture, processing, sale, import, placing on the domestic market and transfer under any title whatsoever of all varieties of asbestos fibers shall be prohibited, regardless of whether these substances have been incorporated into materials, products or devices".

It is further clarified, "on an exceptional and temporary basis, the bans instituted under Article 1 shall not apply to certain existing materials, products or devices containing chrysotile fiber when, to perform an equivalent function, no substitute for that fiber is available".

Canada requests the Panel to find that the Decree favors the national industry of products like chrysotile fiber and chrysotile-cement products, contrary to the national treatment disciplines of Article 3.4.

Panel's Finding

The Panel adopted the approach in the Border Tax Adjustments Report, using the four general criteria mentioned above. After reviewing the first criterion, "properties,

① Source: WTO Appellate Body Report, European Communities–Measures Affecting Asbestos and Asbestos-Containing Products, WT/DS135/AB/R, adopted on 5 April 2001.

nature and quality of the products", the Panel "conclude[d] that … chrysotile fibers are like PVA, cellulose and glass fibers" .

Under the second criterion, "end-use", the Panel stated that it had already found, under the first criterion, that the products had "certain identical or at least similar end-uses" and that it did not, therefore, consider it necessary to elaborate further on this criterion.

The Panel declined to "take a position" on "consumers' tastes and habits", the third criterion, " because this criterion would not provide clear results".

Finally, the Panel did not regard as "decisive" the different "tariff classification" of the fibers.

Appellate Body Report

The Appellate Body considered it was inappropriate for the Panel to express a "conclusion" after examining only one of the four criteria. By reaching a "conclusion" without examining all of the criteria it had decided to examine, the Panel, in reality, expressed a conclusion after examining only some of the evidence.

The Appellate Body said:

For the first element, we note that the carcinogenicity of chrysotile fibers has been acknowledged for some time by international bodies. This carcinogenicity was confirmed by the experts consulted by the Panel, with respect to both lung cancers and mesotheliomas, even though the experts appear to acknowledge that chrysotile is less likely to cause mesotheliomas than amphiboles. We also note that the experts confirmed that the types of cancer concerned had a mortality rate of close to 100%.

This carcinogenicity, or toxicity, constitutes, as we see it, a defining aspect of the physical properties of chrysotile asbestos fibers. The evidence indicates that PCG fibers, in contrast, do not share these properties, at least to the same extent.

For the second element, Canada argued before the Panel that there are some 3,000 commercial applications for asbestos fibers. Canada and the European Communities indicated that the most important end-uses for asbestos fibers include cement-based products, insulation, and various forms of friction lining. Canada noted that 90%, by quantity, of French imports of chrysotile asbestos were used in the production of cement-based products. This evidence suggests that chrysotile asbestos and PCG fibers share a small number of similar end-uses.

There is, however, no evidence on the record regarding the nature and extent of the many end-uses for chrysotile asbestos and PCG fibers which are not overlapping. Thus, we do not know what proportion of all end-uses for chrysotile asbestos and PCG fibers overlap. Where products have a wide range of end-uses, only some of which overlap, we do not believe that it is sufficient to rely solely on evidence regarding the overlapping end-uses, without also examining evidence of the nature and importance of these end-uses in relation to all of the other possible end-uses for the products.

For the third element, we have also stated that, in a case such as this one, where the physical properties of the fibers are very different, an examination of the evidence relating to consumers' tastes and habits is an indispensable—although not, on its own, sufficient—aspect of any determination that products are "like" under Article 3.4 of the GATT 1994.

Finally, we note that chrysotile asbestos fibers and the various PCG fibers all have different tariff classifications. While this element is not, on its own, decisive, it does tend to indicate that chrysotile and PCG fibers are not "like products" under Article 3.4 of the GATT 1994.

Discussions:

1. Why does the Panel conclude that the physical properties of chrysotile fibers and PCG fibers are similar?
2. From the AB report, what do you learn from its reasoning on physical properties of chrysotile fibers and PCG fibers?
3. How did Appellate Body examine the functions of chrysotile fibers and PCG fibers?
4. What do you think is the decisive factor of the like product analysis?

Chapter Review

1. What is the predecessor of the WTO?
2. How was GATT established?
3. Discuss why ITO failed.
4. How many rounds of trade negotiation were hosted after GATT 1947 was adopted?

5. How is WTO different from the GATT?
6. What are the mandates and functions of the WTO?
7. Does WTO's membership only include sovereign states?
8. How to become a Member of the WTO?
9. Who is the supreme body of the WTO?
10. What is the relationship among the General Council, TPRB and DSB?
11. What is the function of the DSB?
12. What does consensus mean?
13. What is the decision rule for the authoritative interpretations of the WTO covered agreements?
14. How does reverse consensus work? Name the difference between consensus and reverse consensus.
15. Name the authorities of Ministerial Conference and General Council.
16. Briefly introduce the covered agreements of the WTO.
17. How is a plurilateral agreement different from a multilateral agreement?
18. Does TRIPS require absolute conformity of Members' domestic regulations?
19. What are the agreements adopted in Doha Round?
20. State briefly the basic principles of the WTO.
21. What need to be established in challenging the MFN treatment?
22. What is the like product analysis in the WTO rules?
23. What obligations do Members have under the principle of transparency?

Key Terms

Appellate Body (AB)	上诉机构
consensus	协商一致
customs union	关税同盟
Director-General	总干事
Dispute Settlement Body (DSB)	争端解决机构
enabling clause	授予条款
free trade area (FTA)	自由贸易区
General Agreement on Tariffs and Trade (GATT)	《关税与贸易总协定》
General Agreement on Trade in Services (GATS)	《服务贸易总协定》
General Council	总理事会

generalized system of preferential treatment to developing countries	授予发展中国家的更优惠待遇
Ministerial Conference	部长级会议
most-favored-nation treatment	最惠国待遇
national treatment	国民待遇
non-discrimination	非歧视
panel	专家组
reverse consensus	反向协商一致
Trade Policy Review Body (TPRB)	贸易政策评审委员会
transparency	透明度
working group	工作组

Further Readings

1. Bossche, Peter van den & Werner Zdouc, *The Law and Policy of the World Trade Organization: Text, Cases and Materials*, 4th ed., Cambridge University Press, 2017.

2. Chow, Daniel C. K. & Thomas J. Schoenbaum, *International Trade Law: Problems, Cases, and Materials*, Wolters Kluwer, 2017.

3. Matsushita, Mitsuo, Thomas J. Schoenbaum, Petros C. Mavroidis & Michael Hahn, *The World Trade Organization: Law, Practice, and Policy*, 3rd ed., Oxford University Press, 2015.

4. https://www.worldtradelaw.net.

5. https://www.wto.org.

Chapter 2
GATT and Regulations on Trade in Goods

Study Guide

This Chapter focuses on the disciplines of trade in goods. The Chapter discusses three key issues in deciding the customs duties of goods, which are the country of origin, customs valuation and tariff classification. After that, the Chapter summaries different types of non-tariff barriers such as quantitative restrictions, overvaluation of imported goods, high standards of quality or performance standard and lengthy licensing procedures. Then it further talks about trade remedies such as anti-dumping measures, subsidy and countervailing measures, and safeguard measures. The disciplines on trade remedies, especially the so-called surrogate country methodology, have led to some disputes among the US, EU and China.

The Chapter further clarifies the meaning of technical trade barriers and discusses the non-discrimination and necessity requirements imposed by the Agreement on Technical Barriers. The knowledge about the general exception, security exception, and exception provided to the free trade agreements and customs union are also given in this Chapter.

1 Customs Duties and Relevant Rules

In multilateral trade negotiation hosted by the GATT or WTO, customs duties have been greatly reduced. And the members have adopted rules in the GATT 1994 for the disciplines of customs duties.

1.1 Concept and types of customs duties

Customs duty is also called tariff, defined as governmental charges imposed on goods at the time they are imported into a country. Tariff increases government funds. Governments mainly impose tariffs on goods to collect revenue and protect domestic industries and employment, as it makes the like imported products become more costly after the imposition of tariff. Customs duties can also function as a retaliation or a trade remedy against foreign government's unfair trade policies such as subsidization or exporters' dumping.

Customs duty can be levied *ad valorem*, that is, based on a percentage of the value of the imported product, or levied as a specific tariff. Specific tariff means that the tax is not concerned with the estimated value of the imported goods, but rather is based on specific amount of the goods. This type may apply to the number of goods imported or to the weight, volume or other measurement of the goods. For some goods, tariffs may have two components, one *ad valorem* and the other specific.

Tariff could be prohibitive or protective. A prohibitive tariff is one that is such as high cost that it keeps the item from being imported. A protective tariff is used to raise the price of imported goods as a protective measure against the competition from foreign markets. A higher tax allows a local company to compete with foreign competition.

Protective tariffs can be advantageous as they can help foster the local economy, but sometimes they can also make the price of the item so expensive that companies must charge more. For example, when gas prices become too high, industries such as the trucking industry may have to charge retailers more for delivering products. The retail industry then has to mark up their items to allow for their increased transportation costs in order to make the same profit they once did. The end result is that consumers pay more for the goods.

Disciplines on tariffs are an important part of multilateral trade agreements. Members are forbidden to raise the tariff on a particular product above its scheduled level without compensation to others. The bound levels of tariffs of a Member are recorded in a table which is called the schedule of the Member. When new members enter the WTO, they also submit their schedule for binding tariffs.

Generally, in negotiating tariff reductions, two approaches are adopted. One is reductions based on some general formula or principle for an across-the-board tariff cut, commonly called the formula approach. The other one is product-by-product negotiation based on requests and offers among countries, which is normally used when a new member entered into the WTO.

1.2 Tariff schedule

The bound rate of duty of a Member on different kinds of merchandized goods is recorded on a tariff schedule. The bound level is the Member's committed highest level of its tariff rate on the product (see Table II-2 below). If the Member wishes to raise the tariff on a product above its bound level, it has to offer compensatory concession on some other items agreed by the other Members. The Member wishing to raise the tariff informs the council for trade in goods about its proposal, and the council authorizes a negotiation for this purpose.

Table II-2 A Sample of Tariff Schedule

Tariff Item Number	Description of Products	Base Rate of Duty	Bound Rate of Duty	International Normalized Ratio (INR)	Other Duties and Charges
7415 10	Nails and tacks, drawing pins, staples and similar articles	6.5	4.0		
7906 00	Zinc tubes, pipes and tube or pipe fittings	8.0	5.0		
7907 10	Gutters, roof capping, skylight frames and other fabricated building components	7.0	5.0		

The tariff schedule also includes the tariff quota on a product, if it exists in the case of the particular Member. The tariff quota is the quantity of import up to which a lower financial charges, other than ordinary customs duties, imposed on, or in the context of, the importation of a good.

The tariff schedule records other duties and charges as well. They are financial charges, other than ordinary customs duties, imposed on, or in the context of, the importation of a good. Such duties and charges include an import surcharge, i.e., a duty imposed on an imported product in addition to the ordinary customs duty, a security deposit to be made on the importation of goods, a statistical tax imposed to finance the collection of statistical information, or a customs fee, i.e., a financial charge imposed for the processing of imported goods by the customs authorities.

It is required by Article 2.1(b) of the GATT 1994, that products shall be exempt from all other duties or charges of any kind imposed on or in connection with the importation in excess of those imposed on the date of this Agreement or those directly and mandatorily required to be imposed thereafter by legislation in force in the importing territory on that date.

This means that the Members may only impose "other duties and charges" that have been properly recorded in their Schedules and at a level that does not exceed the level recorded in their Schedules.

1.3 Tariff escalation

The term tariff escalation is used to indicate that the rate of tariff in a country is higher on a product with a higher level of processing than on one with a lower level of processing or on the basic raw material in a product chain. For example, the customs duties of raw materials in US, EU, Canada and Japan are zero, while the leather is imposed on a duty ranged from 3.1% to 7.0%. When the leather is further processed to be leather products, the tariff raises to 4.3% through 12%.

Table II-3 Tariff Escalation on Leather Products

Products	Canada	European Union	Japan	The United States
Raw materials	0.0	0.0	0.0	0.0
Leather	6.6	3.7	7.0	3.1
Leather products	12.6	4.3	9.4	9.0

Tariff escalation has an important implication for the development of the processing of raw materials in developing countries, as they are usually on the low value-added side of product chain. Tariff escalation ensures the developed countries to keep the processing industry with high value domestically. The phenomenon of tariff escalation indicates that developing countries could gain a comparatively smaller share of benefits from global trade.

1.4 Determination of customs duty

In determining the tariff applied to certain goods, three factors shall be taken into account: the harmonized system (HS) classification of the product, its country of origin and the customs valuation.

1.4.1 Classification of imported goods

The proper classification of the imported goods shall be determined at first. Before the International Convention on the Harmonized Commodity Description and Coding System entered into force on 1 January 1988, most countries maintained their own tariff classification systems, which were dramatically different from each other in terms of tariff nomenclatures. Obviously, comparison of tariffs among different countries was difficult, and it was hard to evaluate whether MFN treatment had been given. The harmonization of various tariff classification systems was finally done by the adoption of harmonized system by the World Customs Organization (WCO), which was recognized as customary international law and adopted by most WTO members. The WCO updates the harmonized system approximately every five years.

The harmonized system consists of 21 sections covering 99 chapters, 1,241 headings and over 5,000 commodity groups, each identified by a six digit code, arranged in a legal and logical structure and is supported by well-defined rules to achieve uniform classification.

For example, Section 1 includes five chapters (Chapter 1–5) and covers tariff codes for live animals and animal products. Section 2 ranges from Chapter 6 to 14, covering vegetable products. Section 20, evidenced by Chapters 94 through 96, includes furniture, toys , miscellaneous manufactured articles.

Table II-4 A Sample of Tariff Codes in Harmonized System

Section	XV	Base Metals and Articles of Base Metal
Chapter	74	Copper & Articles Thereof
Heading	7408	Copper Wire
Subheading	7408.21	Wire of Copper-Zinc Base Alloys-Brass

Based on the Rules 2 and 3 of the harmonized system, the classification of finished and unfinished goods shall be decided as follows.

Incomplete or unfinished goods are classified as finished goods when the goods already have the essential character of the complete or finished goods.

When goods are, *prima facie*, classifiable under two or more headings, classification shall be effected as follows:

(a) the heading which provides the most specific description shall be preferred to headings providing a more general description;

(b) when goods cannot be classified as provided under (a), mixtures, composite goods consisting of different materials or made up of different components, and goods put up in sets for retail sale, shall be classified as if they consist of the material or component which gives them their essential character; and

(c) when goods cannot be classified as provided under (a) or (b), they shall be classified under the heading which occurs last in numerical order among those which equally merit consideration.

Goods which cannot be classified in accordance with the above rules shall be classified under the heading appropriate to the goods to which they are most akin, i.e., with which they bear most likeness.

1.4.2 Customs valuation

Secondly customs valuation affects the amount of tariff. And different methods of customs valuation could also become a barrier. To harmonize the customs valuation methods among the Members, the Customs Valuation Agreement was adopted by the WTO members in Uruguay Round.

According to the Customs Valuation Agreement, the value for customs purpose of imported merchandise should be based on the actual value of the imported merchandise on which duty is assessed, or of like merchandise, and should not be based on the value of merchandise of national origin or on arbitrary or fictious values.

The primary basis for the customs value is thus the transaction value of the imported goods, i.e., the price actually paid or payable for the goods. This price is normally shown in the invoice, contract or purchase order.

The Customs Valuation Agreement provides six methods for determining the customs value. If the transaction value of the imported goods appears to be fake, transaction value of identical goods will be adopted by the customs, or the transaction value of similar goods if there is no other identical goods traded to the importing state. The other methods such as the deductive value method, the computed value method and the fall-back method can also be used when necessary.

1.4.3 Rules of origin

The third element influencing the tariff is the country of origin of the product.

(1) Significance of rules of origin

Rules of origin are the criteria used to define where a product was made, and are also used to compile trade statistics and to determine origin of the goods. In customs valuation, the determination of country of origin of the goods must be ascertained. Although based on the MFN principle, once a tariff rate is set for a given product, it applies to all WTO members. However, due to the exception rules, a Member is allowed to apply different tariff rates on the same given product to different countries on the basis of FTA or Customs Union or preferential schemes (such as GSP Program). Therefore, in practice, WTO members generally have several different categories of tariff rates (for a given product) that vary depending on the country of export.

Preferential tariffs are recorded in the tariff schedule, specifically mentioning the names of the Members for whom these are applicable. These preferential tariffs are usually applied to the products of developing countries under the Generalized System of Preferences or applied among some countries as a result of their forming a regional trading area or a free trade area.

Rules of origin are used in following aspects:

— to implement measures and instruments of commercial policy such as anti-dumping duties and safeguard measures;

— to determine whether imported products shall receive MFN treatment or preferential treatment;

— for the purpose of trade statistics;

— for the application of labelling and marking requirements; and

— for government procurement.

In trade practice, the restrictive rules of origin are one of the major factors that produce the enclosing benefits and regional protectionism, and distort the inter-region trade. The more restrictive the rules of origin are, the more severe the fragmentation of the international trade law will be. Hence simplification of rules of origin is believed to be capable of reducing the disparities among the preferential trade agreements themselves.

(2) Rules of origin in WTO covered agreements

The rules of origin currently applied by Members are given by the Agreement on Rules of Origin adopted in the Uruguay Round of multilateral trade negotiation.

Pursuant to Article 3 of the Agreement on Rules of Origin, the country to be determined as the origin of a particular good is either the country where the good has been wholly obtained or, when more than one country is concerned in the production of the good, the country where the last substantial transformation has been carried out.

It is comparatively easy to determine the country of origin if the product is wholly obtained in one country. In the case that a manufactured product is not fully acquired in one country, the country in which the last substantial transformation has been carried out is decided by the domestic law of the importing country. And most of the countries identify the "substantial change" of product according to the change of tariff classification, meeting required local value contents or adoption of specific manufacturing procedures,[①] among which the value contents criteria are most popular. Lowering the value contents

① 参见周芳文：《欧盟、北美优惠性原产地规则对我国的借鉴》，载《国际贸易问题》2011年第8期，第83页。

criteria could benefit more countries and promote *de facto* multilateralization of regional agreements.

To be more specific, the rules of origin adopted by the US and EU in their free trade agreements are very complex and even trade restrictive, especially in their sensitive areas such as textiles, agricultural products, and automotive parts. The rules of origin in North American Free Trade Agreement (NAFTA) have a general requirement of local value content between 50% to 60% to make a product of NAFTA origin. For textiles, more strict rules of origin are adopted in that the yarns used in the textile products must be planted and harvested in the two North American countries to enjoy the tariff benefits.

In negotiating the TPP, the US also requires high local contents to label a product as originated from TPP states. The general rules of origin in TPP requires a local content of 65%, and for the textile products, it requires that the plantation, fabrication, and manufacturing of the product all take place in the region to acquire TPP identity.[①] The local value contents of the Pan-European rules of origin are also high and set to 50% for many products.

On the contrary, the developing countries from the South America, Africa and Asia incline to adopt looser rules of origin instead. The Western Africa Economic Community recognizes a product as a local product if the local value content reaches 30%. The Agreement between Association of Southeast Asian Nations and China (ASEAN 10+1) concluded between the Association of Southeast Asian Nations (ASEAN) and China and the free trade agreement between the ASEAN and the Republic of Korea both identify a local product when its local value content reaches 40%. The lower the value content requires, the more countries that could benefit from the regional trade agreements, especially the developing countries with incomplete industry chains that can participate in only one or two stages of the manufacture.[②]

In negotiating free trade agreements, countries usually allow accumulation of value contents acquired in different countries and could also reduce the trade distorting effects of the rules of origin. The diagonal accumulation and the complete accumulation as adopted by the EU, allow the importers of its treaty partners to accumulate the domestic

---

① See Raj Bhala, *Trans-Pacific Partnership or Trampling Poor Partners? A Tentative Critical Review*, 11 Manchester Journal of International Economic Law 2, 35 (2014).

② For Asian countries, offshore sourcing and processing in different countries are quite common. If the minimum local value content is high, it will be hard to obtain the local identity and enjoy the preferential tariff treatment.

value with the value acquired in the EU and other countries maintaining preferential trade agreements (PTAs) with EU that implement the same rules of origin, hence benefit the spoke countries who have signed PTAs with EU.① Such accumulation rules are also found in the PTAs signed by the US. For example, the US-CRAFTA-DR allows the central American countries to accumulate the values acquired in the processing of a textile product in Canada and Mexico.

In summary, to access the level of customs duty of a specific country, its rules on tariff classification, customs valuation and country of origin all need to be taken into account.

2 Non-Tariff Barriers and Disciplines

It is commonplace to find non-tariff barriers in most countries in one way or another. As tariff is strictly regulated by the GATT, governments are not free to set tariffs under the WTO scheme. They may be incented to introduce non-tariff barriers to restrict imports and afford protection to domestic industries.

Non-tariff barriers are all other forms of trade barriers instead of tariff that have effects of obstructing trade. They may be quantitative restrictions, overvaluation of imported goods, high standards of quality or performance imposed on imported goods, lengthy licensing procedures, and other restrictions that result from prohibitions, conditions, or specific market requirements which make importation or exportation of products difficult or costly. Non-tariff barriers are usually present in the form of government laws, regulations, policies, conditions, restrictions or specific requirements, and private sector business practices, or prohibitions that protect the domestic industries from foreign competition.

Non-tariff barriers are less transparent than tariff, and are more difficult to be detected as they can hide in rules and practices and be disguised by legitimate proposals. Non-tariff barriers can exclude a product from entry of the market, as well as increasing cost. They can take different forms, varying from quota to inspection procedure, health and environmental standard, and overvaluation. As they usually hide in nature and are versatile

① See Won-Mog Choi, *Defragmenting Fragmented Rules of Origin of RTAs: A Building Block to Global Free Trade*, 13 Journal of International Economic Law 111, 111 (2010).

in forms, they are extensively used by many countries.

In Uruguay Round of multilateral trade negotiation, the abuse of non-tariff barrier has aroused Members' attention widely. Several separate agreements attached to GATT have been concluded in the negotiation to prevent non-tariff barriers. They are Agreement on Subsidies and Countervailing Measures, Agreement on Safeguard, Agreement on Technique Barriers to Trade, Agreement on Customs Valuation, Agreement on Import Licensing Procedures, Agreement on Rules of Origin, Agreement on Preshipment Inspection and Agreement on Trade-Related Investment Measures.

For example, a quantitative restriction is a measure which limits the quantity of a product that may be imported or exported. It can take different forms, such as a prohibition, or ban of a product, a quota, automatic and non-automatic licensing, or other quantitative restrictions, such as a quantitative restriction made effective through state trading operations; a minimum price, triggering a quantitative restriction; and a voluntary export restraint. Article 11 of GATT 1994 disciplines the Members' quantitative restriction measures and sets out a general prohibition on quantitative restrictions whether on imports or exports. But this rule has also been subject to various exceptions such as agriculture products, textiles products, general exception and security exception based on Articles 20 and 21 thereof, and regional trading agreements.

3 Disciplines on Trade Remedies

Trade remedies are designed as instruments used by importing states to offset the economic injury caused by unfair trade measures such as dumping and subsidies. They also provide a safety valve to deal with the sudden and unforeseen increased imports. That is, anti-dumping and countervailing measures allow the importing states to counter the unfair advantage enjoyed by the exporting firms, while safeguards are considered as responses to fair practices because they are aimed at offsetting a temporary and unforeseen injurious situation for the domestic industry regardless of the fairness of the action of the exporters.

However, motivated by political and economic reasons, the use of trade remedies has been intentionally expanded to increase the price of foreign products and offer protection to domestic industries. It is admitted by many scholars that trade remedies, especially anti-dumping measures produce negative consequence and have become the new tools of protectionism. Thus, they could be used as a new barrier to trade, even though they are not intended to be protectionist by nature.

Under the WTO law, all trade remedies address a specific action that has to cause injury to the domestic industry of the importing state and which gives the right to the importing country to adopt trade restrictive measures. This is due to the fact that they are aimed at counteracting a practice which is injurious to their domestic industries. Hence, anti-dumping, countervailing and safeguard measures share a similar structure, which is basically composed of three substantive elements: (a) the existence of a particular action (dumping, subsidy or increased imports), (b) an injury to the domestic industry and (c) a causal link between them.① The following section explains the meaning and basic disciplines of dumping, subsidy and safeguard, and measures that are allowed to be adopted under the WTO.

3.1 Anti-dumping measures

Theoretically, the purpose of the anti-dumping duty is to protect domestic firms from international competitors who intentionally reduce the price of products, even lower than the cost of production, to acquire unfair competition advantage. Such practices are described as a predatory practice to eliminate competition. It appeared in 16th through 17th century, but it was not until 1904 that the first anti-dumping law was established.

3.1.1 Definition of dumping

If a company exports a product to a country at a price lower than the price it normally charges on its own home market or in a third country market (Normal Value), it is said to be "dumping" the product (exporting products at abnormally low prices). The low-priced goods are being exported abroad in quantities that may injure competitors in foreign markets.

It is recognized that dumped prices do not reflect costs of production and other expenses the firm bears for the production and marketing of the exported goods, so their presence in the global trade causes unfair competition among domestic and foreign producers. Against such unfair trade measure, anti-dumping actions are usually initiated by the importing countries. Typical action or measure is to charge extra import duty on the particular product in order to bring its price closer to the normal value of the product.

---

① See Roberto Soprano, *WTO Trade Remedies in International Law: Their Role and Place in a Fragmented International Legal System*, Routledge, 2018, p. 47–48.

3.1.2 Development of anti-dumping rules and agreements

The first domestic anti-dumping law was enacted by Canada in 1903. Following Canadian example, New Zealand, Australia, Great Britain and the United States adopted anti-dumping laws between 1905 and 1921.① In 1920s, the countries with anti-dumping regulations attempted to create an international regulation on anti-dumping under the auspice of the League of Nations, but it was not until 1947 that formal anti-dumping rules were concluded during the negotiations for the conclusion of the GATT 1947.

Drawing from the text presented by the United States proposing the introduction of an article containing general principles on anti-dumping and countervailing measures, Parties adopted Article 6 of the GATT. The Article provided a basic discipline on anti-dumping and countervailing duties by defining dumping and authorizing the Members to adopt anti-dumping measures with broad discretion. As the adoption of the GATT commitments was limited by the so called grandfather clause, technically, the US and Canada, the most frequently users of anti-dumping measures, did not need to abide by the Article 6. There was a worldwide concern of abuse of anti-dumping practices.

In 1958, a panel of experts was set up to study possible solutions to the abuse of anti-dumping measures. The panel examined different domestic legislations in order to provide a common discipline aimed at harmonizing domestic legislation and defining the most critical terms which had not been addressed by GATT 1947. The Panel's report influenced the negotiations of the Kennedy Round. And at Kennedy Round of multilateral trade negotiation (1964–1967), a Decision on the Implementation of Article VI of the GATT was made, which clarified some critical terms such as domestic industry and like product in anti-dumping measures. But the Decision was not ratified by the US.

At Tokyo Round (1973–1979), the Anti-Dumping Code was further adopted to reduce the possibility of abuse of anti-dumping measures with an aim of protecting domestic industries. Developing countries such as Egypt also raised its voice to require a reform of anti-dumping rules to reflect the interest of developing countries. The text agreed upon by Parties became the Agreement on Implementation of Article VI of General Agreement on Tariffs and Trade, which amended the Anti-dumping Code 1967 and introduced basic rules for the settlement of disputes concerning anti-dumping.

At Uruguay Round (1986–1994), after fierce debates among exporter countries

---

① See Greg Mastel, *Antidumping Laws and the U.S. Economy*, Routledge, 1998, p. 18.

requiring a significant reform of anti-dumping rules, importer countries who wanted to maintain the original texts, and developing countries wishing the reform would take into account of their needs of development, the Anti-Dumping Agreement was concluded in 1994. The Agreement provided a detailed, specific and comprehensive frame for anti-dumping measures. The provisions of Article 6 of GATT 1994 still remain valid insofar as these do not conflict with the Agreement.

3.1.3 Disciplines on anti-dumping measures

Based on Article 6 of GATT and Anti-Dumping Agreement, dumping is not prohibited. Instead, the rules permit members affected to conduct anti-dumping investigations and to impose duties subject to certain elaborated principles and parameters set by the WTO. And it is also required that all Members shall bring their anti-dumping legislation into conformity with the Anti-Dumping Agreement.

Furthermore, the WTO imposes an reporting obligation on Members to notify the Committee on Anti-Dumping Practices (ADP) on their relevant laws and regulations, relevant agencies who have authorities to conduct anti-dumping investigations, and twice annually of any new anti-dumping measures imposed as well as any already in force.

(1) Application of anti-dumping measures

To initiate an anti-dumping investigation, there are three basic conditions or requirements which shall be established by the agencies in charge in the importing state. The authorities shall provide positive evidence to show the facts of dumping, existence of material injury or threat of material injury to the domestic industry, and the causal link between the dumping and the material injury.

(2) Determination of dumping

To determine whether there is dumping and how much the dumping margin is, the export price is to be compared with the normal value.

$$\text{Dumping} = \text{Export Price} < \text{Normal Value}$$

If the export price is less than the normal value, dumping is found, and the price differential is known as the dumping margin. The export price will normally be based on the transaction price at which the foreign producer sells the product to an importer in the importing country or the "constructed export price", which is calculated on the basis of the price at which the imported products are first resold to an independent buyer.

The normal value shall be resorted to the comparable price, in the ordinary course of trade, for the like product when destined for consumption in the exporting country. Three methods of determining normal value are provided in the Agreement.

The first method is to use the price of like product in the exporting/producer's country. The weighted average price during the period of investigation, and usually 1.5 years is preferable.

Alternatively, if insufficient quantities of like product are sold in the exporting country, or if the quantity sold within the exporting country is less than 5% of the sales to the importing country, the price of like product sold to third countries could be adopted.

If these two methods are neither available, the constructed value can be taken. The authorities would calculate the cost occurred in the manufacture of the product in the exporting country plus reasonable costs for administrative, selling, and other costs, and for profit. As the normal value is reflected as the prices or costs in exporting countries or third countries, the prices or costs should be converted into the currency of the importing country in order to make comparison. And the exchange rate used for the comparison is on the date of sale.

The following chart shows the normal three methodologies in calculating the normal value.

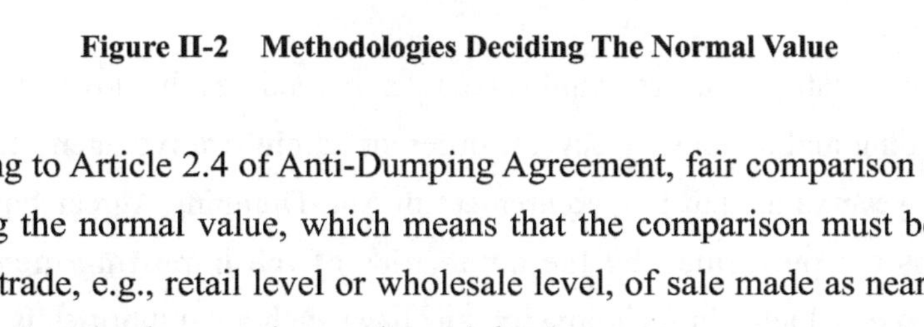

Figure II-2 Methodologies Deciding The Normal Value

According to Article 2.4 of Anti-Dumping Agreement, fair comparison shall be made in determining the normal value, which means that the comparison must be made at the same level of trade, e.g., retail level or wholesale level, of sale made as nearly as possible at the same time, and value or price on the weighted average.

(3) Determination of injury

Injury is a fundamental element that must be positively established in anti-dumping investigation. The Anti-Dumping Agreement divides injury into three types: (a) material injury to a domestic industry of the importing member producing the like product;

(b) threat of material injury to a domestic industry of the importing member producing the like product; (c) material retardation of the establishment of a domestic industry.

The Anti-Dumping Agreement does not define material injury, but it requires that a determination of injury must be based on positive evidence and involve an objective examination of (a) the volume of dumped imports; (b) the effect of the dumped imports on prices on domestic market for the like product; and (c) the consequent impact of the dumped imports on domestic producers of the like product. States are required to examine specific factors which could show whether or not the domestic industry is suffering from the dumping.

According to Article 3.4 of the Anti-Dumping Agreement, the examination of the impact of the dumped imports on the domestic industry concerned shall include an evaluation of all relevant economic factors and indices having a bearing on the state of the industry, including actual and potential decline in sales, profits, output, market share, productivity, return on investments, or utilization of capacity; factors affecting domestic prices; the magnitude of the margin of dumping; actual and potential negative effects on cash flow, inventories, employment, wages, growth, ability to raise capital or investments.

(4) Determination of causal link

To determine the causal link between dumping and injury, the authorities must examine all known factors other than the dumped imports. Those factors at the same time may be injuring the domestic industry (of the like product), including the volume and price of imports not sold at dumping prices, contraction in demand, changes in the pattern of consumption, trade restrictive practices and competition between foreign and domestic producers, developments in technology, the export performance and productivity of the domestic industry.

Dumping investigations are lengthy, complex procedures that involve many hearings, much fact-finding and actions by several different administrative agencies and courts. It could last for years, although the requirement in Anti-Dumping Agreement is 18 months. Investigations are performed by the authorities of the importing member (alleging dumping).Who or which administrative organs have such an authorities is the matter of a national law.

3.1.4 Anti-dumping measures

Anti-dumping measures could be taken by the importing country after a final positive finding of dumping, casual link and material injury has been made, it can also be made before the investigations are complete as provisional measures.

(1) Provisional measures

Provisional measures refer to measures applied before the conclusion of all investigations by the authorities of the importing member after preliminary affirmative determination has been made of dumping and consequent injury to a domestic industry during the period of investigation.

Provisional measures may take one of the following forms: provisional duty or preferably a security by cash deposit or bond equal to the amount of the anti-dumping duty provisionally estimated.

Provisional measures shall not be applied sooner than 60 days from the date on initiation of the investigation, and be limited to as short a period as possible, not exceeding four months, and under special circumstances may be extended to six to nine months.

(2) Final anti-dumping measures

If after the completion of the investigations, all the conditions for applying the anti-dumping measures exist, the authorities of the importing member will take the final anti-dumping measures.

The authorities will issue a final anti-dumping order, which should remain in force only as long as necessary to remedy the dumping that causes the injury and to impose an anti-dumping duty on the dumped imports. The anti-dumping duty is usually a surcharge on the normal tariff charged for that product. The level of the duty may be either the full margin of dumping or less. The Agreement requires Members to collect duties on a non-discriminatory basis on imports from all sources found to be dumped and causing injury, except with respect to sources from which a price undertaking has been accepted.

(3) Price undertaking

The price undertaking is the voluntary action of the foreign exporters or producers (of the dumpling goods) to revise its prices so as to eliminate the dumping margin; or to cease exports at dumped price. If the price undertaking is satisfactory, the anti-dumping duty may not be imposed.

3.1.5 Magnitude of dumping measures

The magnitude of dumping measures cannot be higher than the dumping margin, and is influenced by the *de minimis* rule.

No anti-dumping measure is taken, if dumping is *de minimis*. The *de minimis* limit for the dumping margin is 2% of the export price, and the *de minimis* limit for volume of the dumped import is 3% of the like product in the importing country.

If countries individually account for less than 3% of imports of the like product in the importing country, but they collectively account for more than 7% of imports of the like product in the importing country, *de minimis* rule will not apply and anti-dumping measure may still be taken.

In terms of duration of anti-dumping measure, an anti-dumping duty shall remain in force only as long as and to the extent necessary to counteract dumping which causes injury. Once there is evidence showing that the injury has been offset/eliminated or lessened or the situation has otherwise changed, the interested parties may request the authorities to examine whether the continued imposition of the anti-dumping duty is necessary. If as a result of the review, the authorities determine that the anti-dumping duty is no longer warranted, it shall be terminated immediately.

3.1.6 Challenge of anti-dumping measures before the WTO

Members may challenge the imposition of anti-dumping measures and may raise all issues in compliance with the requirements of the Agreement before a panel established under the DSU.

However, the role of the panel is very much limited, in that, the panel cannot give a finding whether or not a particular measure is inconsistent with the obligation of the Member. The role of the panel is limited to determining whether the authorities of the importing country have established the facts properly and whether they have evaluated the facts in an unbiased and objective manner. China, as an inexperienced user of anti-dumping measures, has also been challenged by other countries when it began to adopt such measures.

For example, on 20 September 2011, the United States requested consultations with China concerning China's measures imposing anti-dumping and countervailing duties on broiler products from the United States.

The United States claimed that the measures appeared to be inconsistent with various provisions of the Anti-Dumping Agreement related to the process of the anti-dumping investigation as well as the anti-dumping duty determination at issue, including improper dumping and injury determination, improper reliance on the facts available, failure to provide access to relevant information, insufficient explanation of the basis for the determinations, absence of proper analysis of the effects of imports under investigation, and absence of objective determination of causality.

The United States claimed that China acted inconsistently with Article 6.2 of the Anti-Dumping Agreement as, despite a specific request from the United States government, the Ministry of Commerce of the People's Republic of China (MOFCOM) did not provide an opportunity for the interested parties with adverse interests to meet and present their views. The Panel upheld the claim as it found that no evidence on the record supported China's assertion that MOFCOM had contacted these Chinese interested parties, and MOFCOM had taken no other action to organize a meeting between the US government and these parties.

The United States also claimed that MOFCOM did not require non-confidential summaries of information in the Petition and thus hampered the US interested parties' ability to defend their interests. The Panel upheld the United States' claims that to the extent the non-confidential version of the Petition constituted non-confidential summaries, which did not satisfy the requirement in Articles 6.5.1 of the Anti-Dumping Agreement and Article 12.4.1 of the SCM Agreement to provide a reasonable understanding of the information submitted in confidence.

The United States claimed that MOFCOM failed to disclose certain essential facts under Article 6.9 of the Anti-dumping Agreement to the individual US respondents and under both Article 6.9 of the Anti-dumping Agreement and 12.8 of the SCM Agreement with respect to the calculation of the "all others" rates. The Panel upheld these claims.

Compared with China, the US and EU are the major users of anti-dumping and countervailing measures. And most of their measures against Chinese exports are not in full conformity with the ADA and SCM Agreement, which has attracted China's challenging before the dispute settlement mechanism of the WTO. The following Section 3.4 shows how China, the US and EU wrested on the utilization of trade remedies.

Case II-2

EU–Footwear (China)①

On 4 February 2010, China requested consultations with the European Union concerning three EU measures in connection with the imposition of anti-dumping

① Source: WTO Panel Report, European Union–Anti-Dumping Measures on Certain Footwear from China, WT/DS405/R, adopted on 22 February 2012.

duties on imports of certain leather footwear from China. In particular, China is challenging Article 9(5) of the Basic EC Anti-Dumping Regulation, which provides that, in cases involving imports from NME countries, the anti-dumping duty shall be specified for the supplying country concerned and not for each individual supplier (countrywide duty rule). According to China, applicable WTO rules require that an individual margin and duty be determined and specified for each known exporter and producer and not for the supplying country as a whole (company specific rule). China states that the Basic Regulation provides that an individual duty will only be specified for exporters that demonstrate that they fulfill the criteria set forth in Article 9(5), the individual treatment rules, and is therefore inconsistent with various provisions of the WTO Agreement, China's Protocol of Accession, the GATT 1994, and the Anti-Dumping Agreement.

The Panel concluded that Article 9(5) of the Basic AD Regulation was "as such" inconsistent with the European Union's obligations under Articles 6.10, 9.2 and 18.4 of the AD Agreement, Article 1.1 of the GATT 1994, and Article 16.4 of the WTO Agreement, and that the application of Article 9(5) of the Basic AD Regulation in the footwear original investigation was inconsistent with Articles 6.10 and 9.2 of the AD Agreement.

The Panel found that the European Union acted inconsistently with Article 2.2.2(iii) of the AD Agreement with respect to the determination of the amounts for SG&A and profit for one producer-exporter in the original investigation, and that the European Union acted inconsistently with its obligations under Articles 6.5 and 6.5.1 of the AD Agreement with respect to the confidential treatment, or the non-confidential summarization, of certain information in the original investigation and the expiration review.

Discussions:

1. What does countrywide duty mean? What does company specific duty mean?

2. Does Anti-Dumping Agreement allow Members to impose "countrywide duty" instead of "company specific" duty on anti-dumping investigations?

3. Did Article 9(5) of EU's Basic AD Regulation conform with the Anti-Dumping Agreement?

4. What is EU's rationale of imposing countrywide duty on China's exported footwear?

3.2 Subsidy and countervailing measures

Subsidies are a very sensitive matter in international trade relations. On the one hand, subsidies are commonly used by governments to pursue and promote important and fully legitimate objectives of economic and social policy. On the other hand, subsidies may have adverse effects on the interests of trading partners whose industry may suffer, in its domestic or export markets, from the unfair competition from subsidized products. Subsidies are considered unfair because subsidized firms practice export prices which are artificially low due to the government's financial contribution.

Subsidies have different effects in the importing country. Imports of subsidized products may harm the domestic producer industry, but may benefit the consumers and user industries.

3.2.1 Concept of subsidy

The official meaning of subsidy is given by Article 1.1 of the SCM Agreement. A subsidy is a financial contribution by a government or any public body that can be a direct transfer of funds, foregone revenue, providing goods and services, or government payments to particular funding mechanisms, or forms of income or price supports, conferring a benefit.

Based on Article 1.1 of the SCM Agreement, there are four elements constituting a subsidy. Firstly, a subsidy must be a financial contribution. Not every form of governmental action can be considered a financial contribution. Article 1.1 of the SCM Agreement restricts the financial contribution to three forms. They can be a direct transfer of funds in forms of grants, loans and infusion of equity, or potential direct transfer of funds or liabilities such as loan guarantees; a government revenue that is otherwise due is foregone or not collected such as tax credits or tax exemption; provision of goods and services (other than general infrastructure), or purchase of goods, or any form of income or price supports in the sense of Article 16 of GATT 1994.

Secondly, a subsidy shall be provided by a government or any public body. Governments include both the central government and local governments of a Member. It is less obscure as compared to the meaning of public body. In *US–Countervailing and Anti-Dumping Measures*, the Appellate Body acknowledged that public body can include enterprises that exercise government authority.

It is possible for a government to circumvent SCM Agreement by directing a private entity to provide subsidies to specific enterprises. In order to avoid this, in *US–*

Countervailing and Anti-Dumping Measures, it was acknowledged by the Panel that the SCM Agreement should be extended to any case in which a government makes payments to a funding mechanism, or entrusts or directs a private body to carry out one or more of the types of functions, which would normally be vested in the government and the practice, in no real sense, differs from practices normally followed by governments.①

Thirdly, a subsidy must confer a benefit to the recipient. In *Canada–Aircraft*, the Appellate Body explained: the word "benefit" implies some kind of comparison. This must be so, for there can be no "benefit" to the recipient unless the "financial contribution" makes the recipient "better off" than it would otherwise have been, absent that contribution. In brief, a benefit arises if the recipient has received a "financial contribution" on terms more favorable than those available to any recipient in the market.

Lastly, it is also required that the subsidy must be specific. Article 2 of the SCM Agreement further restricts the application of the SCM to specific subsidies. A subsidy is specific if access to it is explicitly limited to specific enterprises or specific industries. Thus, the SCM Agreement distinguishes between four types of specificity.

(a) Enterprise specificity, that is, a situation in which a government targets a particular company or companies for subsidization;

(b) Industry specificity, that is, a situation in which a government targets a particular sector or sectors for subsidization;

(c) Regional specificity, that is, a situation in which a government targets producers in specified parts of its territory for subsidization; and

(d) Prohibited subsidies, that is, a situation in which a government targets export goods or goods using domestic inputs for subsidization.

It shall be noted that some scholars think the specificity shall not be regarded as an element of subsidy within the meaning of Article 1.1 of the SCM Agreement, and it is only a requirement for actionable subsidy.

3.2.2 Development of international rules on subsidy

Although subsidies are a widespread practice which was already employed in the mercantilist era, the first international rules were only provided for by Article 16 of GATT in 1974. Before the adoption of the GATT, only domestic rules regulated the use of countervailing measures against subsidies, allowing the importing state the possibility of

① See WTO Appellate Body Report, United States–Definitive Anti-Dumping and Countervailing Duties on Certain Products from China, WT/DS379/AB/R, adopted 11 March 2011, paras. 135–136.

levying duties on imports of allegedly subsidized goods.

At the conclusion of the Tokyo Round in 1979, a specific subsidies code was agreed after years of negotiations delayed by the initial opposition of the United States and the European Communities. The US position was aimed at maintaining its 1930 Tariff Act rules which, by virtue of the grandfather clause, allowed it to levy countervailing measures without showing evidence of injury to its domestic industries. Similarly, the European Communities did not want to commit to any text that could limit its Common Agricultural Policy. One of the main changes in the GATT rules that negotiators achieved during the Tokyo Round was a stringent prohibition against granting of any export subsidies to non-primary products.①

The SCM Agreement entered into force in 1995 and applies to subsidies and countervailing duties on all industrial goods. The SCM Agreement is sufficiently extensive and detailed in setting disciplines for subsidies. There are 32 articles in the Agreement. The basic parts of the new code are:

Part I General Provisions;

Part II Prohibited Subsidies (Red Light);

Part III Actionable Subsidies (Yellow or Amber);

Part IV Nonactionable Subsidies (Green Light); and

Part V Countervailing Measures.

Earlier disciplines include Article 16 of GATT 1994 and countervailing duties by Article 6 of GATT 1994.

3.2.3 Types of subsidy

Subsidies can take different forms. They may be granted to producers or consumers, be specific or general in nature. They can also be direct or indirect. The main distinction in international trade rules is between domestic and export subsidies. A domestic subsidy is granted to a recipient for the production of a good regardless of whether the good will be exported or sold in the domestic market. An export subsidy, on the other hand, is granted to the recipient on the condition that the good be exported. The export subsidies, lower the price of the good in foreign markets and may distort competition in the global market(s) where the subsidized product is exported.②

---

① See Roberto Soprano, *WTO Trade Remedies in International Law: Their Role and Place in a Fragmented International Legal System*, Routledge, 2018, p. 76.

② See Roberto Soprano, *WTO Trade Remedies in International Law: Their Role and Place in a Fragmented International Legal System*, Routledge, 2018, p. 78.

The SCM identifies three different types of subsidy and its disciplines on subsidies adopt the "traffic light approach" to differentiate the rules for prohibited, actionable and non-actionable subsidies. Such approach is significant in setting rules against subsidies, as it shall be noted that the subsidy and countervailing measures do not require the element of wrongfulness. But the differentiation among permissible subsidy, actionable subsidy and prohibited subsidy, somehow reflects the wrongfulness of various subsidies and Members' different attitudes toward them.

(1) Permissible subsidy

"Green light" subsidies mean non-actionable subsidies, which are permissible, indicating Members' willingness to allow governments to intervene in the market by subsidizing their industries. Two types of subsidy are permitted in the sense that no counteraction against them is normally allowed. One is subsidy which is of a general nature, i.e., a subsidy which is not specific to particular enterprises (industrial units) or industries (various industrial sectors); and a subsidy which, though specific, is meant for research or development of disadvantaged regions or environmental purposes.

However, permissible subsidies are no longer in force after the expiration of the time limit provided by Article 31 of the SCM Agreement in 1999, as Members have not reached a further agreement on permissible subsidies.

(2) Prohibited subsidy

Prohibited subsidies are named as "red light" subsidies. Two types of subsidy are identified as prohibited subsidies. There are export subsidies and import substitution subsidies. To be more specific, under Article 3 of the SCM Agreement, a WTO member is prohibited from granting or maintaining subsidies that are: (a) contingent, in law or in fact, whether solely or as one of several other conditions, upon export performance, including those illustrated in Annex I; (b) contingent, whether solely or as one of several other conditions, upon the use of domestic over imported goods. They are prohibited as they distort international trade and competition directly. Prohibited subsidies are per se specific, and the provision of Article 2.3 of the SCM Agreement does not require that in the case of export subsidies a specificity test shall be conducted in order to demonstrate that a subsidy is limited to certain enterprises.

(3) Actionable subsidy

If a subsidy of a Member causes adverse effects to the interests of other Members, action can be taken against the Member.

3.2.4 Requirements of countervailing measures and remedies to counteract the negative effects of subsidy

To impose countervailing duty on the subsidized goods, the authorities in the importing states shall conduct a detailed process of investigation to determine the existence of a subsidy which is prohibited or actionable, the existence of injury to the domestic industry of the affected member, and the existence of a causal link between subsidy and the injury.

Article 5 sets three types of adverse effects as injury to the domestic industry of another WTO member. First, there is injury to a domestic industry caused by subsidized imports in the territory of the complaining Member. This is the sole basis for countervailing action. Second, there is serious prejudice. Serious prejudice usually arises as a result of adverse effects (e.g., export displacement) in the market of the subsidizing Member or in a third country market. Thus, unlike injury, it can serve as the basis for a complaint related to harm to a Member's export interests. Third, there is nullification or impairment of benefits accruing under the GATT 1994. Nullification or impairment arises most typically where the improved market access presumed to flow from a bound tariff reduction is undercut by subsidization.

Adverse effects not only include material injury or threat material injury to an established industry, but also include a material retardation to the establishment of an industry within the territory of another WTO member. Serious prejudice is defined by Article 6.3 of the SCM Agreement as import displacement or impediment, significant price undercutting or suppression, price depression or lost sales in any market or a decrease in world market share.

The assessment of causality in trade remedies includes a positive and negative test. First of all, in order to impose anti-dumping, countervailing or safeguard measures the relevant agreements require that a causal link between the dumping, subsidy and increased imports and injury exists and can be proved. Authorities need to prove that a link of causality exists between the act and injury. They need to prove that there is a link between the cause and effect. In other words, injury is caused by the dumped, subsidized or increased imports.[①]

For prohibited and actionable subsidies, Member can challenge the subsidy through

① See Roberto Soprano, *WTO Trade Remedies in International Law: Their Role and Place in a Fragmented International Legal System*, Routledge, 2018, p. 99.

the dispute settlement process, or impose countervailing duty on the subsidized goods.

In cases where material injury of this threat exists, both options for a remedy are available. But if there is no material injury, only the first remedy can be exercised.

3.2.5 Procedures for conducting a countervailing investigation

Like the anti-dumping investigations, the conduct of countervailing investigations of the importing country also needs to follow certain procedures.

(1) Application of the industry

There must be an application of countervailing investigation by the industry, and such investigation can be initiated in several ways.

The authority can initiate the procedure on receiving a written application given by or on behalf of the domestic industry. If there is sufficient evidence of the existence of a subsidy, injury and a causal linkage between the subsidy and the injury, there is no need for a written application.

(2) Preliminary examination

There is a mandatory provision for a preliminary examination of the application. The accuracy and adequacy of the evidence given in the application must be reviewed by the authorities to determine whether the evidence is sufficient to justify the initiation of an investigation.

The application must contain sufficient evidence about the subsidy and, if possible, its amount, the injury or the threat of injury to the domestic industry, and a causal link between the subsidized imports and the alleged injury.

(3) Consultation

Unlike dumping which is performed by private entities, subsidies are usually governmental behavior, therefore, a proper consultation between the importing country and the exporting country is necessary. After an application is accepted and before initiating the investigation, the initiating Member must consult with the Members whose products are the subject of the application to clarify the facts and arrive at mutually agreed solution. If no agreement is reached, the investigation may start.

3.2.6 Countervailing measures

The SCM Agreement provides for three types of countervailing measures: provisional countervailing measures, voluntary undertakings, and definitive countervailing duties.

(1) Provisional measures

After the expiration of 60 days from the initiation of the investigation and before the final determination is made, the Member can take provisional measures if he meets the conditions, which include, an investigation has been formally initiated; a preliminary determination of the existence of subsidy, injury and causal linkage has been made; the authorities consider such measures necessary to prevent injury being caused during the investigation; these measures may be in the form of a countervailing duty guaranteed by cash deposits or bonds; the period of application must not exceed four months; the measures must not be applied sooner than 60 days from the date of initiation of investigation.

(2) Voluntary undertakings

Investigations may be suspended or terminated without the imposition of provisional measures or countervailing duties upon receipt of satisfactory voluntary undertakings under which: the government of the exporting Member agrees to eliminate or limit the subsidy or to take other measures concerning its effects; or the exporter agrees to revise its prices so that the investigation authorities are satisfied that the injurious effect of the subsidy is eliminated.

(3) Definitive countervailing duties

Members may impose definitive countervailing duties only after making a final determination that a countervailable subsidy exists, and the subsidy causes, or threatens to cause, injury to the domestic industry.

(4) Special provisions for developing countries

The rule-making of subsidy and countervailing measures in WTO leaves the developing countries some policy space and flexibilities.

Developing countries have been divided into two groups. One group is Annex VII developing countries, i.e., the Least Developed Countries (LDCs), and those developing countries which are deemed to have GNP per capita less than USD 1000 per annum. The other group is all other developing countries.

Annex VII developing countries are exempted from the prohibition on subsidies contingent on exports. They can continue with such subsidies and introduce new subsidies of this type. However, they have to phase out such a subsidy on a product eight years after they reach export competitiveness in respect of that product.

Other developing country Members are exempted from the prohibition of export subsidies for a period of eight years from 1 January 1995.

For actionable subsidy, a *de minis* requirement applies, that is, the subsidy level is less than 2% *ad valorem*, or volume of subsidized goods is less than 4% of total imports. They are immuned from the countervailing process.

3.2.7 Judicial review by domestic procedures

The SCM Agreement as well as the ADA requests Members to maintain judicial, arbitral or administrative tribunals or procedures for the purpose, *inter alia*, of the prompt review of administrative actions relating to final determinations and reviews of subsidy and countervailing determinations. Such tribunals must be independent of the authorities responsible for the determination or review in question. It is further required by the SCM Agreement that Members shall provide all interested parties who have participated in the administrative proceedings, and are directly and individually affected by the administrative actions with access to review.

Case II-3

Canada–FIT Program①

The FIT Program is a scheme implemented by the government of the Province of Ontario and its agencies in 2009, through which generators of electricity produced from certain forms of renewable energy are paid a guaranteed price per kilowatt hour (kWh) of electricity delivered into the Ontario electricity system under 20-year or 40-year contracts.

Participation in the FIT Program is open to facilities located in Ontario that generate electricity exclusively from one or more of the following sources of renewable energy: wind, solar PV, renewable biomass, biogas, landfill gas, and waterpower. Under the FIT stream, electricity generation facilities utilizing windpower and solar PV technologies must comply with Minimum Required Domestic Content Levels, which must be satisfied in the development and construction of these facilities.

The Appellate Body explained the benefit in an interesting way. It stated:

A distinction should be drawn between, on the one hand, government interventions that create markets that would otherwise not exist and, on the other hand,

① Source: WTO Appellate Body Report, Canada–Measures Relating to the Feed-in Tariff Program, WT/DS426/AB/R, adopted on 24 May 2013.

other types of government interventions in support of certain players in markets that already exist, or to correct market distortions therein. Where a government creates a market, it cannot be said that the government intervention distorts the market, as there would not be a market if the government had not created it. While the creation of markets by a government does not in and of itself give rise to subsidies within the meaning of the SCM Agreement, government interventions in existing markets may amount to subsidies when they take the form of a financial contribution, or income or price support, and confer a benefit to specific enterprises or industries.

We further note that a comparison between renewable energy electricity generators and conventional energy electricity generators requires consideration of the full costs associated with the generation of electricity. In this respect, if, on the one hand, higher prices for renewable electricity have certain positive externalities, such as guaranteeing long-term supply and addressing environmental concerns, on the other hand, lower prices for non-renewable electricity generation have certain negative externalities, such as the adverse impact on human health and the environment of fossil fuel energy emissions and nuclear waste disposal. Considerations related to these externalities will often underlie a government definition of the energy supply-mix and thus be the reason why governments intervene to create markets for renewable electricity generation.

Discussions:

1. From the above statements, in what circumstances the AB believes that Canadian government has conferred a benefit to the domestic renewable energy electricity generator, and in what circumstances the AB believes that the government has not conferred a benefit to the renewable energy sector?

2. Did the AB take into account the environmental effects of conventional energy electricity generators when it compares the cost of renewable energy electricity with it?

3.3 Safeguard measures

3.3.1 Concept of safeguard measures and their significance

Safeguard measures can be defined as an emergency action in form of import restraint measures that a member may take in order to protect its domestic industry from serious injury due to a sudden increase in the quantity of an imported product.

Safeguard measures are different from anti-dumping and countervailing measures, in that safeguard is an emergency mechanism protecting the importing state's industries from sudden and sharp increase of import, while anti-dumping and countervailing mechanisms are designed as trade remedies against unfair trade measures. Safeguard mechanism is vital for the trading system and inherently accompanies the process of liberalization and of structural adjustment that goes along with enhancing market access for imported products.① Trade liberalization will definitely enhance import flows, but the increase in trade flows may be far more than the expected level of the treaty parties, thereby affecting the domestic industry of an importing country. In facing with the sharp increase of imports, the importing country might have the incentive to withdraw from the trade agreement. In that case, the safeguard mechanism provides it with a safety valve without invoking the treaty exiting procedure. This is the exact impetus for the establishment of the safeguard measures in the WTO.

Safeguard measures are acting in opposition to the general rules of not exceeding the bound rate of duty and not applying any quantitative restrictions on imports. Thus criteria are required and disciplines are needed.

3.3.2 Development of multilateral safeguard disciplines

The US has been an active rule-maker of international safeguard rules. The first multilateral safeguard clause was included in Article 19 of the GATT 1947 and brought from the 1943 Trade Agreement between the United States and Mexico. According to John Jackson, Article 19 was a result of United States desires.② Shortly after, the lack of precise rules for the imposition of safeguard measures led to disputes among the Members. The developed countries wished to use such measures on a selective way, while developing countries wanted the measures to be general and non-discriminatory. In *Norway–Restriction on Imports of Certain Textile Products*, the panel ruled that safeguard measures should be applied in a non-discriminatory manner.③ The result of the dispute caused Members to have recourse to grey area measures such as Voluntary Export Restraints

① See Thomas Cottier, Matthias Oesch & Thomas M. Fischer, *International Trade Regulation: Law and Policy in the WTO, the European Union and Switzerland: Cases, Materials and Comments*, Stämpfli Publishing House, 2005, p. 486.

② See John H. Jackson, *The World Trading System: Law and Policy of International Economic Relations*, MIT Press, 1989, p. 233.

③ Excerpt from WTO Panel Report, Norway–Restriction on Imports of Certain Textile Products, L/4959-27S/119, adopted on 18 June 1980.

(VERs) and Orderly Marketing Arrangements (OMAs) to counter the sudden increase of the imports. These measures were taken by the exporting countries under the pressure of strong importing countries. As they were not formally adopted by the importing countries, so the importing countries avoided all the difficulties and compensation required by Article 19 of the GATT. During the Tokyo Round, negotiations were held to make new rules on safeguards but those negotiations did not lead to a conclusion. The first specific agreement on safeguard was the Agreement on Safeguard (Safeguard Agreement), adopted during the Uruguay Round and entered into force in 1995. In Uruguay Round, the grey area measures such as OMAs and VERs were prohibited.

Currently, safeguard measures are governed by Article 19 of GATT 1994 entitled "Emergency Actions on Imports of Particular Products" and the Agreement on Safeguards which is a part of the WTO covered agreements. In brief, safeguard disciplines are laid down as follows. First, certain measures, known as safeguard measures, are permissible temporarily (for limited time period) in situation when the domestic industry suffers serious injuries because of increase in imports. Second, for measures to be taken, a member is required to follow the prescribed procedure. Third, members bear an obligation on notification to the Committee on Safeguards about the safeguard measures taken by them.

3.3.3 Requirements to adopt a safeguard measure

There are three pre-conditions for taking safeguard action. Firstly, there must be an increase in imports.

Article 2.1 of the Safeguard Agreement sets forth the requirement of increase of imports to legitimize a safeguard measure. According to that Article, a Member may apply a safeguard measure if it has determined that a product is being imported into its territory in such increased quantities, absolute or relative to domestic production, and under such conditions as to cause or threaten to cause serious injury to the domestic industry that produces like or directly competitive products. The increase is not necessarily an actual absolute increase, it can also be an increase relative to the domestic production.

In *Argentina–footwear (EC)* and *US–steel Safeguards*, the Appellate Body clarified the "increased imports" requirement. It noted the difference of increase between safeguard measures and countervailing measures, and stated that the increase in imports in a safeguard measure must have been recent enough, sudden enough, sharp enough, and significant enough, both quantitatively and qualitatively, to cause or threaten to cause serious injury.

Each of these four terms add some textures to the requirements of the safeguard measures. The terms "sharp" and "significant" highlight the magnitude of the increase, requiring the increase must be in huge amounts, and the terms "sudden" and "recent" refer to the duration of the increase, indicating that the increase must occur over a relatively short time span.

Secondly, there must be serious injury, which is a higher threshold than the material injury adopted by the Anti-Dumping Agreement and the SCM Agreement that only requires material injury.

Significant injury means a significant overall impairment in the position of the domestic industry, by evaluating the facts that amount and rate of increase in import of a product, market share taken and changes in other parameters. The Appellate Body has recognized the standard of "serious injury" to be very "high" and "exacting". It is significantly stricter than the standard of material injury of the Anti-Dumping Agreement and the SCM Agreement.

Thirdly, there must be a causal link between the increase in imports and significant injury. The test for establishing causation is twofold. One is a demonstration of the causal link between the "increased imports" and the "serious injury or threat thereof"(the causal link sub-requirement). The other one is an identification of any injury caused by factors other than the increased imports and the non-attribution of this injury to these imports (the non-attribution sub-requirement).

Once the constituent elements of safeguard measures are established, the importing countries can take safeguard measures, which may be in the form of increasing tariff or a quantitative measure of quota.

3.3.4 Prescribed procedures for safeguard measures

Safeguard measures must be taken by importing states following prescribed procedures. The members of the WTO should have rules and procedures in place and should have established a competent authority on safeguard actions.

To initiate a safeguard action, the competent authority of a Member will conduct an investigation over three issues: (a) the increase in import, (b) the existence of serious injury or its threat, (c) a/the causal link between the increased import and injury, and make decisions on these matters.

Public notice shall be given to all interested parties and an opportunity given for their active participations. A report is to be published by the authority which contains its findings and reasoned conclusions on the issues.

Once a decision is made by the authority to take a safeguard measure, a Member has to hold consultation with the Members having substantial export interests for purpose of compensation, as the Member applying a safeguard measure is required to give compensation to other Members which would be affected by such a measure. The compensation would generally be in the form of reduction of duties on some products of export interest to the concerned Members. If no agreement is reached, the concerned Members may retaliate by withdrawal of some other concessions already in place, but cannot do so within the first three years.

The safeguard measures are import restraint measures. They may be in the form of either a tariff type of measure (e.g., import surcharge, levy, increased tariff) or a quantitative restriction on the imports of that product. Discipline of safeguard measures applies only if tariffs have to be raised above the bound level.

Like anti-dumping and countervailing measures, the Members bear the obligations on notification to the Committee on Safeguards as regard to their laws, regulations and administrative procedures concerning safeguard measures; counter-notifications on other Members with respect to their relevant laws, regulations, or other measures, if they failed to do so; the nongovernmental measures taken in the form of order market arrangement or voluntary export restraint.

3.3.5 Duration and magnitude of safeguard measures

The duration of safeguard measures depends on what types of measures are adopted. Provisional measures in the form of tariff increase cannot exceed 200 days. The maximum duration of quantitative restriction in the form of the modulated quota is up to four years. For other forms of safeguard measures, the initial duration is up to four years, yet it can be extended, but the total period of measures must not exceed eight years, which can be treated as the "sunset" provision of safeguard measures.

Like anti-dumping and countervailing measures, *de minimis* rule is also applicable in the safeguard investigation. It is required by the Agreement on Safeguard that no action can be taken against a developing country if its exports volume of the product within *de minimis* rate, that is, 3% for any single country, and 9% collectively for a group of countries, on share of imports of the product in the importing member market.

3.4 China's challenge of anti-dumping and countervailing measures imposed by US and EU

In terms of anti-dumping, countervailing and safeguard measures, trade law in the US and EU witnessed a protectionist shift against Chinese products at the expense of sound, consistent principles, based on their so-called Non-Market Economy (NME) trade remedy rules. China disputed the unfair practice against NME countries. And trade law has corrected some of the most egregious protectionist policies on China.①

After 2008, China actively contested the US and the EU in WTO disputes on five issues: surrogate country methodology, countrywide duty, double counting, out-of-country benchmark, and public body determination. The AB defeated the US and EU overprotective measures, and expanded Member's policy space for redressing market distortion.

3.4.1 Surrogate Country Methodology

Originally, GATT 1947 did not contain NME rules. In 1954–1955, the GATT was reviewed by its Members. For reasons unknown,② Czechoslovakia proposed to amend Article 6.1 of the GATT to legitimatize the importing countries' use of a special anti-dumping pricing methodology on products originating from the centric economy countries, that is, a surrogate country methodology, by which the importing countries adopt the price of like products originating from a Market Economy (ME) country as the normal value of the product in calculating the dumping margin.③

The Members finally added a note to Article 6.1 of the GATT (Second Note, *Ad* Article 6.1) that reads:

"It is recognized that, in the case of imports from a country which has a complete or substantially complete monopoly of its trade and where all domestic prices are fixed by the

---

① See Wentong Zheng, *Trade Law's Responses to the Rise of China*, 34 Berkeley Journal of International Law 109, 111 (2016).

② Some scholars thought that the proposal would not make it worse off as it was always subject to such methodologies. See Alexander Polouektov, *Non-Market Economy Issues in the WTO Anti-Dumping Law and Accession Negotiation: Revival of a Two-tier Membership*?, 36 Journal of World Trade 1, 7 (2002)

③ See Article VI Draft Interpretative Note to Paragraph 1 Proposed by the Czechoslovak Delegation, Spec/93/55, adopted 7 February 1955. The proposed text is "In considering the differences affecting price comparability due regard shall be had for the fact that in a country with a complete or substantially complete state monopoly of its trade and all domestic prices fixed by the state such prices have a different economic function than in countries in which domestic prices are established by private trade".

State, special difficulties may exist in determining price comparability for the purposes of paragraph 1, and in such cases importing contracting parties may find it necessary to take into account the possibility that a strict comparison with domestic prices in such a country may not always be appropriate."

Similar provisions were included in the accession protocols or working party reports when NME countries like Poland, Hungary, Albania, China, and Vietnam entered into the GATT and WTO.

China's commitment of NME rules is contained in Paragraph 15 of its Accession Protocol. Paragraph 15(a)(ii) states that,

"The importing WTO Member may use a methodology that is not based on a strict comparison with domestic prices or costs in China if the producers under investigation cannot clearly show that ME conditions prevail in the industry producing the like product with regard to manufacture, production and sale of that product."

In case producers under investigation can satisfy Paragraph 15 (a)(i) to "clearly show that ME conditions prevail in the industry producing the like product with regard to the manufacture, production and sale of that product", domestic prices and costs shall be adopted. With WTO-minus and WTO-plus provisions in the protocol,① and China's privatization was promising, an exemption and a sunset clause were included in Paragraph 15(d) under China's hard negotiation. They provide that,

"Once China has established, under the national law of the importing WTO Member, that it is a ME, the provisions of subparagraph (a) shall be terminated provided that the importing Member's national law contains ME criteria as of the date of accession. In any event, the provisions of subparagraph (a)(ii) shall expire 15 years after the date of accession."

As it is subject to the importing Member's decision whether China is an ME country, China is more attended to the second sentence as it includes a specific sunset clause for the expiration of Subparagraph (a)(ii).②

In *EU–Footwear*, China mounted its first attack on the surrogate country

① See Julia Ya Qin, *Trade, Investment and Beyond: The Impact of WTO Accession on China's Legal System*, 191 The China Quarterly 720, 723 (2007).

② In the bilateral negotiation regarding China's entry into the WTO, it was first proposed that the surrogate methodology in anti-dumping investigations should remain in force for 20 years after China's entry into the WTO, but China required to reduce it to five years. Finally, both the US and China agreed that the period should be 15 years.

methodology based on the fair comparison principle required by Article 2.4 of the ADA.① The Panel left the US and EU ample space for their choice of surrogate country, opining that the fairness requirement in Article 2.4 referred to the comparison between the normal value and the export price after they were established, while the disputed issue was whether the EU had found a proper normal value. In *EU–Fastener*, China made a comeback by persuading the AB to affirm that the surrogate country methodology in China's accession protocol expired 15 years after the date of China's accession.②

3.4.2 Countrywide duty

In the late 1980s, US petitioners began making the argument that a countrywide anti-dumping duty rate should be assigned to Chinese producers or exporters who could not demonstrate an absence of government control over their business operations. The US Department of Commerce (USDOC) rejected this argument, stating that "the former branches of the national trading companies have separated from the national companies and we found no evidence that the prices the branches charge for exports to the United States are set by or coordinated through the national trading companies". The USDOC also noted that in past anti-dumping investigations, it always calculated separate rates for different Chinese national trading companies even though it treated China as a state-controlled economy. In 1991, however, the USDOC made an about-face on the separate-rate issue and denied, for the first time, a request for separate rates by Chinese exporters. Ironically, the move towards countrywide anti-dumping rates for Chinese companies took place at a time when China was undergoing rapid economic reforms that conferred higher degrees of independence from the government on Chinese firms. Arguably, the adoption of countrywide anti-dumping rates for Chinese products comports not with economic principles, but with protectionist policy needs. In calculating countrywide anti-dumping rates, the USDOC often relies on information provided by petitioners and inferences adverse to respondents.③ The EU NME anti-dumping practice kept up with the US practice in adopting the surrogate country methodology and countrywide duty.

---

① Excerpt from WTO Panel Report, European Union–Anti-Dumping Measures on Certain Footwear from China, WT/DS405/R, adopted on 22 February 2012.

② Excerpt from WTO Appellate Body Report, European Communities–Definitive Anti-Dumping Measures on Certain Iron or Steel Fasteners from China, WT/DS397/AB/R, adopted on 28 July 2011.

③ See Wentong Zheng, *Trade Law's Responses to the Rise of China*, 34 Berkeley Journal of International Law 109, 127–128 (2016).

Countrywide duty, when adopted solely based on the fact that the exporting country is not a market economy country, is arbitrary, as exporters, especially private entities, may not be controlled by the government. In *EU–Fasteners*, China argued that countrywide duty was flawed as it did not conform to Articles 6.10 and 9.2 of the ADA, which require that authorities shall determine an individual margin of dumping for each known exporter or producer.① China emphasized that the term "shall" in Article 6.10 established its mandatory nature.

As the text was free of ambiguity, both the Panel and AB sided with China, agreeing that neither Article 9.2 of the ADA, nor Paragraph 15 of China's Accession Protocol justified the imposition of a countrywide duty.② Nonetheless, the AB shifted its ground and did not rule out the possibility that exporters could be treated as a single entity. That is, authorities shall determine an individual margin for each known exporter, but separate exporters can be treated as a single entity if the authorities establish the existence of structural and commercial relationships between them as a single entity.③ The decision required a thorough analysis before the authorities imposed identical countervailing duty on different exporters. Thus, the EU subsequently amended Article 9(5) of Regulation 1225/2009 and required the authority to specify the duty for each supplier and consider factors such as the existence of structural or corporate links between suppliers and the state or between suppliers, or control or material influence by the state over suppliers with respect to pricing and output, or the economic structure of the supplying country in its individual entity test.④

3.4.3 Double counting

Double counting is also called double remedy. It also becomes a disputed issue after the US and EU imposed both anti-dumping and countervailing duties on NME products, and used surrogate country methodology to calculate the normal value of the dumped

---

① Excerpt from WTO Panel Report, European Communities–Definitive Anti-Dumping Measures on Certain Iron or Steel Fasteners from China, WT/DS397/R, adopted on 28 July 2011.

② See WTO Appellate Body Report, European Communities–Definitive Anti-Dumping Measures on Certain Iron or Steel Fasteners from China, WT/DS397/AB/R, adopted 28 July 2011, para. 290.

③ See Chien-Huei Wu, *Key Issues Regarding The EU'S Concurrent Imposition of Anti-Dumping and Countervailing Duties on Chinese Coated Fine Papers: Analogue Country, Market Economy Treatment, Individual Treatment, and Double Remedy*, 10 Asian Journal of WTO & International Health Law and Policy 263, 287 (2015).

④ The amendments exist in Regulation (EU) No. 765/2012.

products.

Initially, the US agency responsible for assessing anti-dumping and countervailing duties initially chose not to apply countervailing duty law to imports from NMEs. The USDOC once thought that subsidies could not be separated from the amalgam of government directives and controls in Non-Market Economy (NME) countries; thus, it was impossible to conduct countervailing measures on NME products. However, it changed course in 2007 and imposed anti-dumping and countervailing duties simultaneously on the same Chinese product. In 2012, the congress passed a regulation legitimatizing the USDOC's concurrent imposition of countervailing and anti-dumping duties.

Double remedy emerged as an issue after the USDOC conducted the countervailing and anti-dumping investigations simultaneously against Chinese exports after 2007. In *US–Definitive Anti-Dumping and Countervailing Duties*, China contended that where anti-dumping duties were calculated pursuant to a methodology that relied on surrogate market-determined values and countervailing duties were simultaneously applied to the same good, any domestic subsidy bestowed upon that good would be offset twice.[①]

Based on Article 19.3 of the SCM Agreement, which states that the countervailing duty must be applied in "appropriate" amounts, the AB supported China and asserted that double remedy was likely to occur in cases in which an NME methodology was used to calculate the dumping margin. In cases in which an NME methodology was used to calculate the dumping margin, the investigating authorities had an affirmative obligation to determine whether and to what degree double remedy would exist.[②]

Following the decision, the US passed H.R.4105 formally authorizing the USDOC to adopt countervailing measures on NME countries together with anti-dumping measures while requiring the USDOC to adjust the anti-dumping duty to avoid double counting. It is interesting that the USDOC maintained the practice of simultaneous imposition of anti-dumping and countervailing duty even though it needed to subtract the double calculated amount. This "unnecessary" move is actually meaningful, indicating that subsidy and countervailing measures will be explored more thoroughly to combat the market distortion.

---

① See WTO Panel Report, United States–Definitive Anti-Dumping and Countervailing Duties on Certain Products from China, WT/DS379/R, adopted 25 March 2011, para. 14.47.

② See WTO Appellate Body Report, United States–Definitive Anti-Dumping and Countervailing Duties on Certain Products from China, WT/DS379/AB/R, adopted 25 March 2011, paras. 541, 602.

3.4.4 Out-of-country benchmark

Regarding the countervailing measures, there were no similar provisions mentioning the special treatment to NME countries. However, in *US–Soft Lumber (IV)*, the AB opined that the investigating authority could refer to an out-of-country benchmark to decide whether the provision of inputs had been remunerated appropriately when the domestic price was distorted due to the dominance of the government in providing the inputs.① Thus Article 14 of the SCM Agreement makes it possible for the importing members to apply out-of-country benchmarks in countervailing investigations against NME countries. It is further specified by Paragraph 15(b) of China's Accession Protocol to the WTO that if there are special difficulties when Members apply Article 14 of the SCM Agreement, the Members can apply the methodology in evaluating subsidy benefits considering the possibility that Chinese domestic situations and conditions are not always suitable to be proper benchmarks.

Ever since the US imposed countervailing duty on NME products, China has disputed its out-of-country benchmark in the price comparison of Chinese bank loans, land use fees, and inputs in the countervailing process.

In the *US–Definitive Anti-Dumping and Countervailing Duties*, China argued that the US failed to make an entirely separate finding that private prices were distorted by virtue of Chinese government's predominant role in rejecting in-country private prices pursuant to Article 14(d).② The Panel and AB did not support China. The AB distinguished government's significant, predominant, or overwhelming role in the market, and stated that Chinese state-owned enterprises (SOEs) played an overwhelming role in the market of the hot-rolled steel, thus, the US rejection of Chinese domestic prices was supported with sufficient investigation and analysis.③ However, in *US–Countervailing Duty Measures*, China succeeded in impugning the US's inappropriate rejection of using Chinese pricing after identifying China as an NME. The AB ruled that the Panel failed to conduct a case-by-case analysis of whether the USDOC had properly examined whether the relevant

① See WTO Appellate Body Report, United States–Final Countervailing Duty Determination with Respect to Certain Softwood Lumber from Canada, WT/DS257/AB/R, adopted 17 February 2004, para. 90.

② See WTO Appellate Body Report, United States–Definitive Anti-Dumping and Countervailing Duties on Certain Products from China, WT/DS379/AB/R, adopted 25 March 2011, paras. 176, 192.

③ See WTO Appellate Body Report, United States–Definitive Anti-Dumping and Countervailing Duties on Certain Products from China, WT/DS379/AB/R, adopted 25 March 2011, paras. 455–456.

in-country prices were market-determined or were distorted by government intervention.① Obviously, the AB did not deviate from the established practice in which the importing country can refer to the out-of-country benchmark in cases of market distortion, but negated the US arbitrary rejection of in-country prices without reasonable analysis.

3.4.5 Determination of public body

The SCM Agreement constrains the scope of subsidy by requiring the benefits to be provided by the government or a public body. A disputed question between China, the US and EU is whether SOEs and state-owned commercial banks (SOCB) should be considered public bodies and therefore capable of conferring subsidies within the meaning of the SCM Agreement. If the SOE input suppliers and SOCB lenders were considered public bodies, then the USDOC would be able to bypass the requirement to show entrustment or direction for those entities, making it much easier to prove the existence of a countervailable subsidy.

The hybrid nature of the Chinese economy created an opening for the US to interpret the term "public body" in ways that made it easier to prove the existence of a countervailable subsidy. The WTO, however, rejected some of those interpretations and required more evidence than mere government ownership in determining whether a Chinese entity is a public body. To be more specific, to include Chinese state-owned commercial banks and SOEs as subsidy providers, the USDOC adopted government control as the standard of a public body.

China challenged this position in *US–Anti-Dumping and Countervailing Duties* and proposed to identify a public body based on its government authority. China quoted the AB's finding in *Canada–Dairy* that the essence of government was its functions, powers, and authority, and contended that the common practice of the US, EU, and Japan was to identify enterprises established by government as private entities unless the objective of setting up these institutions was to perform some authority or function of the government.②

The Appellate Body first disagreed with the Panel's equation of public body with government control, stating that control of an entity by a government, in itself, is not sufficient to establish that an entity is a public body. The AB acceded that a private body

① See WTO Appellate Body Report, United States–Countervailing Duty Measures on Certain Products from China, WT/DS437/AB/R, adopted 16 January 2015, para. 4.79.

② See WTO Appellate Body Report, United States–Definitive Anti-Dumping and Countervailing Duties on Certain Products from China, WT/DS379/AB/R, adopted 25 March 2011, paras. 24–25.

could be a public body in the sense of Article 1.1 (a)(1)(iv), where a government entrusted or directed it to carry out a function that would normally be vested in the government.① Thus, the AB developed a substantive standard of "meaningful control" in that a public body should have power to force or order other private institutions to act or control its act.②

After *US–Anti-Dumping and Countervailing Duties* and *US–Countervailing Duty Measures*, the US revised its public body determination and placed a Pubic Body Memorandum (PBM) on the record of its countervailing proceedings. The PBM identifies any enterprise in China in which the government has a full or controlling ownership interest as a public body, resting upon the finding that the government is exercising meaningful control over all such enterprises, and these enterprises possess, exercise, or are vested with governmental authority.③ China questioned the consistency of such measure. However, the AB rejected China's request by holding that legal standard for public body determinations under Article 1.1(a)(1) of the SCM Agreement did not prescribe a connection of a particular degree or nature that must necessarily be established between an enterprise and an identified government function.④ The AB's position on public body determination again proves its tolerance to the expansion of market distortion rules through WTO jurisprudence while opposing manifestly unfounded regulatory measures.

4 Disciplines on Technical Trade Barriers and Sanitary and Phytosanitary Measures

4.1 Meaning of technical regulation and standard

Technical regulations and standards are rules or requirements that set out specific characteristics of a product such as its size, shape, design, functions and performance, or

① See WTO Appellate Body Report, United States–Definitive Anti-Dumping and Countervailing Duties on Certain Products from China, WT/DS379/AB/R, adopted 25 March 2011, para. 309.

② See WTO Appellate Body Report, United States–Definitive Anti-Dumping and Countervailing Duties on Certain Products from China, WT/DS379/AB/R, adopted 25 March 2011, paras. 292–294, 346.

③ See WTO Appellate Body Report, United States–Countervailing Duty Measures on Certain Products from China, Recourse to Article 21.5 of the DSU by China, WT/DS437/AB/RW, adopted 15 August 2019, para. 5.7.

④ See WTO Appellate Body Report, United States–Countervailing Duty Measures on Certain Products from China, Recourse to Article 21.5 of the DSU by China, WT/DS437/AB/RW, adopted 15 August 2019, para. 6.2.

the way it is packaged or labelled. The specific characteristics of a product usually derive from its nature, but in some cases, the characteristics of a product are affected by way that such product is produced. Thus, it is argued by some exporters that it is more appropriate to draft technical regulations and standards in terms of a product's process and production methods rather than its characteristics per se.

Technical regulations and product standards vary from country to country. This leaves difficulties and obstacles for producers and exporters in complying with the different requirements. Countries lay technical regulations and standards usually to ensure that the product would meet the requirements of certain safety, health, and environmental standards, but if such technical regulations are set arbitrarily, they could be used as a disguised trade barrier for protectionism.

Technical regulations, standards and its conformity assessment procedures are disciplined by the Agreement on Technical Barriers to Trade (TBT), which apply to both industrial and agricultural products, and related process and production methods (PPMs). The objective of the Agreement on Technical Barriers to Trade is to ensure that regulations, standards, testing and certification procedures do not create unnecessary obstacles while also provide Members with the right to implement measures to achieve legitimate policy objectives, such as the protection of human health and safety, or the environment. Countries usually set technical regulations or standards to make domestic products and imported products comply with their requirements.

The TBT Agreement makes difference between a standard and a technical regulation. The former are mandatory requirements, while conformity with standards is voluntary. Hence they differ in compliance. The differentiation of regulation and standard is meaningful. If an imported product does not fulfill the requirements of a technical regulation, it will not be allowed to be put on sale in the importing country. In case of standards, non-complying imported products will be allowed on the market, but then their market share may be affected if consumers prefer products that meet local standards such as quality or environmental standards for textiles and clothing.

To evaluate whether the products comply with the requirements, the importing country usually adopts a conformity assessment procedure for the exporters and importers to comply with. The conformity assessment procedure is a procedure for inspection, sampling or testing, which is used to verify compliance with the requirements set out in technical regulations or standards.

4.2 Disciplines of Agreement on Technical Barriers to Trade

The TBT Agreement does not require all WTO members to follow the same technical regulation and standard. It takes into account the existence of legitimate divergences of taste, priority, culture, geographical and other factors among countries. For these reasons, the TBT Agreement accords to Members a high degree of flexibility in the adoption and enforcement of their national technical regulations. Evidenced by its Preamble, the TBT Agreement states that "no country should be prevented from taking measures necessary to ensure the quality of its exports, or for the protection of human, animal, and plant life or health, of the environment, or for the prevention of deceptive practices, at the levels it considers appropriate". However, Members' regulatory flexibility is limited by the requirement that technical regulations "are not prepared, adopted or applied with a view to, or with the effect of, creating unnecessary obstacles to trade".

The legitimate objectives of technical regulations usually include protection of human lives and health as disputed in *Australia–Plain Package of Tabaco* and *US–Clove Cigarettes*, protection of animal and plant life or health challenged in *US–Shrimp* and *US–Tuna*, or prevention of deceptive practices such as *US–COOL*.

The most frequently quoted provisions of the TBT Agreement are Article 2.1 that lays a non-discriminatory treatment duty to the Members in enacting and enforcing technical regulations and standards, and Article 2.2 that imposes a necessity obligation of Member's technical regulations and standards in terms of trade restrictiveness.

Article 2.1 of the Agreement states that "in respect of their technical regulations, products imported from the territory of any Member be accorded treatment no less favorable than that accorded to like products of national origin and to like products originating in any other country".

This Article 2.1 consists of three elements. Failing one element would establish inconsistency with this provision. The three elements are:

(a) the measure at issue constitutes a technical regulation within the meaning of Annex 1.1;

(b) the imported products must be "like" the domestic product and the products of other origins; and

(c) the treatment accorded to imported products must be less favorable than that accorded to like domestic products and like products from other countries.

The elements and requirements of Article 2.1 of the TBT Agreement are similar to those listed in Article 1.1 and Article 3 of GATT, while the former applies to the technical regulations. The focus of the non-discrimination analysis also lies in the like product analysis.

Article 2.2 of the TBT Agreement requires that the governments shall adopt technical regulations with the least trade restrictiveness to fulfill its legitimate objective to avoid unnecessary obstacles to trade.

For a government, avoiding unnecessary obstacles to trade means that when it is preparing a technical regulation to achieve a certain policy objective, whether protection of human health, safety, or the environment, the negotiations shall not be more trade-restrictive than necessary to fulfill the legitimate objective. According to Article 2.8 of the TBT Agreement, specifying, whenever appropriate, product regulations in terms of performance rather than design or descriptive characteristics will help in avoiding unnecessary obstacles to international trade. For example, a technical regulation on fire-resistant doors should require that the door passes successfully all the necessary tests on fire resistance. Thus it could specify that "the door must be fire resistant with a 40-minute burn through time", instead of, "the door must be made of high quality steel, two inch thick".

Unnecessary obstacles to trade can result in two situations. One is a regulation that is more restrictive than necessary to achieve a given policy objective. And the other one is the regulation does not fulfill a legitimate objective. In the first scenery, a regulation is more restrictive than necessary when the objective pursued can be achieved through alternative measures which have less trade-restricting effects, taking account of the risks non-fulfillment of the objective would create. In the second scenery, a regulation is unnecessary if it contributes nothing to the legitimate objective that the Member pursues.

Further, it is required by Article 2.4 of the TBT Agreement that where technical regulations are required and relevant international standards exist or their completion is imminent, Members shall use them, or the relevant parts of them, as a basis for their technical regulations. Such international standards or relevant parts would be an ineffective or inappropriate means for the fulfillment of the legitimate objectives pursued, for instance because of fundamental climatic or geographical factors or fundamental technological problems.

The following case *US–Tuna (Ⅲ)* shows as below.

Case II-4

US–Tuna (III)[①]

The US's Dolphin Protection Consumer Information Act (DPCIA) was challenged by the EU based on Articles 2.1 and 2.2 of the TBT Agreement.

The Dolphin Protection Consumer Information Act is codified in Title 16, Section 1385 of the United States Code (USC), which reads:

It is a violation of Section 5 of the Federal Trade Commission Act (15 USC 45) for any producer, importer, exporter, distributor, or seller of any tuna product that is exported from or offered for sale in the United States to include on the label of that product the term "dolphin-safe" or any other term or symbol that falsely claims or suggests that the tunas contained in the product were harvested using a method of fishing that is not harmful to dolphins if the product contains tuna harvested.

With respect to tuna products containing tuna caught inside the Eastern Tropical Pacific (ETP), the use of the term "dolphin-safe" or any analogous term is conditional upon a written statement executed by the captain of the vessel and an observer participating in a national or international program acceptable to the Secretary of Commerce, certifying that no purse seine net was intentionally deployed on or used to encircle dolphins during the particular voyage on which the tunas were caught and no dolphins were killed or seriously injured in the sets in which the tunas were caught.

For tuna caught outside the ETP by a vessel using purse seine nets in any fishery, other than a fishery described in Subparagraph (D) of Subsection 1385(d)(1) of the DPCIA, in accordance with Subparagraph (B)(ii), a written statement executed by the captain of the vessel was required, certifying that no purse seine net was intentionally deployed on or used to encircle dolphins during the particular voyage on which the tuna was harvested.

The tuna protection scheme adopted by the Mexico was different from the US scheme, as Mexico participated in the Agreement on the International Dolphin Conservation Program (AIDCP) scheme that was proposed by an international organization that protects dolphins in harvesting tuna. The Parties to the AIDCP adopted the Resolution to Adopt the Modified System for Tracking and Verification of Tuna. That resolution includes the following definitions:

---

① Source: WTO Panel Report, United States–Measures Concerning the Importation, Marketing and Sale of Tuna and Tuna Products,WT/DS381/R, adopted on 13 June 2012.

"Dolphin safe tuna is tuna captured in sets in which there is no mortality or serious injury of dolphins."

Mexican fishery which uses purse seine net, with certification that no dolphin is injured is not allowed to be label as "dolphin-safe" in the US market, even though it met the conditions of AIDCP.

Panel's Finding

The Panel found that the "dolphin-safe" label had significant commercial value on the market, which agreed with Mexico that access to the "dolphin-safe" label constituted an "advantage" on the US market.

In sum, the participants do not contest the following findings by the Panel. First, setting on dolphins within the ETP may result in a substantial amount of dolphin mortalities and serious injuries and have the capacity of resulting in observed and unobserved effects on dolphins. Further, the use of certain fishing techniques other than setting on dolphins causes harm to dolphins. With respect to tuna fishing outside the ETP, the participants do not contest that the vast majority of tuna caught in the Western Pacific Ocean is caught with fish aggregation devices (FADs), trolls, or gillnets, and that US and foreign vessels use these fishing techniques, other than setting on dolphins outside the ETP.

It is also uncontested that the tuna-dolphin association does not occur outside the ETP as frequently as it does within the ETP, and that there are no records of consistent and widespread fishing effort on tuna-dolphin associations anywhere other than in the ETP.

Finally, the participants do not contest that, as currently applied, the US measure does not address mortality (observed or unobserved) arising from fishing methods other than setting on dolphins outside the ETP, and that tuna caught in this area would be eligible for the US official label, even if dolphins have in fact been killed or seriously injured during the trip.

In these circumstances, we are not persuaded that the United States has demonstrated that the measure is even-handed in the relevant respects, even accepting that the fishing technique of setting on dolphins is particularly harmful to dolphins.

Discussions:

1. Was "dolphin-safe" label mandatory when selling tuna in the US market? Is the label a technical regulation or a technical standard?

2. Can you explain the difference between AIDCP program and the US scheme?

3. Does US's Dolphin Protection Consumer Information Act breach Article 2.1 of the TBT Agreement regarding the fishing method requirement within the ETP? Does it breach the Article regarding the fishing method requirement outside the ETP?

Case II-5

US–Clove Cigarettes[①]

This dispute concerns a tobacco-control measure adopted by the United States that prohibits cigarettes with characterizing flavors, other than tobacco or menthol.

Section 907(a)(1)(A) of the Federal Food, Drug and Cosmetic Act (FFDCA) provides:

"a. IN GENERAL

1. SPECIAL RULES

A. SPECIAL RULE FOR CIGARETTES. Beginning 3 months after the date of enactment of the Family Smoking Prevention and Tobacco Control Act, a cigarette or any of its component parts (including the tobacco, filter, or paper) shall not contain, as a constituent (including a smoke constituent) or additive, an artificial or natural flavor (other than tobacco or menthol) or an herb or spice, including strawberry, grape, orange, clove, cinnamon, pineapple, vanilla, coconut, licorice, cocoa, chocolate, cherry, or coffee, that is a characterizing flavor of the tobacco product or tobacco smoke..."

Indonesia requests the Panel to find that Section 907(a)(1)(A) is inconsistent with: (a) Article 2.1 of the TBT Agreement and, alternatively, Article 3.4 of the GATT 1994, because it results in treatment that is less favorable to imported clove cigarettes than that accords to a like domestic product, menthol cigarettes; (b) Article 2.2 of the TBT Agreement because it is more trade-restrictive than necessary to fulfill a legitimate objective.

Panel's Reasoning and Finding

The Panel conducted a likeness analysis of clove cigarettes and menthol flavored cigarettes. Regarding the physical features of these two products, first, in general, clove and menthol cigarettes are made of tobacco combined with additives contained in a paper wrapper. Second, although both clove and menthol cigarettes are predominantly

① Source: WTO Panel Report, United States–Measures Affecting the Production and Sale of Clove Cigarettes, WT/DS406/R, adopted on 24 April 2012.

composed of tobacco, what appears to differentiate both from regular cigarettes is the presence of an additive, which results in a distinguishing flavor, taste or aroma, other than plain tobacco. Third, the addition of a "sauce" is not exclusive to clove cigarettes, as all cigarettes include a different combination of ingredients that give each cigarette brand a particular and distinct taste.

Several differences are however present between clove and menthol cigarettes, namely, in general, clove cigarettes contain Java tobacco, eugenol and coumarin, while menthol cigarettes generally do not contain these components in significant quantities or at all. However, these differences appear to us as minor or secondary.

Regarding to the end use of clove cigarette and menthol cigarette, the end use of a cigarette is to be smoked. And regarding to the consumers' taste and habits, flavored cigarettes, in addition to being more attractive to young people, make it easier for new smokers to start smoking by masking the unpleasant flavor of tobacco. Studies have also demonstrated that young people believe that flavored tobacco products are safer than unflavored tobacco products.

The evidence submitted by the parties further shows that both types of cigarettes at issue, precisely because of their characterizing flavor which helps mask the harshness of tobacco, appeal to youth and are better vehicles for youth to start smoking than regular cigarettes.

Finally, the tariff classification of cigarettes are under Chapter 24 of the harmonized system, in Heading 2402 for "Cigars, cheroots, cigarillos and cigarettes, of tobacco or of tobacco substitutes". We have found three relevant HS 6-digit codes for cigarettes, namely:

"240210 Cigars, Cheroots, Cigarillos (Containing Tobacco)

240220 Cigarettes (Containing Tobacco)

240290 Other Cigars, Cheroots, Cigarillos, Cigarettes."

Therefore, the 6-digit heading for clove, menthol and regular cigarettes is 2402.20.

Panel found that:

(a) Section 907(a)(1)(A) is a technical regulation within the meaning of Annex 1.1 of the TBT Agreement.

(b) Section 907(a)(1)(A) is inconsistent with Article 2.1 of the TBT Agreement because it accords to imported clove cigarettes treatment less favorable than it accords to like menthol cigarettes of national origin.

Discussions:

1. Was Federal Food, Drug and Cosmetic Act a technical regulation or standard in terms of the TBT Agreement?

2. Did the Panel find clove cigarette and menthol cigarette like products? Please explain.

3. Why did the US exempt menthol flavor from its Federal Food, Drug and Cosmetic Act?

4. How did the Panel conduct the like product analysis in this dispute?

5. What shall be proved if a Member challenges Article 2.1 of the TBT Agreement?

4.3 Sanitary and phytosanitary measures and disciplines

A specific category of measure can be identified within the general category of technical barriers to trade, namely, sanitary and phytosanitary measures (SPS measures). These are measures aimed at the protection of human, animal or plant life or health from certain specified risks.

The WTO members adopted the Agreement on the Application of Sanitary and Phytosanitary Measures (SPS Agreement) to regulate the SPS measures. Based on Article 1 of the SPS Agreement, the Agreement applies to all sanitary and phytosanitary measures which may, directly or indirectly, affect international trade. Such measures shall be developed and applied in accordance with the provisions of this Agreement. Not all measures for the protection of health are SPS measures. Whether a measure is a SPS measure depends on its purpose or aim. If it aims at the protection of human or animal life or health from food-borne risks or aims at the protection of human, animal or plant life or heath from risks of pests or diseases, it is a SPS measure.

It is recognized that Members have the right to take sanitary and phytosanitary measures necessary for the protection of human, animal or plant life or health, provided that such measures are not inconsistent with the provisions of the SPS Agreement. And the basic disciplines of the SPS Agreement impose three obligations on Members. Firstly, a Member has the obligation to take or maintain only those SPS measures necessary to protect human, animal or plant life or health.

Secondly, Members shall take or maintain only SPS measures based on scientific principles and on sufficient scientific evidence. According to Article 5, Members shall ensure that their sanitary or phytosanitary measures are based on an assessment, as appropriate to the circumstances, of the risks to human, animal or plant life or health, taking into account risk assessment techniques developed by the relevant international organizations. In the assessment of risks, Members shall take into account available scientific evidence; relevant processes and production methods; relevant inspection, sampling and testing methods; prevalence of specific diseases or pests; existence of pests—or disease—free area; relevant ecological and environmental conditions; and quarantine or other treatment. In assessing the risk to animal or plant life or health and determining the measure to be applied for achieving the appropriate level of sanitary or phytosanitary protection from such risk, Members shall take into account relevant economic factors: the potential damage in terms of loss of production or sales in the event of the entry, establishment or spread of a pest or disease; the costs of control or eradication in the territory of the importing Member; and the relative cost-effectiveness of alternative approaches to limiting risks.

And thirdly, it shall not adopt or maintain SPS measures that arbitrarily or unjustifiably discriminate or constitute a disguised restriction on trade. Members shall ensure that their sanitary and phytosanitary measures do not arbitrarily or unjustifiably discriminate between Members where identical or similar conditions prevail, including between their own territory and that of other Members. Sanitary and phytosanitary measures shall not be applied in a manner which would constitute a disguised restriction on international trade.

To harmonize sanitary and phytosanitary measures on as wide a basis as possible, it is advised that Members shall base their sanitary or phytosanitary measures on international standards, guidelines or recommendations, where they exist. And sanitary or phytosanitary measures which conform to international standards, guidelines or recommendations shall be deemed to be necessary to protect human, animal or plant life or health, and presumed to be consistent with the relevant provisions of the SPS Agreement and of GATT 1994.

Meanwhile, Members are still allowed to introduce or maintain sanitary or phytosanitary measures which result in a higher level of sanitary or phytosanitary protection than would be achieved by measures based on the relevant international standards, guidelines or recommendations, if there is a scientific justification, or as a consequence of the level of sanitary or phytosanitary protection a Member determines to be appropriate in accordance with the relevant provisions of the SPS Agreement.

Case II-6

EC–Hormones①

The dispute is about the artificial hormones used in cattle farming. The use of these hormones in cattle farming had been studied scientifically in North America for 50 years prior to the EC's ban, and there had been widespread long-term use in over 20 countries. The assertion of Canada and the United States was that this provided empirical evidence both of long-term safety and of scientific consensus.

The EC's ban on hormones may not have been wholly motivated by scientific analysis. The EU was at the time under pressure from its citizens, who, in the light of the mad cow disease crisis, were reluctant to accept the word of scientific authorities on the matter of food safety, in particular where it related to cattle products. It was not producers asking for protectionist measures that were pressuring the EU, but consumers, expressing concerns over the safety of hormone use. The imposition of a general ban was encouraged by the European Parliament, with a 1981 resolution passing by a majority of 177 : 1 in favor of a general ban. Canada and the United States opposed this ban, taking the EU to the WTO Dispute Settlement Body.

The WTO Appellate Body affirmed the WTO Panel's conclusion in a report adopted by the Dispute Settlement Body on 13 February 1998. Section 208 of this report says:

We find that the European Communities did not actually proceed to an assessment, within the meaning of Articles 5.1 and 5.2, of the risks arising from the failure of observance of good veterinary practice combined with problems of control of the use of hormones for growth promotion purposes. The absence of such risk assessment, when considered in conjunction with the conclusion actually reached by most, if not all, of the scientific studies relating to the other aspects of risk noted earlier, leads us to the conclusion that no risk assessment that reasonably supports or warrants the import prohibition embodied in the EC Directives was furnished to the Panel. We affirm, therefore, the ultimate conclusion of the Panel that the EC import prohibition is not based on a risk assessment within the meaning of Articles 5.1 and 5.2 of the SPS Agreement and is, therefore, inconsistent with the requirements of Article 5.1.

---

① Source: WTO Appellate Body Report, European Communities–Measures Concerning Meat and Meat Products (Hormones), WT/DS26/AB/R, WT/DS48/AB/R, adopted on 13 February 1998.

New evidence was released by the EC in 2003 about beef hormones. The EC made the scientific claim that the hormones used in treating cattle remained in the tissue. Despite this evidence the EC declared there was no clear quantifiable link to health risks in humans. The EC has also found high amounts of hormones in areas where there are dense cattle lots. This increase in hormones in the water has affected waterways and nearby wild fish. Contamination of North American waterways by hormones would not, however, have any direct impact on European consumers or their health.

This evidence was introduced. The WTO upheld the earlier decision. The WTO authorized the US and Canada to apply tariffs against products from the EU, equivalent to a maximum of USD 116.8 million for the US and USD 11.3 million for Canada.

Discussions:

1. Is EC's ban on artificial hormones a technical requirement? Is it a SPS measure?

2. Does the SPS Agreement require a risk assessment when the Member adopts a SPS measure?

3. Does EC prove that hormones used in treating cattle produce risk to consumers' health?

5 Exceptions

There are various exceptions provided by the GATT. Although they run counter to the general principles of GATT such as non-discrimination and reduction of tariff, they are nevertheless legitimate if the measures meet certain requirements. These exceptions include general exceptions (Article 20), security exception (Article 21), balance of payment exception (Article 18b), infant industry protection (Articles 18a and 18c), enabling clause, and exceptions provided to safeguard measures (Article 19), free-trade areas and custom unions (Article 24), frontier trade (Article 24.3), and government procurement.

5.1 General exceptions

General exceptions contained in Article 20 of GATT 1994 enable Members to take measures for certain specified purposes and specified reasons, even if such measures are inconsistent with the provisions of GATT 1994. There are 10 circumstances in Article 20 that allow Members to refer to.

Article 20 includes two parts. One is the chapeau, the introduction clause of the Article and the other part is the 10 circumstances. The text is as follows:

"Subject to the requirement that such measures are not applied in a manner which would constitute a means of arbitrary or unjustifiable discrimination between countries where the same conditions prevail, or a disguised restriction on international trade, nothing in this Agreement shall be construed to prevent the adoption or enforcement by any contracting party of measures:

(a) necessary to protect public morals;

(b) necessary to protect human, animal or plant life or health;

(c) relating to the importations or exportations of gold or silver;

(d) necessary to secure compliance with laws and regulations which are not inconsistent with the provisions of this Agreement, including those relating to customs enforcement, the enforcement of monopolies operated under paragraph 4 of Article II and Article XVII, the protection of patents, trademarks and copyrights, and the prevention of deceptive practices;

(e) relating to the products of prison labour;

(f) imposed for the protection of national treasures of artistic, historic or archaeological value;

(g) relating to the conservation of exhaustible natural resources if such measures are made effective in conjunction with restrictions on domestic production or consumption;

(h) undertaken in pursuance of obligations under any intergovernmental commodity agreement which conforms to criteria submitted to the Contracting Parties and not disproved by them or which is itself so submitted and not so disapproved;

(i) involving restrictions on exports of domestic materials necessary to ensure essential quantities of such materials to a domestic processing industry during periods when the domestic price of such materials is held below the world price as part of a governmental stabilization plan; Provided that such restrictions shall not operate to increase export of or the protection afforded to domestic industry, and shall not depart from the provisions of this Agreement relating to non-discrimination.

(j) essential to the acquisition or distribution of products in general or local short supply; Provided that any such measures shall be consistent with the principle that all contracting parties are entitled to an equitable share of the international supply of such products, and that any such measures, which are inconsistent with the other provisions of the Agreement shall be discontinued as soon as the conditions giving rise to them have ceased to exist. The Contracting Parties shall review the need for this sub-paragraph not later than 30 June 1960."

The general exception status of Article 20 of the GATT is affirmed in *US–Section 337*, the Panel noted that Article 20 is entitled "General Exceptions" and that the central phrase in the introductory clause reads: "nothing in this Agreement shall be construed to prevent the adoption or enforcement … of measures …" Article 20(d) thus provides for a limited and conditional exception from obligations under other provisions. The Panel therefore concluded that Article 20(d) applies only to measures inconsistent with another provision of GATT, and that, consequently, the application of Section 337 has to be examined first in the light of Article 3.4. If any inconsistencies with Article 3.4 were found, the Panel would then examine whether they could be justified under Article 20(d).

5.1.1 The two-tiered test of Article 20 of GATT

The provision of Article 20 appears simple, but it is actually complicated. In conducting the analysis of Article 20 of GATT, a two-tiered test is to be followed, which is iterated in *US–Gasoline*.

In that dispute, the Appellate Body states that in order that the justifying protection of Article 20 may be extended to it, the measure at issue must not only come under one or another of the particular exceptions—paragraphs (a) through (j)—listed under Article 20; it must also satisfy the requirements imposed by the opening clauses of Article 20. Thus, the analysis is two-tiered. Firstly, it includes a provisional justification by reason of characterization of the measure under Article 20(g). Secondly, it needs a further appraisal of the same measure under the introductory clauses of Article 20.

In summary, for a GATT-inconsistent measure to be justified under Article 20, it must meet: (a) the requirements of one of the exceptions listed in paragraphs (a) through (j) of Article 20; and (b) the requirements of the chapeau of Article 20.

5.1.2 The Sub-paragraphs of Article 20

Article 20 is composed of 10 sub-paragraphs. The most frequent quoted sub-paragraphs of Article 20 are sub-paragraphs (a), (b), (g), and (d). They afford exceptions to the Members' measures that protect public moral, environmental interest, and human health interest.

(1) Article 20(a)

Article 20(a) exempts Members' trade restrictive measures that protect public moral from GATT obligations. It is not a coincidence that public moral appears in the first subparagraph of Article 20, suggesting that Members have highly concerned about their policy space of protecting public moral.

For a trade restrictive measure to be exempted by Article 20(a), first, it must be adopted to protect public morals; then, the measure shall be necessary to fulfill such objective. The public moral has rich meaning. For example, in *US–Gambling*, measures against the gambling, organized crime, money-laundering are deemed as measures to protect public moral. And in *China–Publication*, measures taking to protect the nationals or the young people from pornography are also considered as a measure protecting public moral.

The core of Article 20(a) analysis is the necessity test, that is, whether the measure is necessary to fulfill its objective. Such necessity test is also required in Article 20(b). In *Thailand–Cigarettes*, the Panel concluded that the import restrictions imposed by Thailand could be considered to be necessary in terms of Article 20(b) only if there were no alternative measures consistent with the GATT, or less inconsistent with it, which Thailand could reasonably be expected to employ to achieve its health policy objectives. The Panel thus concluded that there were in fact various measures consistent with the GATT which were reasonably available to Thailand to control the quality and quantity of cigarettes smoked. It has to be admitted that the "no alternative measure" requirement is highly stringent in evaluating the necessity of the measure.

In *Korea–Beef*, the AB developed three benchmarks in deciding the necessity of the disputed measure, which clarified the requirements in *Thailand–Cigarettes* and were followed by other disputes. It is recognized by the AB that the necessity test is a weighing and balancing process. Firstly, it includes a consideration of the value that the measure pursues, and the more vital or important the common interest or value that the measures pursues, the higher of necessity of the measures. And it is up to the Member to decide the level of protection.

Secondly, it involves an evaluation of the contribution of the measure to the objective, the more contribution to the purposes, the measure is more likely to be acceptable as necessary.

Lastly, the necessity test shall consider the trade restrictiveness of the measure. The less trade-restrictiveness of the measures, the higher of necessity of the measures. In evaluating this benchmark, the Member shall consider whether there is a less trade-restrictive measure to satisfy the objects.

In *EU–Seal Ban*, the Panel considered the necessity of EU's ban on seal products to protect its public moral against excessive cruelty in hunting and killing seals.

Case II-7

EU–Seal Ban[①]

On 2 November 2009, Canada requested consultations with the European Communities concerning Regulation (EC) No. 1007/2009 of the European Parliament and of the EC Council of 16 September 2009 on trade in seal products, and subsequent related measures. According to Canada, the Regulation in question prohibited the importation and the placing on the EU market of all seal products. As public concern in Europe about the pain, suffering, and distress involved in the methods used to kill seals grew, it was reflected in a "massive number of letters and petitions... expressing citizens' deep indignation and repulsion regarding the trade in seal products in such conditions".

Unlike other measures, which are primarily aimed at encouraging humane practices to mitigate or avoid unnecessary suffering in the processes and production methods used for creating agricultural or other tangible (or intangible) products, both the seal product ban's motivation and its object are the same—to seriously discourage, if not eliminate, cruel killing practices applied to living, sentient creatures as an ethical matter.

Although it might be possible to kill and skin seals in such a way as to avoid unnecessary pain, distress, fear or other forms of suffering, given the conditions in which seal hunting occurs, consistent verification and control of hunters' compliance with animal welfare requirements is not feasible in practice or, at least, is very difficult to achieve in an effective way, as concluded by the European Food Safety Authority on 6 December 2007.

Discussions:

1. Is EU's seal ban a technical regulation? Please explain.
2. Why did the EU refer to Article 20(a) or 20(g), rather than Article 20(b) to defend the ban?
3. Do you think *EU–Seal Ban* is necessary to protect EU citizen's moral?

(2) Articles 20(b) and (g)

There are two sub-paragraphs relating to the protection of environment and natural

① Source: WTO Appellate Body Report, European Communities–Measures Prohibiting the Importation and Marketing of Seal Products, WT/DS400/AB/R, WT/DS401/AB/R, adopted on 18 June 2014.

resources. They are Articles 20(b) and 20(g). Article 20(b) permits action which is necessary to protect the life or health of human beings, animals or plants. And Article 20(g) permits action relating to the conservation of exhaustible natural resources.

For measures exempted by Article 20(b), the policy objective pursued by the measure must be the protection of life or health of humans, animals or plants; and the measure must be necessary to fulfill that policy objective. That is, Article 20(b) permits a measure meeting its requirement of policy objective and the necessity of measure in terms of trade restrictiveness.

For measures referring to Article 20(g), the policy objective pursued must be conservation of exhaustible natural resources. The measure must be related to that policy objective and be made effective in conjunction with restrictions on domestic production or consumption. Thus, Article 20(g) requires three elements, apart from the policy objective as required in Article 20(b), the provision requires that the measure has relevance with its objective, which is much lower than the necessity test, and the import or export restrictive measure must also be taken domestically.

Case II-8

US–Shrimp①

Seven species of sea turtles have been identified. They are distributed around the world in subtropical and tropical areas. They spend their lives at sea, where they migrate between their foraging and nesting grounds.

Sea turtles have been adversely affected by human activity, either directly (their meat, shells and eggs have been exploited), or indirectly (incidental capture in fisheries, destruction of their habitats, pollution of the oceans).

In early 1997, India, Malaysia, Pakistan and Thailand brought a joint complaint against a ban imposed by the US on the importation of certain shrimp and shrimp products. The protection of sea turtles was at the heart of the ban.

The US Endangered Species Act of 1973 listed as endangered or threatened the five species of sea turtles that occurred in US waters, and prohibited their take within the US in its territorial sea and the high seas. Under the Act, the US required that US

① Source: WTO Appellate Body Report, United States–Import Prohibition of Certain Shrimp and Shrimp Products, WT/DS58/AB/R, adopted on 6 November 1998.

shrimp trawlers use turtle excluder devices (TEDs) in their nets when fishing in areas where there is a significant likelihood of encountering sea turtles.

Section 609 of US Public Law 101–102, enacted in 1989, dealt with imports. It said, among other things, that shrimp harvested with technology that may adversely affect certain sea turtles may not be imported into the US—unless the harvesting nation was certified to have a regulatory program and an incidental take-rate comparable to that of the US, or that the particular fishing environment of the harvesting nation did not pose a threat to sea turtles.

As disputed by Malaysia, Pakistan and Thailand on the conformity of its Section 609 of the Public Law, the US referred to Article 20(g) for GATT exemption.

Discussions:

1.Why did the US refer to Article 20(g) instead of Article 20(b) for GATT exemption?

2. Is sea turtle a natural resource defined by Article 20(g)? Is it an exhaustible natural resource?

3. Do you think the US measure is relating to the protection of sea turtle? Do you think the measure is necessary to its objective?

4. Do you think the US's import ban of shrimp products would be justified by Article 20(g), and why?

(3) Other Sub-paragraphs

Other sub-paragraphs in Article 20 provide exceptions to measures securing compliance with national law, protection of national treasures, and so on.

To be more specific, Article 20(d) can justify measures necessary to secure compliance with laws or regulations which are not inconsistent with the provisions of this Agreement, including those relating to customs enforcement, the enforcement of monopolies operated under Paragraph 4 of Article 2 and Article 17, the protection of patents, trademarks and copyrights, and the prevention of deceptive practices.

Thus, for a GATT inconsistent measure to be provisionally justified under Article 20(d), the measure must satisfy two requirements: (a) the measure must be designed to secure compliance with national law, such as customs law or intellectual property law, which, in itself, is not GATT-inconsistent; and (b) the measure must be necessary to ensure compliance.

Article 20(e) permits action relating to the products of prison labor. Article 20(f) provides for actions imposed for the protection of national treasures of artistic, historical or archaeological value.

5.1.3 The chapeau of Article 20

When the Member successfully invokes one of the sub-paragraphs of Article 20 to provincially legitimatize its measure, it still needs to go through the chapeau of Article 20 for final justification.

The chapeau of Article 20 is an expression of the principle of good faith, a general principle of law as well as a general principle of international law, which controls the exercise of rights by states. The chapeau by its express terms addresses, not so much the questioned measure or its specific contents as such, but rather the manner in which that measure is applied. The purpose and object of the introductory clauses of Article 20 is generally the prevention of abuse of the exceptions of Article 20. The application of the trade-restrictive measure may not constitute: (a) either arbitrary of unjustifiable discrimination between countries where the same conditions prevail; or (b) a disguised restriction on international trade.

In *US–Shrimp*, it is stated that the challenge to the chapeau of Article 20 needs to prove three things. First, the application of the measure must result in discrimination; second, the discrimination must be arbitrary or unjustifiable in character, and third, the discrimination must occur between countries where the same conditions prevail.

In that very dispute, the AB acknowledged that the US measure could be provincially legitimatized by Sub-paragraph 20(g), but the disputed measure would not survive the chapeau test:

It may be quite acceptable for a government, in adopting and implementing a domestic policy, to adopt a single standard applicable to all its citizens throughout that country. However, it is not acceptable, in international trade relations, for one WTO member to use an economic embargo to require other Members to adopt essentially the same comprehensive regulatory program, to achieve a certain policy goal, as that in force within that Member's territory, without taking into consideration different conditions which may occur in the territories of those other members.

Section 609, in its application, imposes a single, rigid and unbending requirement that countries applying for certification … adopt a comprehensive regulatory program that is essentially the same as the US's program, without inquiring into the appropriateness of that program for the conditions prevailing in the exporting countries. Furthermore, there is little or no flexibility in how officials make the determination for certification pursuant to these provisions.

Therefore, the AB found the US measure arbitrary in that there was no sufficient flexibility to take into account the specific conditions prevailing in any exporting Member. The US failed to engage the appellees in serious, across-the-board negotiations with the objective of concluding bilateral or multilateral agreements for the protection of sea turtles. Furthermore, the US failed to grant different countries different phasing-in periods to comply with the US requirement.

Case II-9

Brazil–Retreaded Tyres①

On 20 June 2005, the European Communities requested consultations with Brazil on the imposition of measures that adversely affected exports of retreaded tyres from the EU to the Brazilian market. The EC would like to address the following measures: (a) Brazil's imposition of an import ban on retreaded tyres; (b) Brazil's exemption of retreaded tyres imported from other Mercosur countries from the import ban and from the abovementioned financial penalties, in response to the ruling of a MERCOSUR Panel established at the request of Uruguay.

The Panel determined that the imports of used tyres through court injunctions resulted in discrimination in favor of domestic retreaders. This was because these imports enabled retreaded tyres to be produced in Brazil from imported casings, while retreaded tyres produced abroad using the same casings could not be imported. Having done so, the Panel went on to examine whether this discrimination was arbitrary or unjustifiable.

The Panel noted that the importation of used tyres into Brazil was prohibited, and that "used tyres have been imported into Brazil in recent years only as a result of injunctions granted by Brazilian courts in specific cases". The Panel found that the discrimination resulting from the imports of used tyres through court injunctions

① Source: WTO Appellate Body Report, Brazil–Measures Affecting Imports of Retreaded Tyres, WT/DS332/AB/R, adopted on 17 December 2007.

was not the consequence of a capricious or random action, and that, to this extent, the Import Ban was not applied in a manner that would constitute arbitrary discrimination.

The AB partly overturned the Panel's finding and gave its reasons. The analysis of whether the application of a measure results in arbitrary or unjustifiable discrimination should focus on the cause or rationale given for the discrimination. For Brazil, the fact that Brazilian retreaders are able to use imported casings is the result of the decisions of the Brazilian administrative authorities to comply with court injunctions that followed the MERCOSUR Panel's decision. The AB observe that this explanation bears no relationship to the objective of the Import Ban—reducing exposure to the risks arising from the accumulation of waste tyres to the maximum extent possible.

The imports of used tyres through court injunctions even go against the objective pursued by the Import Ban. As the AB indicated above, there is arbitrary or unjustifiable discrimination, within the meaning of the chapeau of Article 20, when a Member seeks to justify the discrimination resulting from the application of its measure by a rationale that bears no relationship to the accomplishment of the objective that falls within the purview of one of the paragraphs of Article 20, or goes against this objective. Accordingly, the AB find that the imports of used tyres through court injunctions have resulted in the Import Ban being applied in a manner that constitutes arbitrary or unjustifiable discrimination.

Discussions:

1. Did Brazailian's ban of used tyres aim at protecting health of human being or animal? Was the Import Ban arbitrary or unjustifiable without considering its exemption?

2. Why did Brazil exempt retreated tyres imported from other Mercosur countries from the Import Ban? Do you think Brazil's excuse is appropriate? Please explain.

3. How did the Panel explain "arbitrary and unjustifiable"? Did the Panel think the exemption breach the chapeau of Article 20?

4. Why did the AB disagree with the Panel on the exception of the Import Ban?

5.2 Balance of payment exception

Developing countries have the flexibility to deviate temporarily from specific obligations of the WTO agreements if they face balance-of-payment (BOP) problems. The BOP provisions for developing countries are contained in Article 18(b) of GATT 1994 and are further clarified by two legal instruments. They are the 1979 Declaration on Trade Measures Taken for Balance-of-Payments Purposes, adopted on 28 November 1979, and the Understanding on Balance-of-Payments Provisions, contained in Annex 1A of WTO agreement.

The main purpose of these special provisions for developing countries is to provide them with some relief and flexibility when they face problems of low inflow and small reserves of foreign exchange.

There are no specific criteria for determining whether BOP problems exist. Members take into account the facts and information provided by the IMF. In determining the eligibility of the Republic of Korea for the benefits of BOP provisions, a detailed consideration of this issue took place in 1989. The Panel on *Korea–Restrictions on Imports of Beef* found that the country's reserve was increasing and that the Committee on BOP Restrictions had earlier held the prevailing view that import restrictions were no longer justified. The Panel concluded that the Republic of Korea did not have BOP difficulties.

To invoke the BOP exception, a Member shall establish three conditions: (a) the developing country has a weak economy, so that it can only support low standards of living; (b) it is in the early stages of development; (c) it is experiencing BOP difficulties arising mainly from its efforts to expand its internal markets, and instability of its terms of trade.

The Member experiencing the BOP difficulties may resort to price-based measures such as import surcharges, import deposit requirements, or quantitative restrictions. While applying quantitative restrictions on imports, Members have to justify why price-based measures are not adequate to deal with the problem.

In *India–Quantitative Restrictions*, the Appellate Body upheld the Panel's finding that India could manage its balance-of-payments situation using macroeconomic policy instruments alone, without maintaining quantitative restrictions. India appealed this finding, arguing that the Panel required India to change its development policy. The AB stated that we believe that structural measures are different from macroeconomic instruments, if India were asked to implement agriculture reform, such would probably have involved a change in India's development policy.

The infant industry argument for protection holds that weak industries in developing countries should be promoted through trade or industrial policy measures to allow them to mature and compete with their strong foreign rivals.

The idea of infant industries can be traced back as far as the 17th century. In Book IV of *The Wealth of Nations*, Adam Smith was skeptical that trade restrictions would create new wealth, arguing that they would just divert scarce resources into less productive endeavors. Other writers, such as Alexander Hamilton and Friedrich List, believed that policies to promote manufacturing industries would be beneficial in encouraging economic diversification and growth in developing countries.

The infant industry exception is designed for developing countries, especially the least developed countries. The exception is included in Articles 18(a) and 18(c).

Articles 18(a) and 18(c) permit governments to modify or withdraw concession in order to promote the establishment of a particular industry. When developing countries utilize Article 18(a) or 18(c) , they need to satisfy two elements: (a) it has a weak economy, so that it can only support low standards of living; (b) it is in the early stages of development.

5.3 Security exception

Article 21 of the GATT 1994, entitled "Security Exceptions", states that nothing in the Agreement shall be construed: (a) to require any contracting party to furnish any information the disclosure of which it considers contrary to its essential security interests; or (b) to prevent any contracting party from taking any action which it considers necessary for the protection of its essential security interests (i) relating to fissionable materials or the materials from which they are derived; (ii) relating to the traffic in arms, ammunition and implements of war and to such traffic in other goods and materials as is carried on directly or indirectly for the purpose of supplying a military establishment; (iii) taken in time of war or other emergency in international relations; or (c) to prevent any contracting party from taking any action in pursuance of its obligations under the United Nations Charter for the maintenance of international peace and security.

Compared with other exceptions, Article 21 is unique in that this national security exception is "self-declaratory". That is, each WTO member is able to determine and define what it considers to be its own "essential security interests" without the need to meet an objective standard and to take any action it considers necessary to protect such interests. This makes Article 21 distinct as all other exceptions are subject to certain objective requirements. The major reason for the lack of objectivity inherent in Article 21 is because the sovereign governments are reluctant to let other bodies review what they deem to be in their country's security interests. But such "self-declaratory" feature also allows the provision to be abused by the Members.

For example, in 1975, Sweden recoursed to Article 21 to justify its imposition of a global import restriction on certain footwear. Sweden alleged that a significant decrease in domestic production of footwear would result in a critical threat to the emergency planning of its economic defense, thus justified the imposition of an import ban. Considering the fact that use of general exceptions found in Article 20 requires justification of both specific situations given by the sub-paragraphs and the chapeau, the broad application of Article 21 seems especially problematic.

In another case, the United States relied on Article 21 in 1985 to justify measures prohibiting all imports of goods and services of Nicaraguan origin in addition to all US exports to Nicaragua. The United States argued that Article 21 left it to each contracting party to judge what action it considered necessary for the protection of its own essential security interests. In response, Nicaragua initiated a complaint and sought a GATT Panel resolution. The United States was successful in arguing for the terms of reference that precluded the Panel from examining the validity of the US invocation of Article 21. While the Panel was critical of actions taken by the US and stated that a party relying on the exception must balance its need to do so against the more fundamental need for stable trade regulation, the process itself lent support to the general and still predominant view that a GATT Panel cannot or simply does not have jurisdiction to review a state's decision to invoke Article 21.

In 2018, the Trump administration raised tariffs by 10% on goods originated from China and defended the measures on national security exception. It appeared that this exception has become an excuse for Members' trade protection measures. The question becomes, how a proper balance can be struck between maintaining a state's sovereignty to protect itself in true cases of national security and preventing abuse and the imposition of trade-barriers for purely commercial or political reasons.

Apart from the exceptions listed here, there are also other exceptions mentioned before, such as exception provided by Article 24 of GATT, which allows the formation of a customs union or of a free-trade area or the adoption of an interim agreement necessary for the formation of a customs union or of a free-trade area. Article 19 of GATT allows Members to adopt safeguard measures in case of sharp increase in import. And, 1979 GATT Decision on Differential and More Favorable Treatment, Reciprocity, and Fuller Participation of Developing Countries also establishes the generalized system of preferences exception.

Chapter Review

1. Why is tariff escalation significant to the developing countries?
2. What are the rules of origin, and how do we identify the origin of a good?
3. In what situations that preferential tariff can be afforded to members of the WTO?
4. What are the rules deciding the customs value of a product?
5. What does non-tariff barrier mean?
6. What are the usual forms of non-tariff barriers?
7. What are the disciplines for quantitative restriction in GATT?
8. What are the functions of customs duties?
9. What does tariff quota mean?
10. What is dumping? Does dumping distort competition?
11. How to determine whether there is dumping and if there is, and how much is the dumping margin?
12. State briefly the development of international anti-dumping disciplines.
13. What does subsidy mean in SCM?
14. What are the positive and negative consequences caused by subsidy?
15. Explain the difference between the domestic subsidy and export subsidy?
16. What are the different types of subsidies in the SCM, and what are the specific rules for each type?
17. To impose countervailing duties, what need to be established by the authorities of the importing states?
18. State briefly the procedure of countervailing investigation.
19. Explain the magnitude of countervailing measures.
20. What are the special rules in SCM for developing countries?
21. State briefly the special provisions of countervailing investigations in dealing with developing countries.
22. What are the main issues challenged by China against the US and EU's countervailing measures?
23. What is the function of safeguard mechanism?
24. Are safeguard measures taken to counter unfair trade measures taken by the exporters?
25. What are the requirements for adoption of safeguard measures?
26. What do OMA and VER mean? Are they legitimate in WTO covered agreements?
27. What is technical trade barrier, and what is a sanitary and phytosanitary measure?

28. What is the difference between technical regulation and technical standard?
29. Can Article 2.1 of the TBT be interchanged by Article 1 and Article 3 of the GATT?
30. What is the relationship between the necessity test of Article 20 of GATT 1994 and the Article 2.2 of the TBT?
31. What is the relationship between the TBT Agreement and the SPS Agreement?
32. What are the disciplines set by the SPS Agreement on sanitary and phytosanitary measures?
33. What is the nature of Article 20?
34. What is the function of the chapeau of Article 20 of GATT?
35. What is the two-tier test of Article 20 of GATT?
36. Who shall bear the burden of proof if a Member wishes to invoke Article 20 for defense?
37. Compare the elements of Articles 20(b) and 20(g).
38. Explain the necessity test in Articles 20(a) and 20(b).
39. State briefly the elements of Article 20(a).
40. In *US–Shrimp*, why did the US invoke Article 20(g) instead of 20(b) to defend its case?
41. Discuss the elements of Article 20(d).
42. What does the balance of payment difficulty mean?
43. What are the elements for a Member to invoke the BOP exception?
44. What remedies can be adopted by the Member experiencing the BOP difficulties?
45. Explain the infant industry exception. Which article authorizes the Member to adopt national security exception?
46. Explain the national security exception and its features.

Key Terms

actionable subsidy	可诉补贴
ad valorem tariff	从价关税
anti-dumping	反倾销
balance-of-payment exception	收支平衡例外
chapeau	序言条款
countervailing duties	反补贴税
de minimis	微量不计
dumping margin	倾销幅度

general exception	一般例外
non-actionable subsidy	不可诉补贴
non-tariff barrier	非关税壁垒
normal value	正常价值
prohibited subsidy	禁止性补贴
quantitative restriction	数量限制
safeguard measures	保障措施
security exception	安全例外
specific duty	从量关税
surrogate country methodology	替代国方法
tariff escalation	关税升级
tariff quota	关税配额
technical regulation	技术法规
technical standard	技术标准
technical trade barriers	技术贸易壁垒
trade remedy	贸易救济

Further Readings

1. Bossche, Peter van den & Werner Zdouc, *The Law and Policy of the World Trade Organization: Text, Cases and Materials*, 4th ed., Cambridge University Press, 2017.

2. Chow, Daniel C. K. & Thomas J. Schoenbaum, *International Trade Law: Problems, Cases, and Materials*, Wolters Kluwer, 2017.

3. Matsushita, Mitsuo, Thomas J. Schoenbaum, Petros C. Mavroidis & Michael Hahn, *The World Trade Organization: Law, Practice, and Policy*, 3rd ed., Oxford University Press, 2015.

4. World Trade Organization, *The WTO Agreements: The Marrakesh Agreement Establishing the World Trade Organization and its Annexes*, 2nd ed., Cambridge University Press, 2017.

5. https://www.worldtradelaw.net.

6. https://www.wto.org.

Chapter 3
GATS and Rules on Trade in Service

Study Guide
This Chapter is about the rules and disciplines on trade in service. The service in GATS has been defined in four modes: cross-border supply of service, consumption abroad, commerce presence and presence of natural person. Unlike the GATT, Members' commitments in GATS include general commitments and specific comments. The former includes Members' obligations of most-favored-nation treatment and transparency, while the latter encompasses the duty of market access, national treatment. The distinction of general and specific obligations is supposed to let the Members to liberalize their service market and offer national treatment progressively. This Chapter also illustrates the contents of a Member's schedule in trade in service.

International trade in service, or transboundary service, means the sale or delivery of a service exchanged between residents and non-residents of a country. Trade in service accounts for almost half of world exports when the full value of service inputs is properly accounted for in the final output of goods. Services include transport (both freight and passengers), travel, communications services (postal, telephone, satellite, etc), construction services, insurance and financial services, computer and information services, royalties and license fees, other business services (merchanting, operational leasing, technical and professional services, etc), and cultural and recreational services. Unlike trade in goods that is usually restricted by tariff, trade in services is often restricted by domestic regulations. The General Agreement on Trade in Services (GATS) is the first multilateral trade agreement on transboundary service, which came into effect on 1 January 1995. As one of the three pillars to the world trading system, GATS is far less liberalized than GATT.

The creation of the GATS was one of the landmark achievements of the Uruguay Round. The GATS was inspired by essentially the same objectives as its counterpart in merchandise trade, while the GATT was aimed at creating a credible and reliable system of international trade rules, ensuring fair and equitable treatment of all participants (principle of non-discrimination), stimulating economic activity through guaranteed policy bindings, and promoting trade and development through progressive liberalization.

The GATS consists of three parts. The Agreement, as the first part, contains basic rules and disciplines that cover all service sectors and are applicable to all Members. There are several sectoral annexes dealing with specific sectors such as financial service and telecommunication, which form the second part of the GATS. Then each Member submits its Schedules to state its specific commitments that it has agreed to undertake.

1 Definition of Service and Modes of Service Supply

The GATS covers all trade in service in any sector, for example, banking, telecommunications, tourism, professional services, except those supplied in the exercise of governmental functions and air transport services. Article 1.3 of the GATS excludes services supplied in the exercise of governmental authority. These are services that are supplied neither on a commercial basis nor in competition with other suppliers. Cases in point are social security schemes and any other public service, such as health or education, that is provided at non-market conditions. Furthermore, the Annex on Air Transport Services exempts from coverage measures affecting air traffic rights and services directly related to the exercise of such rights.

It is interesting that the GATS does not define the service. Instead, it divides the supply of service in four modes. Based on Article 1 of GATS, trade in services is defined as the supply of a service in four modes: (a) from the territory of one Member into the territory of any other Member (cross-border supply) (Mode 1); (b) in the territory of one Member to the service consumer of any other Member (consumption abroad) (Mode 2); (c) by a service supplier of one Member, through commercial presence in the territory of any other Member (commercial presence) (Mode 3); (d) by a service supplier of one Member, through presence of natural persons of a Member in the territory of any other Member (presence of natural persons) (Mode 4).

Thus, services could be supplied in four ways among members. Cross-border supply means services are supplied from one country to another. International courier service and international phone calls are typical cross-border supply of services. Consumption abroad means consumers or firms transport to another country and use a service there. Tourism and education abroad belong to such mode. Commercial presence means a natural person or a firm establishes an entity in another country to provide service there, which is also a manifestation of investment. Presence of natural persons means individuals travel from their own country to supply services in another country. For example, a lawyer travel abroad to provide legal counseling service would be deemed as a provision of service in the form of presence of natural person.

The supply of many services often involves the simultaneous physical presence of both producers and consumers. There are thus many instances in which, in order to be commercially meaningful, trade commitments must extend to cross-border movements of the consumer, the establishment of a commercial presence within a market, or the temporary movement of the service provider.

2 General Obligations in GATS and Exemptions

Members' obligations under the GATS are divided into two categories. One is general obligations and the other is specific obligations. The general obligations apply to all WTO members, including most-favored-nation (MFN) treatment and transparency.

2.1 MFN treatment in GATS

The GATS seeks to ensure that each Member in sectors where commitments exist, takes measures that are administered impartially and in a reasonable and objective manner.

Article 2.1 of GATS describes the MFN treatment in service sectors as follows:

(a) With respect to any measure covered by this Agreement, each Member shall accord immediately and unconditionally to services and service suppliers of any other Member's treatment no less favorable than that it accords to like services and service suppliers of any other country.

(b) A Member may maintain a measure inconsistent with paragraph 1 provided that such a measure is listed in, and meets the conditions of, the Annex on Article II Exemptions.

(c) The provisions of this Agreement shall not be so construed as to prevent any Member from conferring or according advantages to adjacent countries in order to facilitate exchanges limited to contiguous frontier zones of services that are both locally produced and consumed.

Considering unfair treatment exists not only among like services, but also exists among like service suppliers, the likeness analysis in service sectors is more complicated than its counterpart in trade in goods.

Although treated as a general obligation to the Member, GATS allows Members' initial derogation and exemptions from MFN treatment, considering the complexity of services trade. This derogation was supposed to be temporary in nature when GATS was negotiated, with a duration of 10 years. But many exemptions in the Schedule did not specify the duration, condition, and special treatment of MFN inconsistent measures, which undermined the openness and liberalization of service sectors.

The exceptions to the MFN treatment under the GATS are very complex. There are country specific exemptions or so-called Article II-exemptions based on accession reservation under the GATS when Members were allowed to seek such exemptions before the Agreement entered into force. And there are general exceptions under GATS such as frontier trade exemption, regional integration exception, which are given by Article 5 of the GATS. Furthermore, there are exemptions by way of a waiver under Article 6.3 of the WTO Agreement as well.

Pursuant to the GATS provision, general exceptions to the MFN treatment include the following:

(a) Frontier trade exemption. The exemption is based on Article 2.3 of GATS and allows a Member to confer advantages to adjacent countries in order to facilitate exchanges limited to contiguous frontier zones of service.

(b) Regional economic integration exception. The Article 24 exemption in GATT finds its twins in Article 5 of GATS. Hence, a Member adopted an FTA to further liberalize the trade in service among the FTA or customs union parties and such an agreement that has substantial sectoral coverage, would be exempted from MFN treatment.

(c) Labor markets integration exemption.

(d) General exception. Article 14 of GATS permits Members in specified circumstances to introduce or maintain measures in contravention of their obligations under the Agreement, including the MFN requirement or specific commitments. The relevant article covers, among other things, measures necessary to protect public morals or maintain public order, protect human, animal or plant life or health; or secure compliance with laws or regulations not inconsistent with the Agreement including, among other things, measures necessary to prevent deceptive or fraudulent practices.

(e) Sectoral exception. The Annex on Financial Services entitles Members, regardless of other provisions of the GATS, to take measures for prudential reasons, including for the protection of investors, depositors, policy holders or persons to whom a fiduciary duty is owed by a financial service supplier, or to ensure the integrity and stability of the financial system.

(f) BOP exception. Finally, in the event of serious balance-of-payments difficulties Members are allowed to temporarily restrict trade, on a non-discriminatory basis, despite the existence of specific commitments.

If a Member's measure is not covered by the exemption mentioned above, it shall conform to the general requirement of MFN treatment.

2.2 Transparency

GATS members are required, among other things, to make public all measures of general application and establish national enquiry points mandated to respond to other Members' information requests. More specifically, the GATS provides that governments must publish all relevant laws and regulations affecting trade in service, and the changes to these laws, and shall respond promptly to any requests by any other Members for specific information on any of its measures of general application or international agreements. Members also need to set up enquiry points within their bureaucracies.

Apart from MFN treatment and transparency, other generally applicable obligations include the establishment of administrative review and appeals procedures and disciplines on the operation of monopolies and exclusive suppliers.

3 Progressive Liberalization and Specific Obligations in GATS

The notion of progressive liberalization is one of the basic tenets of the GATS. Article 19 provides that Members shall enter into successive rounds of negotiations, beginning not later than five years from the date of entry into force of the WTO Agreement and periodically thereafter, with a view to achieving a progressively higher level of liberalization. Such negotiations shall be directed to the reduction or elimination of the adverse effects on trade in services of measures as a means of providing effective market access and the process of liberalization shall take place with due respect for national policy objectives and Members' development levels, both overall and in individual sectors. Therefore, market access and national treatment commitments are regarded as specific obligations of Members that allow them to liberalize domestic service sectors gradually.

3.1 Market access

Market access is a negotiated commitment in specified sectors. With respect to market access through the modes of supply identified in Article 1, each Member is required to accord services and service suppliers the market access as committed in its Schedule and may subject such commitments to various types of limitations that are enumerated in Article 16.2.

For example, limitations may be imposed on the number of services suppliers, the value of service transactions or assets, the number of service operations or employees in the sector, the legal form of the service suppliers, or the participation of foreign capital.

3.2 National treatment

In the sectors inscribed in its Schedule, and subject to any conditions and qualifications set out therein, each Member shall accord to services and service suppliers of any other Member, in respect of all measures affecting the supply of services, treatment no less favorable than that it accords to its own like services and service suppliers.①

A commitment to national treatment implies that the Member concerned does not operate discriminatory measures benefiting domestic services or service suppliers. The key requirement is not to modify, in law or in fact, the conditions of competition in favor of the Member's own service industry. Again, the extension of national treatment in any particular sector may be made subject to conditions and qualifications.

Members are free to tailor the sector coverage and substantive content of such commitments as they see fit. The commitments thus tend to reflect national policy objectives and constraints, overall and in individual sectors. While some Members have scheduled less than a handful of services, others have assumed market access and national treatment disciplines in over 120 out of a total of 160-odd services.

The existence of specific commitments triggers further obligations concerning, among other things, the notification of new measures that have a significant impact on trade and the avoidance of restrictions on international payments and transfers.

4 Members' Schedules

Each WTO member is required to have a schedule of specific commitments which identifies the services for which the Member guarantees market access and national t reatment and any limitations that may be attached. With respect to sectors where such commitments are undertaken, each Schedule shall specify: (a) terms, limitations and conditions on market access; (b) conditions and qualifications on national treatment; (c) undertakings relating to additional commitments; (d) where appropriate the time-frame for implementation of such commitments; and (e) the date of entry into force of such commitments.②

The Schedule may also be used to assume additional commitments regarding, for

① See GATS, Article 17.1.

② See GATS, Article 20.

example, the implementation of specified standards or regulatory principles. Commitments are undertaken with respect to each of the four different modes of service supply.

Most schedules consist of both sectoral and horizontal sections. The "Horizontal Section" contains entries that apply across all sectors subsequently listed in the Schedule. Horizontal limitations often refer to a particular mode of supply, notably commercial presence and the presence of natural persons. The "Sector-Specific Section" contains entries that apply only to the particular service.

Table II-5 EC's Schedule for Professional Service①

Sector or Sub-sector	Limitations on Market Access	Limitations on National Treatment	Additional Commitments
II. SECTOR-SPECIFIC COMMITMENTS			
1. BUSINESS SERVICES A. Professional Services a) All Members except CZ, EE, FI, HU, LV, PL, SI, SK: Legal advice home country law and public international law (excluding EU law) HU:Legal advisory services concerning home country law (part of CPC 861) FI: Legal Services (CPC 861): public international law and home country law CZ, EE, LV, PL, SI, SK: Legal Services (CPC 861).	1) All Members except CY, EE, FR, MT, PT, SE, SI: None CY, MT: Unbound EE: Unbound for CPC 861 other than CPC 86190 FR, PT, SI: Unbound for drafting of legal documents SE: An "advokat" (see next column) may not practice his profession neither in cooperation with other persons than other "advokats", nor in the form of a limited liability company (joint stock company). 2) All Members except CY, MT: None CY, MT: Unbound	1) All Members except AT, CY, DK, EE, FR, MT, PT, SE, SI: None AT: Foreign legal advisors are required to be members of their national Bar Association; they may use their professional title only with reference to the place of registration in their home country. CY, MT: Unbound DK: Marketing of legal advice activities is restricted to lawyers with a Danish licence to practise and law firms registered in Denmark. EE: Unbound for CPC 861 other than CPC 86190 FR, PT, SI: Unbound for drafting of legal documents SE: None except for the protection of the use of the Swedish title "advokat" (lawyer/solicitor/barrister), which requires membership in the Swedish Bar Association. Swedish law exam or equivalent education and practical experience, citizenship and residency are required for such membership. 2) All Members except CY, MT: None CY, MT: Unbound	

① Source: https://www.wto.org/english/tratop_e/serv_e/serv_commitments_e.htm.

Case II-9

China–Publication and Audiovisual Products[①]

On 10 April 2007, the United States requested consultations with China concerning certain measures that restricted trading rights with respect to imported films for theatrical release, audiovisual home entertainment products.

Among all its claims and requests, the United States claimed that China did not provide national treatment for imported reading materials, sound recordings intended for electronic distribution, and films for theatrical release by subjecting them to more burdensome content review requirements than like domestic products. Regarding reading materials, the United States claimed that Chinese measures restricted distribution channels for certain imported reading materials by requiring their distribution to be conducted exclusively through subscription, and by Chinese wholly state-owned enterprises, unlike for like domestic reading materials. Similarly, the United States also pointed out that Chinese measures limited the distribution of certain imported reading materials (which could be distributed other than through subscription) to wholly Chinese-owned enterprises, while the distribution of like domestic reading materials could be effected by other types of enterprises, including foreign-invested ones.

China defended itself by alleging that its commitment on market access and national treatment of sound recordings in its GATS Schedule only referred to the sound recordings through physical media. The commitment was made in 2001 and China had no intention to liberalize the audio-visual sector by electronic means when it had not yet developed in China. But the Panel regarded that the ordinary meaning of the term "sound recording distribution services" in China's GATS Schedule encompassed the distribution of sound recordings through both physical and non-physical media and concluded that these measures were inconsistent with China's obligations under Article 3.4 of the GATT 1994. China disputed the Panel's finding and submitted the dispute to the Appellate Body, while the AB upheld Panel's finding on the issue.

Discussions:

1. What were the US' arguments?

---

① Source: WTO Appellate Body Report, China–Measures Affecting Trading Rights and Distribution Services for Certain Publications and Audiovisual Entertainment Products, WT/DS363/AB/R, adopted on 19 January 2010.

2. Are sound recordings intended for electronic distribution like products of sound recordings in physical form?

3. Do you agree with the Panel and AB that "sound recording distribution services" in China's Schedule in 2001 includes sound recordings in both physical and electronic forms when the latter has not developed or even occurred in China?

4. What do you learn from the dispute on treaty interpretation in *China–Publicaiton and Audiovisual Products*?

Chapter Review

1. What are the different modes of supply of service given by the GATS?
2. What kind of service is excluded from the GATS?
3. Explain the MFN treatment in the GATS.
4. State briefly the general obligations in the GATS.
5. Explain the general exceptions in the GATS.
6. What are the three parts that compose the GATS?
7. Explain the transparency requirement in the GATS.
8. What are the disciplines included in the specific requirements in the GATS?
9. What does national treatment requirement mean in the GATS?
10. State briefly the specific obligations in the GATS. What does progressive liberalization mean?
11. What is the relationship between specific obligations and progressive liberalization principle?
12. On Members' schedules of services, what shall be specified?
13. What do you learn from EC's Schedule for Professional Service? Do all its Members give identical commitments?

Key Terms

commercial presence	商业存在
consumption abroad	境外消费
cross-border supply	跨境提供

general obligation	一般义务
market access	市场准入
presence of natural person	自然人流动
progressive liberalization	逐步自由化
schedule	（承诺）减让表
specific obligation	特定义务

Further Readings

1. Godsoe, Harold, *The Depth of Trade in Services Agreement*, International Law & Management Review, Vol. 10: 1, 2014.

2. Kelsey, Jane, *Serving Whose Interest?: The Political Economy of Trade in Services Agreements*, Routledge-Cavendish, 2008.

3. Peng, Shin-yi, *Is the Trade in Services Agreement (TiSA) a Stepping Stone for the Next Version of GATS?*, Hong Kong Law Journal, Vol. 43: 611, 2013.

Chapter 4
TRIPS and International Intellectual Property Conventions

Study Guide

This Chapter is about the international rules of intellectual property. This Chapter introduces the most important international intellectual property treaties to the students and their key provisions. The Agreement on Trade-Related Intellectual Property (TRIPS or TRIPS Agreement) was concluded in Uruguay Round of multilateral negotiation. The Agreement has laid down the minimum standard of intellectual property protection rules on patents, trademarks, copyrights, geographical indications, industrial designs, layout-designs of integrated circuits and undisclosed information. Any breach of duties in TRIPS may be brought to the WTO's dispute settlement mechanism.

The other well-known intellectual property treaties include Paris Convention on Industrial Property Protection and Berne Convention on Copyright Protection, the Madrid system on trademark registration concluded under the auspice of World Intellectual Property Organization and Anti-Counterfeiting Trade Agreement. The general rights given to the intellectual property owners and duties imposed by the these conventions and treaties will be given in this Chapter.

Intellectual property rights are the rights given to persons over the creations of their minds. They usually give the creator an exclusive right over the use of his/her creation for a certain period of time. Before the WTO was established, most of the multilateral intellectual property treaties were drafted by the World Intellectual Property Organization (WIPO), including the Paris Convention on Industrial Property Protection and the Berne Convention on Copyright Protection.

When the WTO was established in 1995, the TRIPS Agreement became the Annex 1C of the Marrakesh Agreement. A large number of countries participating in the negotiations had initially objected to the inclusion of IPRs in GATT on the grounds that the subject was covered by WIPO and also because GATT had jurisdiction only in the field of trade. As a compromise, the subject of the negotiations was termed TRIPS. But finally, the link with trade has almost vanished, yet the original name remains. This Chapter discusses the basic disciplines given by TRIPS and other conventions relating to intellectual property.

1 TRIPS

The extent of protection and enforcement of intellectual property rights varied widely around the world, and as intellectual property became more important in trade, these differences became a source of tension in international economic relations. New internationally-agreed trade rules for intellectual property rights were seen as a way to introduce more order and predictability, and to settle disputes more systematically. The Uruguay Round achieved that. The WTO's TRIPS Agreement is an attempt to narrow the gaps in the way these rights are protected and enforced around the world, and to bring them under common international rules. It establishes minimum standards of protection and enforcement that each government has to give to the intellectual property held by nationals of fellow WTO members. The TRIPS Agreement plays a critical role in facilitating trade in knowledge and creativity, in resolving trade disputes over intellectual property, and in assuring WTO members the latitude to achieve their domestic objectives. The Agreement is legal recognition of the significance of links between intellectual property and trade.

1.1 Types of intellectual properties protected by TRIPS

The inclusion of intellectual property rights (IPRs) in the Uruguay Round of Multilateral Trade Negotiations under the GATT has created widespread unease among the developing countries because it is feared that that this would lead to the absolute dominance of the developed countries on trade and technology matters with far reaching implications for self-sufficiency and long-term growth performance of the developing countries.

The Agreement finally prescribes minimum standards for members in various areas of intellectual property. One of the significant achievements made by the TRIPS Agreement is that it provides a set of uniform global standards for the protection of intellectual property rights.

The TRIPS includes seven types of intellectual property: patents, copyrights, trademarks, geographical indications, industrial designs, layout-designs of integrated circuits and undisclosed information.

1.1.1 Copyrights

Copyright refers to the exclusive legal right to reproduce, publish, sell, or distribute the matter and form of something, such as a literary, musical, or artistic work. In a wider sense, copyright also includes "related rights": the rights of performers, producers of phonograms and broadcasting organizations.

It is given by TRIPS, whenever the term of protection of a work, other than a photographic work or a work of applied art, is calculated on a basis other than the life of a natural person, such term shall be no less than 50 years from the end of the calendar year of authorized publication, or, failing such authorized publication within 50 years from the making of the work, 50 years from the end of the calendar year of making.

The TRIPS Agreement ensures that computer programs will also be protected as literary works under the Berne Convention and outlines how databases should be protected. Based on Article 10, computer programs, whether in source or object code, shall be protected as literary works under the Berne Convention. It is required that compilations of data or other material, whether in machine readable or other form, which by reason of the selection or arrangement of their contents constitute intellectual creations shall be protected as such. Such protection, which shall not extend to the data or material itself, shall be without prejudice to any copyright subsisting in the data or material itself.

The authors of computer programs and cinematographic works shall have rental rights under the TRIPS. Members shall provide authors and their successors in title the right to authorize or to prohibit the commercial rental to the public of originals or copies of their copyright works. A Member shall be excepted from this obligation in respect of cinematographic works unless such rental has led to widespread copying of such works which is materially impairing the exclusive right of reproduction conferred in that Member on authors and their successors in title. In respect of computer programs, this obligation does not apply to rentals where the program itself is not the essential object of the rental.

There is one article in TRIPS protecting the performers, producers of phonograms and broadcasting organizations. Performers of phonograms shall be given the possibility of preventing the fixation of their unfixed performance and the reproduction of such fixation, or the broadcasting by wireless means and the communication to the public of their live performance. Producers of phonograms shall enjoy the right to authorize or prohibit the direct or indirect reproduction of their phonograms.

Given by Article 14, broadcasting organizations shall have the right to prohibit the fixation, the reproduction of fixations, and the rebroadcasting by wireless means of broadcasts, as well as the communication to the public of television broadcasts of the same without their authorization. The term of the protection available under this Agreement to performers and producers of phonograms shall last at least until the end of a period of 50 years computed from the end of the calendar year in which the fixation was made or the performance took place. The term of protection granted pursuant to paragraph 3 shall last for at least 20 years from the end of the calendar year in which the broadcast took place.①

1.1.2 Patents

What shall be offered patent protection is always disputable among WTO members as it might conflict with a Member's provision of public goods for safety and health. It is stipulated by TRIPS that patents shall be available for any inventions, whether products or processes, in all fields of technology, provided that they are new, involve an inventive step and are capable of industrial application. They must be protected for at least 20 years.

However, it is also recognized that Members may exclude from patentability inventions, the prevention within their territory of the commercial exploitation of which is necessary to protect *ordre public* or morality, including to protect human, animal or plant life or health or to avoid serious prejudice to the environment, provided that such exclusion is not made merely because the exploitation is prohibited by their law. And Members may also exclude from patentability of: (a) diagnostic, therapeutic and surgical methods for the treatment of humans or animals; (b) plants and animals other than micro-organisms, and essentially biological processes for the production of plants or animals other than non-biological and microbiological processes. However, Members shall provide for the protection of plant varieties either by patents or by an effective sui generis system or by any combination thereof. The provisions of this subparagraph shall be reviewed four years after the date of entry into force of the WTO Agreement.

As a patent owner, he shall have exclusive rights for the use of its patent and shall have the right to assign, or transfer by succession, the patent and to conclude licensing contracts. Where the subject matter of a patent is a product, to prevent third parties not having the owner's consent from the acts of: making, using, offering for sale, selling, or importing for these purposes that product. Where the subject matter of a patent is a process, to prevent third parties not having the owner's consent from the act of using the process, and from the acts of: using, offering for sale, selling, or importing for these purposes at least the product obtained directly by that process. The term of protection available shall not end before the expiration of a period of 20 years counted from the filing date.

TRIPS recognizes Members' right to compulsory license in facing with public

---

① See TRIPS, Article 14.

health emergency. Where the law of a Member allows for other use of the subject matter of a patent without the authorization of the right holder, such use may only be permitted if, prior to such use, the proposed user has made efforts to obtain authorization from the right holder on reasonable commercial terms and conditions and that such efforts have not been successful within a reasonable period of time. This requirement may be waived by a Member in the case of a national emergency or other circumstances of extreme urgency or in cases of public non-commercial use. In situations of national emergency or other circumstances of extreme urgency, the right holder shall, nevertheless, be notified as soon as reasonably practicable. In the case of public non-commercial use, where the government or contractor, without making a patent search, knows or has demonstrable grounds to know that a valid patent is or will be used by or for the government, the right holder shall be informed promptly, the scope and duration of such use shall be limited to the purpose for which it was authorized, and the right holder shall be paid adequate remuneration.①

1.1.3 Trademarks

Trademarks as defined by the TRIPS, include any signs or any combination of signs, capable of distinguishing the goods or services of one undertaking from those of other undertakings. Such signs, in particular words including personal names, letters, numerals, figurative elements and combinations of colors as well as any combination of such signs, shall be eligible for registration as trademarks. Where signs are not inherently capable of distinguishing the relevant goods or services, Members may make registrability depend on distinctiveness acquired through use. Members may require, as a condition of registration, that signs be visually perceptible, but actual use of a trademark shall not be a condition for filing an application for registration.②

Once registered, a trademark shall be protected for a term of no less than seven years. And its registration can be renewable indefinitely. During such protected period, the trademark owner has the exclusive right to prevent all third parties not having the owner's consent from using in the course of trade identical or similar signs for goods or services which are identical or similar to those in respect of which the trademark is registered where such use would result in a likelihood of confusion. In case of the use of an identical sign for identical goods or services, a likelihood of confusion shall be presumed. The rights described above shall not prejudice any existing prior rights, nor shall they affect the

---

① See TRIPS, Articles 27–31.

② See TRIPS, Article 15.

possibility of Members making rights available on the basis of use.

For well-known trademark protection, there is a link between TRIPS and Paris Convention. It is required that the Members in Article 6bis of the Paris Convention (1967) shall apply, *mutatis mutandis*, to services. In determining whether a trademark is well-known, Members shall take account of the knowledge of the trademark in the relevant sector of the public, including knowledge in the Member concerned which has been obtained as a result of the promotion of the trademark.

Article 6bis of the Paris Convention (1967) shall apply, *mutatis mutandis*, to goods or services which are not similar to those in respect of which a trademark is registered, provided that use of that trademark in relation to those goods or services would indicate a connection between those goods or services and the owner of the registered trademark and provided that the interests of the owner of the registered trademark are likely to be damaged by such use. Thus, the TRIPS has incorporated the provision of well-known trademark protection stipulated by Paris Convention into the Agreement.

1.1.4 Geographical indications

Geographical indications are place name used to identify the origin and quality, reputation or other characteristics of products.

TRIPS protects indications that identify a good as originating in the territory of a Member, or a region or locality in that territory, where a given quality, reputation or other characteristic of the good is essentially attributable to its geographical origin. Members are required by Article 22 of TRIPS to provide the legal means for interested parties to prevent the use of any means in the designation or presentation of a good that indicates or suggests that the good in question originates in a geographical area other than the true place of origin in a manner which misleads the public as to the geographical origin of the good, or any use which constitutes an act of unfair competition within the meaning of Article 10bis of the Paris Convention. If a trademark contains or consists of a geographical indication with respect to goods not originating in the territory indicated and causes confusion, a Member shall refuse or invalidate the registration of the trademark as requested by the interested party.

A higher or enhanced level of protection for geographical indications are given by TRIPS for wines and spirits. Pursuant to Article 23, each Member shall provide the legal means for interested parties to prevent use of a geographical indication identifying wines for wines not originating in the place indicated by the geographical indication in question or identifying spirits for spirits not originating in the place indicated by the geographical indication in question, even where the true origin of the goods is indicated or the geographical indication is used in translation or accompanied by expressions such as "kind", "type", "style", "imitation" or the like. Thus, the registration of a trademark for wines which contains or consists of a geographical indication identifying wines or for spirits which contains or consists of a geographical indication identifying spirits shall be refused or invalidated.

The protection of geographical indications is not without limits. In some cases, geographical indications do not have to be protected or the protection can be limited. Among the exceptions that the Agreement allows are: when a name has become the common (or "generic") term (for example, "cheddar" now refers to a particular type of cheese not necessarily made in Cheddar, in the UK), and when a term has already been registered as a trademark.①

1.1.5 Industrial designs

Members shall provide for the protection of independently created industrial designs that are new or original. Members may provide that designs are not new or original if they do not significantly differ from known designs or combinations of known design features. Members may provide that such protection shall not extend to designs dictated essentially by technical or functional considerations. The owner of a protected industrial design shall have the right to prevent third parties not having the owner's consent from making, selling or importing articles bearing or embodying a design which is a copy, or substantially a copy, of the protected design, when such acts are undertaken for commercial purposes. And the duration of protection available shall amount to at least 10 years.

Each Member shall ensure that requirements for securing protection for textile designs, in particular in regard to any cost, examination or publication, do not unreasonably impair the opportunity to seek and obtain such protection. Members shall be free to meet this obligation through industrial design law or through copyright law.②

1.1.6 Layout designs of integrated circuits

Members shall consider unlawful the following acts if performed without the

---

① See TRIPS, Articles 22–24.

② See TRIPS, Articles 25–28.

authorization of the right holder: importing, selling, or otherwise distributing for commercial purposes a protected layout-design, an integrated circuit in which a protected layout-design is incorporated, or an article incorporating such an integrated circuit only in so far as it continues to contain an unlawfully reproduced layout-design.①

In Members requiring registration as a condition of protection, the term of protection of layout-designs shall not end before the expiration of a period of 10 years counted from the date of filing an application for registration or from the first commercial exploitation wherever in the world it occurs. In Members not requiring registration as a condition for protection, layout-designs shall be protected for a term of no less than 10 years from the date of the first commercial exploitation wherever in the world it occurs.②

1.1.7 Undisclosed information

Undisclosed information includes trade secrets and test data. TRIPS protects information that is secret, has commercial value because it is secret, and has been subject to reasonable steps to keep it secret. Natural and legal persons shall have the possibility of preventing information lawfully within their control from being disclosed to, acquired by, or used by others without their consent in a manner contrary to honest commercial practices.③ Test data submitted to governments in order to obtain marketing approval for new pharmaceutical or agricultural chemicals must also be protected against unfair commercial use and disclosure. Extended transition periods continue to apply to least developed country members.

1.2 Non-discriminatory principles of TRIPS

As in the GATT and the GATS, the starting point of the TRIPS Agreement is basic principles. And as in the two other Agreements, non-discrimination features are national treatment and most-favored-nation treatment. National treatment is also a key principle in other intellectual property agreements outside the WTO. The TRIPS Agreement has an additional important general objective: intellectual property protection should contribute to technical innovation and the transfer of technology, and both producers and users should benefit, and economic and social welfare should be enhanced.

① See TRIPS, Article 36.
② See TRIPS, Article 38.
③ See TRIPS, Article 39.

1.3 Enforcement of TRIPS

Intellectual property protection requires robust and stringent domestic enforcement mechanisms. TRIPS has made mandatory duties on enforcement of Member's intellectual property law, covering issues of administrative and judicial procedure, evidence, injunction, damages, and so on.

Members shall ensure that their enforcement procedures are available to permit effective action against any act of infringement of intellectual property rights covered by TRIPS, including expeditious remedies to prevent infringements and remedies which constitute a deterrent to further infringements.

These procedures shall be fair and equitable, and they shall not be unnecessarily complicated or costly, or entail unreasonable time-limits or unwarranted delays. The procedures shall be applied in such a manner as to avoid the creation of barriers to legitimate trade and to provide for safeguards against their abuse.

When the administrative bodies make decisions on intellectual property registration or annulment, decisions are preferably in writing and reasoned. They shall be made available at least to the parties to the proceeding without undue delay. Decisions on the merits of a case shall be based only on evidence in respect of which parties are offered the opportunity to be heard.

After an administrative decision is made, it is required by the TRIPS that parties to a proceeding shall have an opportunity for review by a judicial authority of final administrative decisions and, subject to jurisdictional provisions in a Member's law concerning the importance of a case, of at least the legal aspects of initial judicial decisions on the merits of a case. However, there shall be no obligation to provide an opportunity for review of acquittals in criminal cases.

Members shall make available to right holders civil judicial procedures concerning the enforcement of any intellectual property right covered by TRIPS. Defendants shall have the right to written notice which is timely and contains sufficient detail, including the basis of the claims. Parties shall be allowed to be represented by independent legal counsel, and procedures shall not impose overly burdensome requirements concerning mandatory personal appearances. All parties to such procedures shall be duly entitled to substantiate their claims and to present all relevant evidence. The procedure shall provide a means to identify and protect confidential information, unless this would be contrary to existing constitutional requirements.

Concerning evidence, the judicial authorities shall have the authority, where a party has presented reasonably available evidence sufficient to support its claims and has specified evidence relevant to substantiation of its claims which lies in the control of the opposing party, to order that this evidence be produced by the opposing party, subject in appropriate cases to conditions which ensure the protection of confidential information.①

TRIPS requires the Members to provide injunctions as a remedy for IP infringement. The judicial authorities shall have the authority to order a party to desist from an infringement, *inter alia*, to prevent the entry into the channels of commerce in their jurisdiction of imported goods that involve the infringement of an intellectual property right, immediately after customs clearance of such goods. Members are not obliged to accord such authority in respect of protected subject matter acquired or ordered by a person prior to knowing or having reasonable grounds to know that dealing in such subject matter would entail the infringement of an intellectual property right.②

Concerning the damages, the judicial authorities shall have the authority to order the infringer to pay the right holder damages adequate to compensate for the injury the right holder has suffered because of an infringement of that person's intellectual property right by an infringer who knowingly, or with reasonable grounds to know, engaged in infringing activity.

The judicial authorities shall also have the authority to order the infringer to pay the right holder expenses, which may include appropriate attorney's fees. In appropriate cases, Members may authorize the judicial authorities to order recovery of profits and/or payment of pre-established damages even where the infringer did not knowingly, or with reasonable grounds to know, engage in infringing activity.

In order to create an effective deterrent to infringement, it is required by the TRIPS that the judicial authorities shall have the authority to order that goods that they have found to be infringing be, without compensation of any sort, disposed of outside the channels of commerce in such a manner as to avoid any harm caused to the right holder, or, unless this would be contrary to existing constitutional requirements, destroyed. The judicial authorities shall also have the authority to order that materials and implements the predominant use of which has been in the creation of the infringing goods be, without compensation of any sort, disposed of outside the channels of commerce in such a manner

① See TRIPS, Article 43.
② See TRIPS, Article 44.

as to minimize the risks of further infringements. In considering such requests, the need for proportionality between the seriousness of the infringement and the remedies ordered as well as the interests of third parties shall be taken into account. In regard to counterfeit trademark goods, the simple removal of the trademark unlawfully affixed shall not be sufficient, other than in exceptional cases, to permit release of the goods into the channels of commerce.①

To sum up, although the TRIPS only stipulates the minimum standard of intellectual property protection for its Members, it enhances the awareness of intellectual property protection in the developing countries and provides a legal framework for them.

1.4 Anti-competitive practice and technology transfer

More generally, the TRIPS Agreement recognizes that right holders could use their rights to restrict competition or impede technology transfer. The Agreement gives governments the right to take action against anti-competitive practices. In certain situations, the TRIPS Agreement also waives some conditions required for the compulsory license of a patent in cases where the government grants the compulsory license in order to remedy a practice determined to be anti-competitive.

Developing country members in particular see technology transfer as part of the bargain in which they have agreed to protect intellectual property rights. The TRIPS Agreement aims for the transfer of technology and requires developed country members to provide incentives for their companies to promote the transfer of technology to least-developed countries in order to enable them to create a sound and viable technological base.

Case II-10

Australia–Tobacco Plain Package Requirements②

The tobacco plain packaging measures were apt to make a meaningful contribution to Australia's objective of improving public health by reducing the use of, and exposure to, tobacco products. The measures required tobacco products and

① See TRIPS, Articles 45–46.

② Source: WTO Panel Report, Australia–Certain Measures Concerning Trademarks, Geographical Indications and Other Plain Packaging Requirements Applicable to Tobacco Products and Packaging, WT/DS435/R, WT/DS441/R, WT/DS458/R, WT/DS467/R, adopted on 29 June 2020.

their retail packaging to appear in a uniform manner and no trademarks and logos were allowed to be printed on the package or on the products themselves. On 3 May 2013, Cuba requested consultations with Australia concerning certain Australian laws and regulations that allegedly imposed trademark restrictions and other plain-packaging requirements on tobacco products. Cuba claimed that Australia's measures appeared to be inconsistent with Australia's obligations under Articles 2.1, 3.1, 15.4, 16.1, 20, 22.2(b) and 24.3 of the TRIPS Agreement, Articles 2.1 and 2.2 of the TBT Agreement, and Articles 3.4 and 9.4 of the GATT 1994.

On 8 May 2013, Canada and New Zealand requested to join the consultations. On 13 May 2013, Honduras and Norway requested to join the consultations. On 14 May 2013, Ukraine requested to join the consultations. On 16 May 2013, the European Union requested to join the consultations. On 17 May 2013, Brazil, the Dominican Republic, Guatemala, Nicaragua and Uruguay requested to join the consultations. On 5 May 2014, the Director-General composed the panel. On 10 October 2014, the Chair of the Panel informed the DSB that the Panel expected to issue its final report. Hereunder is the Panel's findings on the measures' conformity with TRIPS.

Panel's Findings

(1) Paris Convention Art. 6 quinquies (registration of trademarks): The complainants did not demonstrate that the tobacco plain packaging measures were inconsistent with Australia's obligation to accept for filing and protect "as is" every trademark duly registered in the country of origin.

(2) TRIPS Art. 15.4 (an obstacle to registration of a trademark): The complainants did not demonstrate that the nature of the goods to which the tobacco plain packaging measures applied ("tobacco products") formed an obstacle to the registration of trademarks contrary to Art. 15.4.

(3) TRIPS Art. 16.1 (rights conferred to an owner of a registered trademark): The complainants did not demonstrate that the tobacco plain packaging measures were inconsistent with Australia's obligation to allow the owner of a registered trademark to prevent unauthorized use of identical or similar trademarks on identical or similar products, where such use would result in a likelihood of confusion.

(4) TRIPS Art. 16.3 (well-known trademarks): Cuba and Indonesia did not demonstrate that the tobacco plain packaging measures were inconsistent with Australia's obligation to protect well-known trademarks under Art. 16.3.

(5) TRIPS Art. 20 (other requirements): The complainants did not demonstrate that the tobacco plain packaging measures unjustifiably encumbered the use of trademarks in violation of Art. 20.

(6) Paris Convention Art. 10bis (unfair competition): Cuba and Indonesia did not demonstrate that the tobacco plain packaging measures compelled market actors to engage in acts of unfair competition of such a nature as to create confusion within the meaning of para. 3(1) or to engage in acts amounting to misleading indications or allegations within the meaning of para. 3(3); Honduras, the Dominican Republic and Cuba did not demonstrate that the tobacco plain packaging measures required market actors to engage in such acts of unfair competition against which Australia was bound to assure effective protection pursuant to para. 1.

(7) TRIPS Art. 22.2(b) [use of geographical indications (GIs) constituting unfair competition]: The complainants did not demonstrate that the tobacco plain packaging measures compelled market actors to engage in acts of unfair competition that would amount to misleading indications or allegations about product characteristics within the meaning of Paris Convention Art. 10bis(3)(3) in respect of GIs.

(8) TRIPS Art. 24.3 (pre-existing domestic protection of GIs): The complainants did not demonstrate that the protection that GIs enjoyed under Australian law immediately had been diminished as a result of the tobacco plain packaging measures or that the tobacco plain packaging measures were inconsistent with Art. 24.3.

Discussions:

1.What duty does TRIPS Art. 16.1 impose on the WTO members? Did plain packaging measures in Australia breach Art. 16.1 of TRIPS?

2. What are the TRIPS' requirements on well-known trademark protection? Did plain packaging measures breach these requirements?

2 Paris Convention on Industrial Property Protection

The Paris Convention for the Protection of Industrial Property (Paris Convention) was signed in Paris on 20 March 1883. The Convention was one of the first intellectual property protection treaties in the world and it established a Union to protect the intellectual property for its Members. The substantive provisions of the Convention mainly include national treatment and priority right. Besides, it makes some common rules of industrial property protection for the Union members.

2.1 National treatment

According to Articles 2 and 3 of the Convention, judicial and natural persons who are either national of or domiciled in one contracting state to the Convention shall, as regard to the protection of industrial property, enjoy in all the other countries of the Union, the advantages that their respective laws grant to nationals.

In other words, when an applicant files an application for a patent or a trademark in a foreign country of the Union, the application receives the same treatment as if it came from a national of this foreign country. Furthermore, if the intellectual property right is granted, the owner benefits from the same protection and the same legal remedy against any infringement as if the owner was a national owner of this right.

2.2 Priority right

The priority right is established by Article 4 of the Paris Convention, and is regarded as one of the cornerstones of the Convention. It provides that an applicant from one contracting state shall be able to use its first filing date in one of the contracting states as the effective filing date in another contracting state, provided that the applicant, or his successor in title, files a subsequent application within a period of time. In terms of industrial designs and trademarks, it shall be six months, while in terms of patents and utility models, it shall be 12 months from the date of its first filing.

Article 11(1) of the Paris Convention requires that the Members of the Union grant temporary protection to patentable inventions, utility models, industrial designs, and trademarks, in respect of goods exhibited at official or officially recognized international exhibitions held in the territory of any of them.

If a patent or trademark registration is applied for during the temporary period of protection, the priority date of the application may be counted "from the date of introduction of the goods into the exhibition" rather than from the date of filing of the application, if the temporary protection referred to in Article 11(1) has been implemented in such a manner in national law. There are, however, other means for the countries of the Union to implement in their national law the temporary protection provided for in Article 11 of the Paris Convention.

It is also possible, for example, in the case of exhibited patentable inventions, to make provision for temporary protection by other means, namely, by prescribing that, during a certain period, such exhibition will not reduce the novelty of the invention and that the person who exhibits the invention will also be protected against usurpation of his invention by third parties. Still another possibility of protection consists in the recognition of a right of prior use in favor of the exhibitor as against possible rights acquired by third parties.

2.3 Mutual independence of patents and trademarks in different countriesof the Union

According to Articles 4bis and 6 (for patents and trademarks respectively), for foreigners, the application for a patent or the registration of a trademark shall be determined by the Member in accordance with their national law and not by the decision of the country of origin or any other countries. Patent applications and trademark registrations are independent among contracting countries.

3 Berne Convention for the Protection of Copyright Literary and Artistic Works

The Paris Convention provides a scheme for the Union members to protect their industrial property, while the International Convention for the Protection of Literary and Artistic Works (Berne Convention) protects literary and artistic works. The Berne Convention was adopted in 1886 and was modified several times after its adoption (Berlin, 1908; Rome, 1928; Brussels, 1948; Stockholm, 1967; and Paris, 1971).

The core of the Berne Convention lies in that each of its Members shall provide automatic protection for works first published in other countries of the Berne Union and for unpublished works whose authors are citizens of or resident in such other countries.

Each country of the Berne Union must guarantee to authors who are nationals of other member countries the rights that its own laws grant to its nationals. If the work has been first published in a Berne Union country but the author is a national of a nonunion country, the Berne Union country may restrict the protection to the extent that such protection is limited in the country of which the author is a national. The works protected by the Rome revision of 1928 include every production in the literary, scientific, and artistic domain, regardless of the mode of expression, such as books, pamphlets, and other writings; lectures, addresses, sermons, and other works of the same nature; dramatic or dramatic musical works, choreographic works and entertainments in dumb show, the acting form of which is fixed in writing or otherwise; musical compositions; drawings, paintings, works of architecture, sculpture, engraving, and lithography; illustrations, geographical charts, plans, sketches, and plastic works relative to geography, topography, architecture, or science. It also includes translations, adaptations, arrangements of music, and other reproductions in an altered form of a literary or artistic work, as well as collections of different works. The Brussels revision of 1948 added cinematographic works and photographic works. In addition, both the Rome and Brussels revisions protect works of art applied to industrial purposes so far as the domestic legislation of each country allows such protection.

The protection of the Berne Convention mainly extends to authors who are nationals of one of the countries of the Union, for their works, whether published or not, and authors who are not nationals of one of the countries of the Berne Union, for their works first published in one of those countries, or simultaneously in a country outside the Berne Union and in a country of the Union. But this does not mean that authors who are not nationals of one of the countries of the Berne Union will not be protected. If they have their habitual residence in one of them shall, for the purposes of this Convention, be assimilated to nationals of that country, they are nevertheless protected.

For cinematographic works and architecture, the Berne Convention shall apply, to authors of cinematographic works the maker of which has his headquarters or habitual residence in one of the countries of the Berne Union and authors of works of architecture erected in a country of the Union or of other artistic works incorporated in a building or other structure located in a country of the Berne Union.

The term of protection granted by this Convention shall be the life of the author and 50 years after his death. In case of joint authorship, the provisions of the preceding Article shall also apply in the case of a work of joint authorship, provided that the terms measured from the death of the author shall be calculated from the death of the last surviving author.

However, in the case of cinematographic works, the countries of the Berne Union may provide that the term of protection shall expire 50 years after the work has been made available to the public with the consent of the author, or, failing such an event within 50 years from the making of such a work, 50 years after the making.

The rights protected by the Berne Convention include authorship, right of translation, right of reproduction, right of adaptation, arrangement and other alteration, broadcasting and related rights, and so on.

4 Other Treaties on Intellectual Property Protection

Other well-known treaties on intellectual property protection include Madrid system for trademark registration and Anti-Counterfeiting Trade Agreement.

The Madrid system for trademark registration consists of two treaties. One is the Madrid Agreement and the other one is Madrid Protocol. The system offers an international registration of trademarks for countries. It is a convenient and cost-effective solution for registering and managing trademarks worldwide, as filing a single application and paying one set of fees will allow its trademark being protected in up to 122 countries. Moreover, the application can be conducted in only one language and in one office.

Apart from the convenience and simplicity of trademark registration in different countries, the Madrid Protocol also simplifies the subsequent management of the mark, since a simple, single procedural step serves to record subsequent changes in ownership or in the name or address of the holder with World Intellectual Property Organization's (WIPO) International Bureau. The International Bureau administers the Madrid System and coordinates the transmittal of requests for protection, renewals and other relevant documentation to all Members.

The greatest value of Madrid System is that it provides an opportunity of international registration for its Members. An application for international registration may be filed only by a natural person or legal entity having a connection—through establishment, domicile or nationality—with a Contracting Party to the Madrid Agreement or the Madrid Protocol. A mark may be the subject of an international application only if it has already been registered with the trademark office of the Contracting Party with which the applicant has the necessary connections. However, where all the designations are effected under the Protocol, the international application may be based simply on an application for registration filed with the office of origin. An international application must be presented to the International Bureau of WIPO through the intermediary of the office of origin.

An application for international registration must designate one or more Contracting Parties in which protection is sought. Further designations can be effected subsequently. A Contracting Party may be designated only if it is the party to the same treaty as the Contracting Party whose office is the office of origin. The latter cannot itself be designated in the international application.

The designation of a given Contracting Party is made either under the Madrid

Agreement or the Madrid Protocol, depending on which treaty is common to the Contracting Parties concerned. If both Contracting Parties are parties to the Madrid Agreement and the Madrid Protocol, the designation will be governed by the Madrid Protocol.

Once the International Bureau receives an international application, it carries out an examination for compliance with the requirements of the Protocol. This examination is restricted to formalities, including the classification and comprehensibility of the list of goods and/or services. If there are no irregularities in the application, the International Bureau records the mark in the International Register, publishes the international registration in the WIPO Gazette of International Marks, and notifies it to each designated Contracting Party. Any matter of substance, such as whether the mark qualifies for protection or whether it is in conflict with a mark registered previously in a particular Contracting Party, is determined by that Contracting Party's trademark office under the applicable domestic legislation.

The Anti-Counterfeiting Trade Agreement (ACTA) is a proposed international trade agreement negotiated by the US, the EU, Switzerland, Canada, Australia, New Zealand, Mexico, Singapore, Morocco, Japan, and The Republic of Korea from 2007 to 2010. Eight out of the eleven negotiating countries signed this Agreement in October 2011. Judged from its name, the aim of the Agreement is to curtail commercial scale counterfeiting and piracy of intellectual property.

The negotiation of ACTA was a secret, and domestic policy makers, NGOs and citizens were kept out of the negotiation. The text was first released in 2010, once it had already been finalized following eight rounds of closed-door negotiations.

The ACTA includes six chapters and 45 articles. The Agreement applies to pirated copyright goods, which are copies made without the permission of the rights holder, and counterfeit trademark goods, which are packages and goods bearing a trademark identical to the registered trademark without authorization. The ACTA text purports to strengthen intellectual property enforcement against pirates and counterfeits. In order to provide the adequate legal protection and effective legal remedies, the signatory parties shall provide protection at least against the unauthorized circumvention of an effective technological measure carried out knowingly or with reasonable grounds to know; and the offering to the public by marketing of a device or product, including computer programs, or a service, as a means of circumventing an effective technological measure; and the manufacture, importation, or distribution of a device or product, including computer programs, or provision of a service that is primarily designed or produced for the purpose of circumventing an effective technological measure, or has only a limited commercially significant purpose other than circumventing an effective technological measure.

States participating in the ACTA scheme shall also ensure their enforcement procedures against intellectual property infringement apply to infringement of copyright or related rights over digital networks. A country may provide, in accordance with its laws and regulations, its competent authorities with the authority to order an online service provider to disclose expeditiously to a right holder information sufficient to identify a subscriber whose account was allegedly used for infringement, where that right holder has filed a legally sufficient claim of trademark or copyright or related rights infringement, and where such information is being sought for the purpose of protecting or enforcing those rights. These procedures shall be implemented in a manner that avoids the creation of barriers to legitimate activity, including electronic commerce, and, consistent with that Party's law, preserves fundamental principles such as freedom of expression, fair process, and privacy.①

Parties to ACTA shall provide that its competent authorities have the authority to order the seizure of suspected counterfeit trademark goods or pirated copyright goods, any related materials and implements used in the commission of the alleged offense, documentary evidence relevant to the alleged offense, and the assets derived from, or obtained directly or indirectly through, the alleged infringing activity.

They shall also provide its competent authorities with the authority to order the forfeiture or destruction of materials and implements predominantly used in the creation of counterfeit trademark goods or pirated copyright goods and, at least for serious offenses, of the assets derived from, or obtained directly or indirectly through, the infringing activity. Each Party shall ensure that the forfeiture or destruction of such materials, implements, or assets shall occur without compensation of any sort to the infringer.② In cases where counterfeit trademark goods and pirated copyright goods are not destroyed, the competent authorities shall ensure that, except in exceptional circumstances, such goods shall be disposed of outside the channels of commerce in such a manner as to avoid causing any harm to the right holder. Each Party shall ensure that the forfeiture or destruction of such goods shall occur without compensation of any sort to the infringer.

① See ACTA, Article 27.
② See ACTA, Article 25.

Under the ACTA, each signatory party shall also allow access to the courts of its country to any party infringed under the terms of the Agreement. The courts of any signatory country may order the infringing party to pay appropriate damages, including legal fees, to the rights holder. ACTA allows judicial authorities of the signatory countries to issue orders to stop the infringement and to have the pirated or counterfeited goods destroyed.

The Parties established the ACTA Committee to review the implementation and operation of ACTA, and to consider proposed amendments and any other matter that may affect the implementation and operation of this Agreement.

Chapter Review

1. What are the subject matters protected by TRIPS?
2. Does TRIPS protect the performers and producers? How does it protect them?
3. What kind of information is protected by TRIPS?
4. What are the rules for well-known trademarks protection under the TRIPS?
5. What kind of industrial designs will be protected by TRIPS?
6. State briefly the rules of patent protection in TRIPS.
7. How does TRIPS require when geographic indication protection conflicts with trademark protection?
8. What are the rules of enforcement of intellectual property right required by TRIPS?
9. Does Member need to provide a distinct judicial procedure for intellectual property protection apart from ordinary civil procedure?
10. What is the full name of Paris Convention, and what are the mandates of it?
11. How do you explain the rule of national treatment of Paris Convention?
12. What does priority right mean? How is it protected by Paris Convention?
13. Who determines the applicability of patent registration pursuant to Paris Convention?
14. What is the Madrid system for trademark registration? What are the merits of such System?
15. What does international registration mean? How does a trade mark owner apply for an international registration?
16. Does International Bureau examine the substance of a mark's registrability in the process of international registration?
17. What is the Anti-Counterfeiting Trade Agreement? Who are the parties of it?

18. How does Anti-Counterfeiting Trade Agreement strengthen intellectual property enforcement among its parties?
19. When signatory countries of ACTA require destruction of materials used to produce counterfeited goods, shall compensation of any sort be paid to the infringer?
20. What kind of intellectual property is protected by Berne Convention?
21. Are translations and adaptations of original work protected by Berne Convention?
22. Which revision of Berne Convention added cinematographic works and photographic works into its coverage?
23. Briefly explain the Rome revision and Brussels revision of Berne Convention.
24. What is the term of authorship granted by Berne Convention?
25. Must the author be a national of one of members of Berne Union for Berne Convention?

Key Terms

Anti-Counterfeiting Trade Agreement (ACTA)	《反假冒贸易协定》
Berne Convention for the Protection of Literary and Artistic Works	《保护文学与艺术作品伯尔尼公约》
copyright	版权
geographical indications	地理标志
industrial design	工业设计
layout designs of integrated circuits	集成电路拓扑设计
Madrid System	马德里体系
Paris Convention for the Protection of Industrial Property	《保护工业产权巴黎公约》
patent	专利
trademark	商标
undisclosed information	未披露信息（商业秘密）

Further Readings

1. Fitzgerald, Brian, Sampsung Xiaoxiang Shi, Cheryl Foong & Kylie Pappalardo, *Country of Origin and Internet Publication: Applying the Berne Convention in the Digital Age*, in Brian Fitzgerald & John Gilchrist eds., Copyright Perspectives:

Past, Present and Prospect, Springer, 2015.

2. Helfer, Laurence R., *Regime Shifting: The TRIPs Agreement and New Dynamics of International Intellectual Property Lawmaking*, Yale Journal of International Law, Vol. 29: 1, 2004.

3. https://www.wipo.int/portal/en/index.html.

Chapter 5
The Crisis of the WTO and Proliferation of PTAs

Study Guide

This Chapter includes some academic discussions on the crisis of the WTO and fragmentation of international economic law, which is supposed to shed light on the reasons causing the WTO's current deadlock, different ways of reforming the WTO and the difficulties faced by the international community. The contents in this Chapter is rather inspiring with an aim to encourage students to think profoundly about the problems inherent in the world trade law and form their own opinions.

The Chapter also discusses the proliferation of preferential trade agreements (PTAs). The rising number of PTAs suggests not only the vitality of regional cooperation on trade and relevant issues, but also indicates that the multilateral cooperation will be influenced by these regional agreements. Poor countries will be further marginalized in the world trading system.

The GATT has acted as an engine for global free trade governance since the end of World War II. Its highest achievement is the establishment of the WTO. However, the trade negotiations under the WTO are far from successful, as it missed the major agendas set in the Seattle, Cancun, and Hong Kong ministerial conferences. Trade negotiations failed to liberalize members' markets in sensitive sectors, such as agriculture and trade in service, and only achieved success in the Bali and Nairobi conferences.

As the WTO gradually loses momentum and influences, its status is challenged by preferential trade agreements (PTAs), especially by the so-called mega-PTAs or high-standard PTAs. Such PTAs would exert only peripheral influence in global trade governance but are gaining more attention now.

To keep global trade governance working, both the WTO and PTAs are undergoing reforms. The WTO needs to reestablish its erstwhile position, not at the center but near the center of world commerce, sharing power and responsibility with PTAs in their respective spheres of influence.① The peripheral reforms led by high-standard PTAs are taking steps forward in updating international trade rules. Apart from these rule-based reforms, the Belt and Road initiated by China, shows another method of reform, which is far from

---

① See Mitsuo Matsushita, *A View on Future Roles of The WTO: Should There be More Soft Law in The WTO?*, 17 Journal of International Economic Law 701, 705 (2014).

rule-based and shares little commonality with the high-standard PTAs. However, it has immense potential to revitalize international trade and investments in Asia. Such regional cooperation contributes to the peripheral reforms of global trade and investment law and provides us with a new angle of observing and analyzing the effectiveness of regional trade cooperation.

Hence, the future global trade governance will progress with the co-influence of the central and peripheral reforms hosted by the WTO, PTAs, or other innovative regional cooperative platforms.

1 Crisis Faced by the WTO and Possible Reforms

The global trade governance of the GATT and the WTO has been applauded by the members for multilateralism, free trade, and non-discrimination since 1947. A half century later, however, it has lost its viability and driving force toward more comprehensive trade and investment. What has exhausted the WTO's vitality and crippled its treaty negotiation function?

1.1 Factors frustrating the WTO's trade negotiation and dispute settlement functions

The most significant factor is the power shift among its members. Before the Uruguay Round, the power of trade governance was assumed by the top four countries, the "Quad" (US, EU, Japan and Canada), as led by the US and followed by the EU, Canada, and Japan. The multilateral trade negotiations were concessions among the Quad and their trade-affiliated countries. At the end of the 20th century, however, the members of the Quad were declining due to their overseas wars, economic downturns, and the Euro crisis. The financial and economic crisis in 2008 spread rampant protectionism across trading nations, and dragged the global economy and fragmented the world of developed countries. In many countries around the globe stock markets have fallen, financial institutions have collapsed and governments have adopted rescue packages to bail out their financial systems.

The Quad's global trade shares have been significantly taken up by emerging economies, such as China, Brazil, and India. The decline of the original big powers and the rise of newly emerging economies give rise to new clashes and make consent-based solutions harder. And 2/3 of the 164 WTO members are developing countries. These countries are aligning and forming the counter-power to contest the rules once set by the big powers.①

Apart from the power shift, the reconstruction of the global value chain and international trade constrains the trade negotiations of the WTO. The offshore sourcing and trading of semi-finished products requires comprehensive integration of the value chain among the trading nations, producing the needs for multilateral law-making in investment, trade in service, intellectual property, rules of origin, competition, etc. Hence, the negotiation agendas in the Doha Round are far more complex than in former rounds. With the increased flow of international trade and investment, members' statuses in the international value chain also change. The developed countries are losing their comparative advantage in manufacturing industries but are reimbursed by the high yields derived from foreign direct investment, trade in service, and technology transfer. Therefore, liberalizing developing countries' markets of trade in service and investment and strengthening overseas intellectual property protection and competition rules, labor, and environmental protection standards clearly become the mandates of new treaty negotiation in pushing the reform of global trade governance. The global value chain revolution has also altered the nature of trade barriers. The so called behind-the-border trade measures and trade barriers imposed by third parties may affect upstream or downstream flow of international trade, which further complicate the trade administration and regulation.

The next major factor that changes global trade governance is the development of information technology. The General Agreement on Trade in Services (GATS) became obsolete just a few years after its conclusion due to the rapid development of information technology. Today, free data flow is indispensable for the development of electronic commerce and transboundary trade in service, which makes data a new production factor apart from the raw material, land, labor, and capital. Shortly after the International Technology Product Agreement was entered into force in 1997, the developed countries intended to renew the GATS by negotiating the so-called GATS 2000 to reap the benefits of fast development of information technology. However, the consensus was not adopted due to the North-South division in their control of information technologies and each

① See Mitsuo Matsushita, *Japanese Policies toward East Asia Free Trade Agreements: Policy and Legal Perspectives*, in Ross Buckley et al. eds., Challenges to Multilateral Trade: The Impact of Bilateral, Preferential and Regional Agreements, Kluwer Law International, 2008.

member's different concerns of national security and consumer privacy. Just free data flow continues to be a core issue in the negotiation of the Trade in Service Agreement (TISA).

Despite these challenges, the WTO's institutional structure remains unchanged. It has failed to adapt to new economic and societal needs and has often been criticized for not having provided solutions to current economic troubles. The debacle of the Doha Round negotiations, which instilled a sense of helplessness into the WTO, reveals the fatal flaw of WTO's institutional structure. The biggest obstacle for reaching consensus is the members' veto power. It would prevent the WTO from adopting new treaties or amending old ones.① When developed countries try to export their domestic rules to less-developed countries without cutting their agriculture subsidies and tariffs to reimburse the developing countries for the direct and inherent costs and risks of rule integration, the developing countries' grievances accumulate, and they refuse to cooperate with their developed partners.

Apart from the consensus requirement, the WTO's government-driven nature is criticized by civic society for its lack of democracy and transparency as well as ignorance of non-trade values. The legitimate authority and *opinio juris* in the 21st century are no longer derived from diplomatic fiat, but from the consent of citizens, their democratic representatives, and from progressive clarification of principles of justice by impartial and independent courts of justice limiting intergovernmental power politics. The concept of "thick stakeholders consensus" is thus proposed to reshape multilateral and regional trade governance. According to Joost Pauwelyn, the traditional democracy of allowing the consensus of governments joining in the trade negotiation relies on "thin state consent", only producing thin validation and democracy, while the decision-making process allows experts, intellectuals, and stakeholders to influence the decision, which is known as "thick stakeholders consensus".② In pursuing a thick stakeholder consensus, civil society demands more participation in the trade negotiations of the WTO, but the current government-driven WTO cannot accommodate such demands without institutional reforms.

---

① E.g., the July Package, aiming to reach new agreements on agricultural and non-agricultural market access and to revise the rules of more preferential and special treatment of the developing countries, was first negotiated in 2004, but the negotiators failed to reach a meaningful agreement in the following years.

② See Joost Pauwelyn, Ramses A. Wessel & Jan Wouters, *When Structures Become Shackles: Stagnation and Dynamics in International Lawmaking*, 25 European Journal of International Law 733, 735–742 (2014).

1.2 Suggestions on reforms of the WTO

1.2.1 "Critical mass" negotiations in enhancing decision-making efficiency

The plurilateral negotiation, or the *à la carte* approach, which was once popular in the Tokyo Round, was suppressed by the single-taking requirement in the Uruguay Round. As today's trade negotiations consistently let members down, reforms to this rigid decision-making process are proposed by more scholars. Some propose to give up the single-undertaking requirement and to allow the members to pick up the treaties as they wished, thereby encouraging variable geometry, which embodies the members' different priorities in setting their trade policies through plurilateral agreements and PTAs.[①] Others suggest that the WTO adopt the weighted voting rule as the IMF. Although negotiating plurilateral agreements instead of multilateral agreements or adopting weighted voting rules could compensate for the inefficiency of WTO's decision making, these reforms deviate too much from the WTO's current institutional structure and from the ideology of the multilateralism of developing countries.[②] Instead, the "critical mass approach", as proposed by the Warwick Commission, could bridge certain elements of variable geometry with the principle of consensus to build new and flexible multilateral cooperative networks.

The Information Technology Agreement and the Agreement on Basic Telecommunications are founded on such an approach. In 1996, 29 members signed the draft of the Information Technology Agreement in the Singapore Ministerial Conference and submitted the draft for other members to ratify. Later, the Agreement was ratified by 82 members, representing 97% of the market share of computer appliances and computer services, meeting the requirement of critical mass. This Agreement later became a covered one of the WTO on 1 April 1997. The Agreement on Basic Telecommunications followed suit. In 1998, 69 members ratified the Agreement with trade flows in the sector of basic telecommunications, which reached 90%. Satisfying the requirement of critical mass, the Agreement finally became the fourth protocol of GATS. Because both the Information Technology Agreement and the Agreement on Basic Telecommunications adopted "critical mass" decision-making processes, the parties negotiated and made concessions

---

① See Rafael Leal-Arcas, *The Fragmentation of International Trade Law: Is Now the Time for Variable Geometry?*, 12 The Journal of World Investment & Trade 145, 177 (2011).

② Excerpt from *Framework for the International Services Agreement*, in Peterson Institute for International Economics Policy Brief, edited by Gary C. Hufbauer, J. Bradford Jensen & Sherry Stephenson.

on a plurilateral basis but conferred the benefits to all members in accordance with unconditional MFN treatment. As a result, this would persuade the others who have not participated in the negotiations to accept the deal and add new multilateral agreements to the WTO scheme.

The idea of negotiating critical mass agreements first was proposed by Moisés Naím, who advocated simplifying the decision-making process of treaty negotiation within the smallest number of countries to solve issues more effectively.[①] As the WTO membership was increasing to 164, either a consensus or a 2/3 majority became burdensome for any new treaty negotiation, incurring tremendous costs and uncertainties. Critical mass approach only requires trade negotiation among a small number of countries that hold substantial market share and can make concessions, while conferring the market access benefits to all. By avoiding Pareto sanction as caused by consensus, eventually, it will enhance the efficiency of members' decision-making processes. In this course, an agreement will only be reached when participants are convinced that no one is worse off by the agreement.[②] The critical mass negotiations enable a multi-speed WTO. Here, 90% is deemed to be the magic number[③] for the most efficient trade governance among the members.

The critical mass negotiation would have the potential to speed up the WTO's decision-making process. The question then may arise: can we count on this approach to revitalize WTO's treaty negotiation function? Although the critical mass relieves the burden of the WTO's decision making, it also has limits. In negotiating a market-access issue, members' trade flows could be easily quantified to determine whether the critical mass requirement has been met. In negotiating the trade regulation[④] or rule-integration issues, such as intellectual property, environmental protection, labor standards, and competition policy, however, it will be difficult to quantify the influence of trade flows.

Moreover, is 90% really the magic number that reaches the Pareto efficiency in balancing the members' participation and the efficiency of their decision making? This is doubtful because 90% is rather a high benchmark to accomplish in many negotiations. To

---

① Excerpt from *Minilateralism: The Magic Number to Get Real International Action* in Foreign Policy.

② See Bernard M. Hoekman & Petros C. Mavroidis, *WTO 'à la carte' or 'menu du jour'? Assessing the Case for More Plurilateral Agreements*, 26 European Journal of International Law 319, 319 (2015).

③ See Stephen J. Powell & Trisha Low, *Is WTO Quietly Faded Away? The New Regionalism and Global Trade Rules*, 9 Georgetown Journal of Law & Public Policy 261, 265 (2011).

④ See Thomas Cottier, *The Common Law of International Trade and the Future of the World Trade Organization*, 18 Journal of International Economic Law 3, 13 (2015). Professor Cottier mentioned that the core of WTO's decision-making has been shifted from market access to trade regulation.

receive support from the members of the critical mass, the negotiating issues should be carefully chosen to avoid those with sporadically distributed trade flows. The successful achievement of the Information Technology Agreement is due to the high concentration of the trade flows relating to computer services and computer appliances, which gives the US sufficient incentives to propose the negotiation and seek support from other trade alliances.[①] 28 parties negotiating the Government Procurement Agreement only covers 50% of the trade flows in the sector of government procurement, making it a plurilateral agreement. The critical mass negotiation also raises the concerns of fairness in trade negotiations. As compared to the conventional multilateral negotiation, variable geometry would give preference to certain issues above others, so that it would respond to the interests of the selective WTO members.

If the magic number of the critical mass is not as high as 90%, more critical mass agreements could be adopted and could save the WTO's treaty negotiation function. Thus, why can critical mass not suffice through a substantial coverage of trade flows in question to reap more benefits of mini-multilateral negotiation but stay at 90%? There may be no substantiated evidence proving that the perfect Pareto state of critical mass should be 90%. Instead, it is safer for the critical mass to stay at 90% by preventing emerging economies from freeriding the benefits of any new agreements.

1.2.2 Soft law-making to break the constraints of formal legislation

As the mandates of multilateral trade negotiations led by the WTO are to make mainly formal laws, such as treaties, there is little room for soft law-making. However, the formal legislative structure of the WTO has become a constraint, preventing the adoption of new rules in international trade, which not only blocks the new agreements on substantive issues but also fails to push the reform of procedure issues, such as dispute resolution. It is suggested that the WTO should be more attentive to informal law-making and learn from the experience of other economic cooperative platforms in forming cooperation through soft laws. One example of this is the Santiago Principles, as proposed by the IMF in developing the best practice of management of sovereign funds, which are voluntarily adopted by more sovereign funds of developed and developing countries. The International Competition Network advocated by the United States also functions well

① As IBM held dominant market shares in trade in computer services and computer appliances, it lobbied its home country to launch the negation of the Information Technology Agreement.

in coordinating the competition rules among 120 countries by making model laws and principles. The success of soft law is derived from its informality, flexibility, and *esprit de corps*,① which might remedy the deficiencies of formal law-making in international law, as they are persuasive in adducing countries' voluntary efforts even while having no enforcement.

On 22 June 2016, Canada once suggested to amend the dispute resolution rules of the WTO through the soft law-making approach by voluntarily adopting the Informal Procedure Innovation Framework Agreement. Although the dispute settlement mechanism is regarded as the crown jewel of the WTO, its confidentiality, close nature, and exclusiveness to third parties and nongovernmental organizations (NGOs) are criticized to run counter to the idea of the thick stakeholder consensus. The Informal Procedure Innovation Framework Agreement, as proposed by Canada, could make the dispute resolution procedure more open and responsive to outsiders. Canada also suggested that the dispute settlement body applied the Informal Procedure Innovation Framework Agreement to those members signing the Agreement after the exchange of the opinions or on an *ad hoc* basis upon disputing members' approval of an application in a certain dispute.

As the Informal Procedure Innovation Framework Agreement is not a treaty, no formal ratification is needed for the Members to adopt it. Therefore, the Dispute Settlement Understanding (DSU) does not have to be amended. Such soft law-making also offers a kind of variable geometry to the Members, especially in dealing with the rule-integration issues, as not all Members are ready for further integration of domestic laws on intellectual property protection or competition rules. For these issues, the significant North-South discrepancies have made a consensus difficult. Albeit the critical mass approach is impossible, the soft law approach might be more workable for the Members to update their trade rules gradually from a bottom-up approach. However, the soft law approach is less helpful in liberalizing market-access issues, as it might not incentivize Members to open their markets voluntarily if no benefits are given back, especially in the case where no measure is taken to avoid freeriding by outsiders. Lack of enforceability is another shortcoming of these soft rules, as disobedience of the rules cannot be handled through dispute settlement, and the soft laws are not covered agreements of the WTO.②

---

① See Eleanor M. Fox, *Linked-in: Antitrust and the Virtues of a Virtual Network*, 43 International Lawyer 151, 151–174 (2009).

② See DSU Article 1.1 (Appendix 1).

1.2.3 Multi-Party Interim Appeal Arbitration Arrangement to substitute the dispute settlement mechanism

The robust performance of the WTO dispute settlement mechanism was always applauded by its members and scholars as the "crown jewel" before it was defunct to deadlock in 2019.

In 2016, the US vetoed the renewal of the Korean appellant judge, and the US deliberately obstructed the appointment of judges later on. On 11 December 2019, the AB mechanism has only one judge left, suggesting that the Appellate Body has actually collapsed. In order to maintain a rule-based global trading system, EU and China, together with other WTO members began to take alternative measures in October 2019. On 15 April of 2020, the European commission approved the Multi-Party Interim Appeal Arbitration Arrangement (MPIA).

This Arrangement implements the political commitments reached at the Davos ministerial meeting in January. 15 members, including Australia, Brazil, Canada, China Chile, Colombia, Costa Rica, the EU, Guatemala, Mexico, New Zealand, Norway, Singapore, Switzerland and Uruguay have ratified the Arrangement. At present, the establishment of MPIA is conducive to keep the WTO dispute settlement mechanism and the multilateral trade system based on rules. China works with other participants to promote its formal implementation as soon as possible, and welcome other WTO members to participate.

According to the MPIA's rules, the MPIA applies to any future dispute between any two or more participating Members, including the compliance stage of such disputes, as well as to any such dispute pending on the date of this communication, except if the interim panel report, in the relevant stage of that dispute, has already been issued on that date.[①]

In order to render the appeal arbitration procedure operational in particular disputes, the participating Members indicate their intention to enter into the arbitration agreement (the appeal arbitration agreement) contained in Annex 1 to this communication and to notify that agreement pursuant to Article 25.2 of the DSU within 60 days after the date of the establishment of the panel. For pending disputes where, on the date of this communication, the panel has already been established but an interim report has not yet been issued,

---

① See Multi-Party Interim Appeal Arbitration Arrangement Pursuant to Article 25 of the DSU, paragraph 9.

the participating Members will enter into the appeal arbitration agreement and notify that agreement pursuant to Article 25.2 of the DSU within 30 days after the date of this communication.

The appeal arbitration procedure will be based on the substantive and procedural aspects of appellate review pursuant to Article 17 of the DSU, in order to keep its core features, including independence and impartiality, while enhancing the procedural efficiency of appeal proceedings. The appeal arbitration procedure is set out in Annex 1.

In particular, the participating Members envisage that, under the appeal arbitration procedure, appeals will be heard by three appeal arbitrators selected from the pool of 10 standing appeal arbitrators composed by the participating Members in accordance with Annex 2 (hereinafter as the "pool of arbitrators"). The pool of arbitrators will comprise persons of recognized authority, with demonstrated expertise in law, international trade and the subject matter of the covered agreements generally. They will be unaffiliated with any government. They will not participate in the consideration of any disputes that would create a direct or indirect conflict of interest. The composition of the pool of arbitrators will ensure an appropriate overall balance.①

It is hoped that the current crisis encountered by the WTO will offer an opportunity to reflect about the role and functioning of WTO and its born defect in institution-setting. The financial turmoil had offered an opportunity to transform the crisis into a chance to better the WTO.

2 Evolvement and Proliferation of PTAs

As the prospect of trade negotiation under the WTO is unlikely, both the developed countries and newly emerging economies place more resources on the peripheral reforms by signing high-standard PTAs to reshape the trade rules and develop other routes of regional economic cooperation. The following discussion first analyzes the rule-based PTAs to see what reforms have been taken and whether they are effective.

The high-standard PTAs, such as TPP and CETA, effectively respond to the newly emerging needs of international trade. Here, it not only complements the multilateral

① See Multi-Party Interim Appeal Arbitration Arrangement Pursuant to Article 25 of the DSU, paragraphs 3, 4.

trading system by making breakthroughs and breaking the deadlock in negotiating new rules but also establishes the new high land for trade liberalization, despite the withdrawal of US from TPP.

The peripheral reform led by the high-standard PTAs brings more unconventional trade issues covered by the PTAs. What is or is not a trade issue is becoming more blurred as the mega-PTAs extend the boundaries to the domestic domains, which were previously not covered by the PTAs. Global trade governance is no longer just coping with the discriminatory measures taken alongside the border. Instead, it is responding to the pre- and post-entry issues. Today's trade negotiation in a PTA covers issues like trade in merchandise goods, trade in service, investment, intellectual property, government procurement, competition, and anti-bribery, among which many of the issues are not even trade relevant. Henrik Horn, Petros Mavroidis, and André Sapir once conducted research on the subject matter signed by the two main hubs (the EU and the US) between 1992 and 2008. They have found over 50 areas that are subject to provisions in one or more PTAs.①

In addition, many new areas are included to respond to the new economic and societal needs. For example, the US-led PTA set a new chapter for electronic commerce to shelve its dispute with the EU on whether e-commerce should be in the domain of trade in goods or trade in service. Such a chapter is later found in the EU's PTAs. These rules respond to the needs of economic cooperation with advanced information technology. The in-depth integration of the value chain requires simplification of administrative procedures in trade regulation and enhancement of fairness and transparency of administrative procedures through rules of anti-corruption, transparency, digitalized administration measures, and judicial review of disputed administrative measures. Such new areas not only blur the boundaries of international trade law and administrative law but also make more effective regulation on non-tariff barriers.

The rule updates of both market-access and trade regulation issues were successful, especially compared to the multilateral trade negotiations. The market access of trade in service in the newly concluded mega-PTAs far exceeds members' commitments in negotiating the GATS 2000. The intellectual property protection of the PTAs has never yet stood upon the minimum standard as required by the Agreement on Trade-Related Aspects

---

① See Henrik Horn, Petros C. Mavroidis & André Sapir, *Beyond the WTO? An Anatomy of EU and US Preferential Trade Agreements*, 33 The World Economy 1565, 1565 (2010).

of Intellectual Property Rights (TRIPS). They keep pushing the coverage of intellectual property protection and pushing the boundaries to reach the TRIPS-plus standard. The Singapore issues, such as government procurement and competition policy, as dropped by the WTO in the Doha Round, have also reached consensus in many high-standard PTAs, thereby providing a basis for the negotiation of TISA.

Furthermore, the mega-PTAs reshape our conceptions of the regulation of non-tariff barriers. Beyond the anti-discrimination governance, the high-standard PTAs set up the best practice for the central and local governments and enterprises, providing effective measures targeting parties' weaknesses in enforcing trade rules. The regulation on East Asian countries' commercial fishery of marine mammals and consumption of shark fins, and Malaysia's minimum age of child labor in TPP are such examples. The pre-entry governance through negative lists and pre-establishment of national treatment further liberalize members' trade in services and investments. The regulatory cooperation, uniform technology standards, and rule integration on intellectual property protection and competition rules help harmonize various domestic laws to reduce the trade costs and uncertainties caused by the behind-the-border barriers.

Finally, stakeholders' participation in negotiating and enforcing PTAs is more welcomed. It suits civil society's needs better and develops a more open, competitive, and market-oriented trade cooperative structure. The environmental attachment of the North American Agreement on Environmental Cooperation (NAAEC) to the North American Free Trade Agreement (NAFTA) establishes citizens' rights of supervising and reporting government's rule-breaching measures. In the TPP, governments are required to inform stakeholders, including foreign investors and traders, and to allow stakeholders to express their concerns and opinions in the decision-making process before the technology standards are made. The participation and transparency of the investor-state dispute settlement mechanism are also improved in the PTAs.

The recent PTAs have been successful in reforming the international trade rules by covering more trade-related issues, regulating the trade barriers more effectively, and providing more room for citizens to participate. Could these reforms then be consistent with each other, although different PTAs might have very different rules?

The development and evolution of the PTAs demonstrate a more open and liberalized tendency, while developing countries tend to adopt more sophisticated rules mirroring PTA models from developed countries. Such tendency could be explained by the export of legal norms from the developed countries to their developing partners via PTAs. Among all the factors, the competitive liberalization as generated by high-standard PTAs, exerts the most significant influence on developing countries to accept the rules as proposed by the developed countries.

Moreover, NAFTA offers a good example to analyze the effects of competitive liberalization. While NAFTA should have been ratified by its three members, the negotiation of the Uruguay Round was struck, as the European Commission (EC) intended to withdraw from the negotiations. The negotiation and ratification of NAFTA by three members showed a practical North-South cooperative framework for the EU and the developing members, with integrated rules governing trade in goods, trade in services, and intellectual property in a single package. The EC returned to the negotiations and the Uruguay Round finally succeede.① This competitive liberalization effect inspired the US trade representative Zoellick to adopt PTAs as a strategy.

The competitive liberalization of NAFTA produced further repercussions in the formation of similar PTAs in Central America, Europe, and Asia. After concluding NAFTA, Mexico's huge trade benefits made Central American countries frustrated because their export to the US remained flat in the following ten years. It finally pushed them to sign a similar PTA with the US in 2003. The Agreement also influenced Europe. As the trade flow between the EU and Mexico dropped to 6.5% in 1994 from 10.6% in 1991, it was believed that the EU-Mexico PTA was put on the agenda and was adopted to combat such negative effects. The formation of the Asia-Pacific Economic Cooperation (APEC) was also believed to be relevant to NAFTA's competitive liberalization.②

Furthermore, NAFTA shows that, once a high-standard PTA is formed, the trade advantage caused by cutting tariffs and removing non-tariff barriers inside the trade bloc will strengthen the rule advantage of such a PTA. It further attracts other countries to copy the rules and triggers formation of similar PTAs. With competitive liberalization, the global, regional, and bilateral trade agreements could complement and reinforce each other. In addition, each PTA could be a foundation for the further liberalization of other trade rules, so that it will finally update less liberalized trade rules.

The rule evolution of PTAs not only updates trade rules but also enlarges the

① See C. O'Neal Taylor, *Of Free Trade Agreements and Models*, 19 Indiana International & Comparative Law Review 569, 571–572 (2009).

② See Mohammad F. Nsour, *Regional Trade Agreements in the Era of Globalization: A Legal Analysis*, 33 North California Journal of International Law & Commercial Regulation 359, 365 (2008).

imbalance of comparative advantage among nations. It may result in forcing countries with fewer resources to pay dearly and become an advantage for countries with plenty of resources. To generate such competitive liberalization, even big powers usually have the following contributing factors for their PTAs.

First, it is vital to choose the right partner to negotiate a high-standard PTA. A big power usually chooses trade-affiliated countries who are willing to make political and economic reforms with a high-standard PTA. Then, the big power will offer tariff benefits to the export products of the parties in exchange for their acceptance of high-standard rules on investment, service, intellectual property, and competition. Once they sign it, the PTA diverts the trade within and beyond its treaty parties, triggering the non-parties who lose export shares to surrender their disputes and sign similar treaties with the big power.

Second, in producing the competitive liberalization, the PTA needs to adopt conditional MFN treatment and restrictive rules of origin to lock in trade benefits inside the region to avoid free riders. Eventually, most of the US-led PTAs maintain strict rules of origin that require high levels of local content, some of which even burden the parties to keep a record and certificate of the rules of origin for five years.[①]

Then, to further strengthen the rule advantage of such high-standard PTAs, the big power will guarantee the consistency of its trading rules with different countries because competitive liberalization might be interfered by contesting PTAs adopted by other big trading nations. Since the 1990s, the US has insisted on their adoption throughout its negotiations, developing NAFTA and the WTO Plus model. These two models ensure consistency and integrity of the US trade rules around the world and allow each PTA signed by the US to act as a precedent, or serve as a catalyst and benchmark for broader trade agreements.

When the global economy is in recession, however, emerging economies' rising advantage in manufacturing industries has pressured the developed countries, such as the US, to abandon the TPP and renegotiate NAFTA. It is worried that once the achievements are obtained by the high-standard PTAs, they would roll back, and even the further liberalization of global trade would be influenced by the emerging anti-globalization sentiments.

---

① See William J. Kovatch, Jr., *The NAFTA's Rules of Origin, Certificate of Origin, and Record-Keeping Requirements: The Disadvantage to Small Business*, 12 The Transnational Lawyer 403, 414 (1999).

Chapter Review

1. What is the deficiency of the WTO decision-making process?
2. What are the suggestions to reform the WTO decision-making process?
3. What happened to the WTO's dispute settlement mechanism?
4. What is MPIA? How does it work?
5. What are the advantages of negotiating PTAs?
6. What are the disadvantages of negotiating PTAs? Will PTAs divert trade?

Key Terms

Multi-Party Interim Appeal Arbitration Arrangement (MPIA)	多方临时上诉仲裁安排
North American Agreement on Environmental Cooperation (NAAEC)	《北美环境合作协定》(《北美自由贸易协定》的环境附属协议)
North American Free Trade Agreement (NAFTA)	《北美自由贸易协定》
preferential trade agreements (PTAs)	特惠贸易协定
Understanding on Rules and Procedures Governing the Settlement of Disputes (DSU)	《关于争端解决规则与程序的谅解》

Further Readings

1. Matsushita, Mitsuo, *A View on Future Roles of The WTO: Should There be More Soft Law in The WTO?*, Journal of International Economic Law, Vol. 17: 701, 2014.

2. Pauwelyn, Joost, Ramses A. Wessel & Jan Wouters, *When Structures Become Shackles: Stagnation and Dynamics in International Lawmaking*, European Journal of International Law, Vol. 25: 733, 2014.

3. Petersmann, Ernst-Ulrich, *Multilevel Governance Problems of the World Trading System beyond the WTO Conference at Bali 2013*, Journal of International Economic Law, Vol. 17: 233, 2014.

4. Wang Yan, *Central and Peripheral Reforms of Global Trade Governance*, China and WTO Review, Vol. 2: 289, 2017.

Part III International Investment Law

Chapter 1

Domestic Rules Administrating Inward and Outward Investments

Study Guide
International investment law in Part III includes three chapters. Among which, Chapter 1 is about the domestic rules administrating inward and outward investment. This Chapter introduces a country's domestic rules administrating inward investments and its rules administrating outward investment. Its inward investment administration usually includes restrictions on inward investments in forms of equity ownership, screening process, business forms and performance requirements. Its outward administration usually includes measures promoting overseas investments such as governmental guarantees to the political risks in foreign direct investment. This Chapter also introduces the development of China's inward and outward investment policies and its investment administration measures to let the students have a better understanding of the evolvement of Chinese foreign direct investment policies.

1 Domestic Rules Administrating Inward Investments

The regulations governing foreign investment are usually included in investment law or investment regulations in developing countries. Most of the countries maintain a screen process to direct foreign investors to invest in those sectors that host states wish to acquire capital.

1.1 Restrictions on inward investments

Investment restrictions take different forms. The most frequently adopted restrictions are usually relevant to equity ownership, business forms, sectoral or geographical requirements. These restrictions may work for legitimate purpose such as environmental protection, but they could also act as barriers.

1.1.1 Restrictions on equity ownership

Restrictions on foreign ownership are one of the most frequently appeared restrictions in domestic policies. They typically limit the share of companies' equity capital in a target sector that non-residents are allowed to hold. For example, countries may allow foreign investors to hold less than 50% of equity capital in an invested company in energy sector, or even prohibit any foreign ownership. Even in developed countries, such restrictions are not scarce. Majority domestic ownership requirements include airlines in the European Union and North American countries, telecommunications in Japan, and coastal and freshwater shipping in the United States. Exclusive domestic ownership is often applied to natural resource sectors with the aim of giving citizens access to the associated rents. For example, foreign ownership is banned in the fishing and energy sectors in Iceland, and in the oil sector in Mexico.①

1.1.2 Restrictions in form of screening process

In many countries, foreign investments are subject to screening and approval procedures, which can also be used to limit foreign direct investment (FDI) though their constraining effects depend on the implementation of such practices.

In Brazil, no governmental authorization is needed unless a foreign investor wants to take advantage of certain industrial incentives. The Board of Investment of the Philippines screens all new investments in which foreigners have a 40% or greater share and all expansions or additional investments in existing firms that have foreign ownership of 40% or more.

In Argentina, investments of less than USD 5 million do not require approval unless a majority of the shares in a locally owned company is to be bought by foreigners. In Algeria, the prefect of the department concerns screen investments that do not exceed

① See Stephen S. Golub, *Measures of Restrictions on Inward Foreign Direct Investment for OECD Countries*, 36 OECD Economic Studies 88, 90 (2003).

500,000 Algerian dinars and that do not contain a request for financial incentives. Otherwise, the Secretariat of the National Investment Board must review the application. France has a similar arrangement.① The screen process, if non-transparent, will hamper the flow of investments.

1.1.3 Restrictions on business forms

Many countries will restrict the business forms of investments in their foreign investment law. For example, before China adopted the new Foreign Investment Law (2018), there were three forms of foreign investments: Chinese-foreign equity joint ventures, Chinese-foreign cooperative joint ventures, and wholly foreign-owned enterprises.

Among all the forms, most countries generally prefer the foreigners to invest in their countries through joint ventures. Thus, the local entities and entrepreneurs will be fostered. And it is also possible for the technology transfer from foreign investors to the local entities. Therefore, the host states may provide some incentives to direct the investors to cooperate with local entities. Saudi Arabia, for example, allows a foreign company to set up a local branch without any Saudi participation, but the company is not eligible for any of the incentives, such as tax holidays and other incentives that are available only to investors who form a local company and register with the Saudi Ministry of Commerce.②

1.1.4 Restrictions in form of performance requirements

Performance requirements include any requirements that the host countries impose on the foreign investment or the foreign investors during the period of investment. Such restrictions usually require that foreign investment shall fulfill certain economic benefits to the host country, hire certain number of employees, or export certain percentage of products in the overseas market.

Stipulations that foreign investors must show economic benefits will increase the cost of entry and therefore may discourage the inflow of foreign capital. Such provisions apply, for instance, for a few industries in Japan and for the acquisition of more than 49% of any existing enterprise in Mexico. Prior approval of FDI, such as mandated for all FDI projects in a few OECD countries, could also limit foreign capital inflow if it is taken as a sign of

① 参见曾文革主编：《国际经济法》（双语版），对外经济贸易大学出版社 2012 年版，第 217 页。
② 参见曾文革主编：《国际经济法》（双语版），对外经济贸易大学出版社 2012 年版，第 219 页。

an ambivalent attitude towards free FDI, even though it may not be vigorously enforced. Simple pre- or post-notification (as required in e.g. Japan) is, however, unlikely to have much direct impact on capital inflows, but could have a negative signaling effect.①

1.1.5 Sectoral and geographic limitation

Most countries do not allow the foreign investment in their countries in certain sectors. These prohibited or restricted areas include public utilities such as postal service, financial service, radio and television, transportation, energy, educational and health care industries. Such restrictions may be combined with the equity restrictions. For example, Australia limits foreign investment in its radio and television companies to 20%. Canada restricts the amount of equity ownership that foreigners may have in television broadcasting, insurance, local and trust companies, fishing, newspapers, banks and federal oil, gas, and mining leases.②

Apart from sectoral restrictions, some developing countries may also limit the geographic areas in which foreign investors may conduct business or encourage the investors to invest in special economic zones.

1.1.6 Other restrictions

Other formal restrictions that affect FDI inflows include constraints on the ability of foreign nationals either to manage or to work in affiliates of foreign companies and other operational controls on these businesses. There may also be stipulations that nationals or residents must form a majority of the board of directors, as in insurance companies in member countries of the European Union, in financial services industries in Canada and in transport industries in Japan. All these measures may undermine foreign owners' control over their holdings and hence make them more hesitant to invest under such circumstances. Similarly, if regulations restrict the employment of foreign nationals (as in Turkey), investors may judge that they cannot make use of the necessary expertise to make their investment worthwhile. Also, operational requirements, such as the restrictions *vis-à-vis* non-members on cabotage in most European Union countries for maritime transport may limit profits of foreign-owned corporations, and hence the amount of funds foreign

---

① See Stephen S. Golub, *Measures of Restrictions on Inward Foreign Direct Investment for OECD Countries*, 36 OECD Economic Studies 88, 91 (2003).

② 参见曾文革主编：《国际经济法》（双语版），对外经济贸易大学出版社 2012 年版，第 221 页。

investors are willing to commit.①

1.2 Promotion and facilitation measures for inward investment

Most governments, including sometimes at the sub-national level, now actively promote foreign investment through agencies mandated to this effect and offer a range of inducements to attract foreign investments. Shown by an OECD report, measures to promote and facilitate investment can be successful if they take place within the broader context of an overarching strategy for improving the investment environment, which involves mainstreaming investment across a broad range of policy areas that affect the investment climate. Once a country is establishing a generally sound investment climate, governments can take additional steps to promote and facilitate investment. These would include establishing an investment promotion agency, one-stop shop, policy advocacy and investment incentives.

1.2.1 Investment promotion agency

A common institutional approach to such promotion is to create an investment promotion agency (IPA) or other institutional facility. Not only can the IPA help simplify administrative procedures, improve regulatory transparency and focus investment promotion, it can also serve as a conduit for private sector input into the reform process itself. In many cases, the IPA is also used as a vehicle for expanding linkages between foreign investors and domestic suppliers.

As part of the South East Europe Compact for Reform, Investment, Integrity and Growth, the OECD has formulated Strategic Guidelines on Investment Promotion addressed to IPAs based on practices developed in some of the most successful host countries for foreign investment. These include: the establishment of an investment promotion agency (IPA) or other institutional facility, as well as its objectives and the relevant legislative and governance structures; to inculcate within the IPA a professional management and service culture, result-oriented ethos and innovative marketing approach in order to compete successfully in attracting new investment and to ensure satisfactory continuity of the organization culture; and to define strategic policy options and set out the corporate strategy and marketing plan of the IPA to build competitive strength and achieve

---

① See Stephen S. Golub, *Measures of Restrictions on Inward Foreign Direct Investment for OECD Countries*, 36 OECD Economic Studies 88, 91 (2003).

selected policy options.[①]

1.2.2 Investment facilitation and the one-stop shop

One-stop shops can deliver substantial savings in time and costs for users by providing seamless, integrated and easily accessible points of contact. Many host governments seek to alleviate the administrative burden on potential investors through a one-stop shop which provides information on the necessary steps to start a business in that country—in effect a "tourist office for investors". To the extent that informational barriers hinder the global flow of direct investment, a one-stop shop—whether as an office or a website—can help to facilitate such flows.

As well as providing information, one-stop shops are sometimes conceived as a way to centralize the approval process for foreign investment. This was particularly the case in the past when investments were screened. But allowing one agency to grant all licenses, permits, approvals and clearances has often proved unworkable. In worst cases, the one-stop shop becomes one more stop, adding to the red tape facing the investor. Governments are rarely willing to vest decision-making authority within one single organization, especially concerning an issue as politically sensitive as foreign direct investment. Line ministries also resist ceding their regulatory authority to another agency.[②]

1.2.3 Image building

Image building is a foundation block in the process of attracting FDI. Its role is primarily that of focusing investor interest on the location and overcoming negative perceptions rather than directly persuading a multinational company to invest. Indeed, it has been argued that the perceived investment climate is as important as the actual one and so addressing negative perceptions is an important part of encouraging investment. As with any brand, the agency needs to create an image of the host country in the eyes of investors. This is particularly important for countries with little track record in attracting foreign investment, those undergoing rapid political or economic reform or emerging from a period of civil unrest, and those countries which are too small to attract the attention of home country media and hence are not even on the map for multinational investors. In

---

① See OECD Secretariat, *A Policy Framework for Investment: Investment Promotion and Facilitation*, 2005, p. 3–5, available at https://www.oecd.org/investment/investmentfordevelopment/35635304.pdf.

② See OECD Secretariat, *A Policy Framework for Investment: Investment Promotion and Facilitation*, 2005, p. 5–7, available at https://www.oecd.org/investment/investmentfordevelopment/35635304.pdf.

this context, regional promotion can play an important complimentary role to country-level promotion since many prospective investors think in regional terms (e.g. "Should we invest in South East Europe or in the Baltic?"). The recognition of this fact has motivated the growing interest in regional promotion networks.①

1.2.4 Policy advocacy

Foreign investment is often associated with more general market-opening policies and the private provision of infrastructure, both of which can prove unpopular within host countries. Allied to more general discontent, government ministries, regional governments and lower level civil servants have often resisted relinquishing their regulatory powers over foreign investors.

An IPA or a one-stop shop is not a substitute for regulatory reform. It can nevertheless serve as a useful exercise by indicating to the host government the extent to which business licensing requirements are cumbersome or redundant. It can also send valuable signals to foreign and domestic investors that the government is serious about reform and promoting investment. A more direct approach to simplifying procedures would be to improve the efficiency of each individual ministry responsible for particular aspects of investment approval. In Tanzania, for example, a "no objection" provision in the Investment Code means that unless a ministry objects within 14 days, the Tanzania Investment Centre is entitled to approve the application.②

1.2.5 Investment promotion through specific incentives

The usage of financial and other specific incentives directed at attracting foreign investors is not substitute for pursuing the appropriate general policy measures. In some circumstances, incentives may serve either as a supplement to an already attractive enabling environment for investment or as a compensation for proven market imperfections that cannot be otherwise addressed. However, OECD Investment Committee work finds that authorities engaging in incentive-based strategies face the important task of assessing these measures' relevance, appropriateness and economic benefits against their budgetary and other costs, including long-term impacts on domestic allocative efficiency.

---

① See OECD Secretariat, *A Policy Framework for Investment: Investment Promotion and Facilitation*, 2005, p. 7–8, available at https://www.oecd.org/investment/investmentfordevelopment/35635304.pdf.

② See OECD Secretariat, *A Policy Framework for Investment: Investment Promotion and Facilitation*, 2005, p. 9, available at https://www.oecd.org/investment/investmentfordevelopment/35635304.pdf.

The relevance and appropriateness of FDI incentive strategies should be examined at regular intervals. Transparency and accountability at all levels of governments greatly increases the success of such evaluations. Investment incentives have effects beyond the jurisdiction that offers them, which need to be carefully considered.①

The significance of investment promotion measures have been recognized by some international investment agreements (IIAs), thus regional cooperation to provide a better investment environment is included in the treaties. For example, in RCEP, it is advised that each Party shall endeavor to facilitate the investments among them by simplifying its procedures for investment applications and approvals, promoting the dissemination of investment information, including investment rules, laws, regulations, policies, and procedures; and establishing or maintaining contact points, one-stop investment centers, focal points, or other entities in the respective Party to provide assistance and advisory services to investors, including the facilitation of operating licenses and permits.②

1.3 China's domestic rules administrating inward investments

The foreign investment policy in China has been developing since China adopted opening-up policy in 1979 and evolved from time to time to provide a level playing field for foreign investors.

1.3.1 The period between 1979 to 2001

In 1979, China adopted its opening-up policy with the motive of attracting investment. However, with scarce experience in foreign investment administration, and worries that powerful foreign investors would interfere with China's domestic affairs, China dared not to open its market to foreign investors comprehensively. The most significant step on the history of the construction of foreign investment law was the enactment of the *Law of the People's Republic of China on Chinese-Foreign Equity Joint Ventures* in 1979, and after implementing this Law, several relevant notices and regulations were promogulated, suggesting the start of the attracting of foreign investment.

During this period, the sectors that foreign investors could invest in and forms of foreign investment were restricted by the Central Government. Specifically, foreign

---

① See OECD Secretariat, *A Policy Framework for Investment: Investment Promotion and Facilitation*, 2005, p. 9, available at https://www.oecd.org/investment/investmentfordevelopment/35635304.pdf.

② See RCEP, Article 10.17.

investments were subject to various restrictions such as limit access to raw materials, high prices of land rental fees, import and export restrictions.

The sectors that allowed to be invested by foreigners were limited and the scale of foreign investments was small. The industrial sectors invested by foreign investors were mainly real estate projects in tourism hotels, entertainment facilities in the tertiary industry, and manufacturing sectors such as textiles, clothing, food, beverages, and plastics. The joint ventures in this period were mainly labor-intensive small and medium-sized enterprises, as the government was eager to attract foreign investment and raise employment rates.

Generally, China's investment policies were two fold in this period. On one hand, China maintained various investment restrictive measures to direct foreign capital into the sectors that China mostly needed, acquiring foreign technologies and managing experience in the process of cooperation. On the other hand, China offered super-national treatment to foreign investors, especially in terms of taxation. China issued the *Provisions of the State Council on the Encouragement of Foreign Investment*. The Provisions not only highlighted the vital industries that should be invested most, but also improved the investment conditions from various measures, offering the foreign investors super-national treatment.

From 1987 to 2001, Chinese legal system improved, and a large number of laws and regulations on governing the foreign investment were issued. As a result, the legal foreign investment environment became better than before, and the foreign investors could receive more accountable protections. Economically, the government realized the importance of the market economy, and pushed forward the reform and opening-up policy, especially after 1992, leading to more industries and areas opened up and more restrictions on the foreign investment reduced. All reflected governmental abilities on managing the foreign investment were better. The government still offered more preferential policies in a number of aspects, including tax breaks, import and export rights, priorities in purchasing scarce materials, and acquiring foreign exchange, etc. However, the foreign investors still would receive a few restrictions on the industries, permitting procedures, and operations requirements, which meant the sub-national treatment also existed. In fact, both the super-national treatment and the sub-national treatment the foreign investors received were the measures the government took to guide the foreign investors to invest.

In 1990s, the scope of the foreign investment was clearer and larger. The government enacted the Catalog of Industries for Guiding Foreign Investment (the Catalog) in 1995 and amended it in 1997, which categorized the industries into three kinds: sectors encouraged to be invested in, sectors restricted to be invested in, and sectors prohibited to be invested in. For those not listed in the Catalog, they were sectors allowed to be invested in, with no special screen requirements or investment incentives. With these catalogs, the government gave clear instructions to foreign investors on market access in China. At this period, the government opened up the financial, insurance and other industries that were prohibited to invest before and reduced more restrictions on the real estate, hotel, restaurant industries. Thus, the foreign investors could invest in more industries and were clear of what the industries were prohibited to invest.

In the 1990s, the areas that the foreign investors could invest were greatly enlarged. When China began to open up its market in 1979, only four Special Economic Zones, and 14 Coastal Open Cities were opened up for the foreign investors to invest. While in the 1990s and early 21st century, Hainan Special Economic Zone and inland cities opened up, the Coastal Economic Open Areas and Pudong New Area were founded, the government opened up more cities and areas for foreign investors to invest in. Gradually, China had opened almost all the important cities and areas to the foreign investors.

1.3.2 After 2001

The entry of the WTO is a milestone on China's path of implementing the reform and opening-up policy, marking the further integration of China and the world. After entering the WTO, China needed to make a series of changes according to its commitments in the Accession Protocol to the WTO. For this reason, around 2001, three codes on foreign investment, i.e., the *Law of the People's Republic of China on Chinese-Foreign Equity Joint Ventures*, the *Law of the People's Republic of China on Chinese-Foreign Contractual Joint Ventures*, and the *Law of the People's Republic of China on Foreign-Capital Enterprises*, were adopted. The three codes divided China's foreign investment policies based on the type of foreign enterprises.

As the WTO members need to provide non-discriminatory treatment to exporters or service suppliers from different countries, China began to eliminate its super-national tax treatment to foreign investors. Since 2007, the government promulgated the Enterprise Income Tax Law, which regulated that all the enterprises shall be taxed at the same level. By 2010, China has unified the tax on the urban maintenance and construction and education surcharge for domestic and foreign enterprises.

There were several significant moves of Chinese government in liberalizing the investment market after 2012. One is establishment of the several free trade zones to administer market access of foreign investment through a negative list. In 2012, China and the United States launched bilateral investment treaty negotiation, and China promised to implement the pre-establishment national treatment with the negative list system. The BIT negotiation between the United States and China also helped to shorten the negative list used in Pilot Free Trade Areas. As China always maintains a positive list to regulate the entry of foreign investment and has no experience in providing pre-entry national treatment and negative list, China has to try this policy in the municipality level to make sure that the government can respond to the changes caused by such rule.

In 2013, the first Pilot Free Trade Area was established in Shanghai to enforce new investment access policy. The government enacted the *Special Administrative Measures for the Access of Foreign Investment in Pilot Free Trade Zones* (the Negative List 2013) for the Pilot Free Trade Area. Both the Catalog of Industries for Guiding Foreign Investment and the Negative List 2013 applied to the special area for the access of foreign investment. The Negative List 2013 included 190 special measures in total, among which 152 measures were investment restricted measures and 38 were investment prohibited measures.

A year later, a new Negative List 2014 was enacted to replace the Negative List 2013. Compared with the old list, the new list for investment restricted and prohibited measures was cut short. For one thing, there were only 139 special measures, among which 29 measures were prohibited measures and 110 measures were restricted measures in 16 categories and 51 industries. For another thing, it provided national treatment to the foreign investments explicitly in the negative list.

In 2015, Guangdong, Tianjin and Fujian were also named as Pilot Free Trade Areas to admit foreign investments through negative lists. The Central Government made the Negative List 2015. One of the changes of the Negative List 2015 compared with Negative List 2014 is the classification approach: it abandoned the way it used before, but had a clearer one. It classified the special measures into 15 industries, 50 areas, and the List was further abbreviated to include 38 prohibited measures and 84 restricted measures. The 2015 Negative List contains more detailed regulations on special measures in the financial industry, such as restrictive measures on the qualification requirements and stock ratio requirements of the banking industry, and has made significant changes in the real estate and construction industries adjustment.

In 2017, the Pilot Free Trade Areas had been expanded to include another seven provinces and municipalities, including Liaoning, Zhejiang, Henan, Hubei, Chongqing, Sichuan and Shanxi. The total number of Pilot Free Trade Areas rose to 11. There were

95 investment restrictive or prohibitive measures in Negative List 2017 scattered in 14 industries and 39 areas. The limitations to invest are lesser, especially on the manufacturing industry and service industry.

In the Negative List 2018, the number of investment restrictive or prohibitive measures was further reduced to 45. Meanwhile, with reference to international standard, most of the investment restrictive measures listed in the Negative List 2018 related to the foreign investors' share ratio in key industries and requirements on the nationality of executives.

With several years of pilot enforcement of negative lists in admitting foreign investments in both open municipalities and less liberalized provinces, Chinese government has equipped itself with experience in providing pre-entry national treatment to foreign investors and screening foreign investments through negative list.

The second significant move of Chinese government in liberalizing investment market is to adopt a uniform foreign investment law to replace the three investment codes on China-foreign joint ventures, China-foreign contractual joint ventures and wholly foreign-owned enterprises. Thus, foreign policies become more coherent and consistent.

In 2018, the new Foreign Investment Law was passed and a year later, it took effect. The Foreign Investment Law (2018) has liberalized the investment market in China significantly and has provided pre-entry national treatment to the foreign investors for the first time at the national level. Pursuant to Article 4, China promises to maintain a system of pre-entry national treatment plus a negative list management for foreign investment. The pre-entry national treatment defined by the Foreign Investment Law refers to the treatment given to foreign investors and their investment at the stage of investment admission no less than that to domestic investors and their investments, and the so-called negative list refers to the special management measures that are adopted for the admission of foreign investment in specific areas. The State gives national treatment to foreign investment outside the negative list.

As a response to the impunity from United States on China's acquisition of technology in attracting foreign investment, the Foreign Investment Law (2018) has made it clear that government agencies shall not demand technology transfer in reviewing foreign investment applications. It is acknowledged that the State encourages technical cooperation based on the voluntariness principle and commercial rules in the process of foreign investment. The conditions for technical cooperation are determined by equal negotiation between the parties to the investment in accordance with the principle of fairness. Administrative agencies and their staff are prohibited to use administrative means to force any technology transfer.

Meanwhile, the law commits to protect the intellectual property rights of foreign investors and foreign-invested enterprises, protect the legitimate rights and interests of intellectual property rights holders and related rights holders, and hold intellectual property rights infringers legally accountable in strict accordance with the law. The administrative organs and their staff will not disclose confidential business secrets known to them, of foreign investors and foreign-invested enterprises during the performance of their duties.[①]

But the new Foreign Investment Law (2018) is not an imitation of the western investment policies. In terms of expropriation and compensation, China insists on its always standing that compensation for expropriation shall not be paid in full amount.

Article 24 of the Foreign Investment Law (2018) promises that Chinese government will not expropriate foreign investment in normal situation. The State will only expropriate and requisition the investment of foreign investors in accordance with the law and for the needs of the public interest. The expropriation and requisition will be conducted in accordance with legal procedures and timely and reasonable compensation will be given.

2 Domestic Rules Administrating Outward Investments

Investment provisions also include rules administrating outward investments. An investment in a foreign nation is often subject to risks which are not a significant concern for domestic investment. A foreign investor in the business suffers from the risk of military conflict, uncompensated expropriation, and inconvertible currency. The private insurance is very limited to cover such political risk, so various government programs have been developed to reduce such risk and provide finance to promote outbound investment.

2.1 Measures promoting outward investment in the world

Generally, measures adopted by capital-exporting countries for encouraging overseas investment mainly include measures encouraging corporate financing, technical assistance and insurance or guarantee against political risks incurred in overseas investments.

After the World War II, the US became the biggest capital exporting country in the

① See Foreign Investment Law of the People's Republic of China, Articles 21–24.

world. The independence and the Third World movement had led many newly independent countries to cease their concession agreements with the foreign investors, which had caused huge losses to the transnational corporations in the US. Lobbied by these big companies, the US Congress adopted the Economic Corporation Act in 1948 and created its insurance system for offshore investment based on this Act. During the two decades afterward, the US made multiple rounds of revision to relevant acts so as to cater to new development and requirements of such investment. The essence of such an insurance system lied in the undertaking of non-commercial risks related to US overseas investment by special administrations set up by the US government. This practice lasted until 1969 when the US government thoroughly changed it with the 8th revised edition of the Foreign Assistance Act. The core of the new practice is to establish a government-run Overseas Private Investment Corporation (OPIC).①

The Corporation is actually a US government agency that assists businesses looking to invest abroad. Operated out of Washington D.C., OPIC helps companies investing overseas analyze and manage risk, and tries to promote development in emerging markets in addition to supporting domestic foreign policies.

OPIC supports projects that reinforce and are aligned with current US foreign policy. These are projects that are believed to foster political stability and free market ideals. OPIC also offers political risk insurance for businesses and investors as protection from expropriation risks, political violence, and other country risks. To aid development in underserved areas that are unable to raise sufficient commercial financing, OPIC offers direct loans and guarantees of a few million dollars up to USD 350 million for as long as 20 years. Other functions of this Corporation include promoting communication between foreign governments and US investors, avoiding direct confrontation between the US government and host governments and seeking commercial solutions to political issues.

Inspired by the US, other capital exporting countries, such as Japan and Germany, also establish their own domestic insurance institutions to provide governmental guarantee for overseas investments.

2.2 Development of China's outward investment and its policies

Chinese overseas FDI flows have been rising strongly in the last decade. China became an increasingly import source of investment for many countries in Africa,

① 参见盛建明编著：《国际经济法》（英文版），对外经济贸易大学出版社 2017 年版，第 277 页。

Central Asia and Latin America. In addition, Chinese firms experience increasingly fierce competition in the home market, pushing these firms to internationalize rapidly. Chinese banks have started to acquire shares in the financial sector in developed countries. Also, Chinese high technology companies such as Lenovo, Huawei make significant investments abroad.

After 1999, China adopted a series of policies and regulations to promote outbound investment. These policies include the *Notification on Encouraging Enterprises to Undertake OEM and the Pilot Measures for Fund Management of Small and Medium-Sized Enterprises that Pioneer into International Market*, and the *Regulations on Items that Require Examination and Approval Regarding Investment and Business Incorporation Overseas.*

China also established an agency to provide guarantee to domestic companies investing abroad. In 2001, the China Export and Credit Insurance Corporation (SINOSURE) was established to provide guarantee to certain political risks that occurred in investment.

SINOSURE is a state-funded policy-oriented insurance company with independent status of legal person, established for promoting China's foreign trade and economic cooperation. It began operations on 18 December 2001. Presently SINOSURE has formed a nationwide service network. Its business guideline is by means of insurance service for foreign trade and investment, fully supporting the development of foreign trade and economic cooperation and promoting the economic growth, the employment and the equilibrium of international balance of payment.

SINOSURE is mandated, in accordance with the Chinese government's diplomatic, international trade, industrial, fiscal and financial policies, to promote Chinese exports of goods, technologies and service, especially high-tech and high value-added capital goods like electromechanical products, and national enterprises' overseas investment, by means of export credit insurance against non-payment risks.

SINOSURE's main products include medium and long-term export credit insurance, overseas investment (leasing) insurance, short-term export credit insurance, inbound investment insurance, domestic trade credit insurance, bonds and guarantees concerning foreign trade, investment and cooperation, reinsurance concerning credit insurance, investment insurance, bonds and guarantees, insurance fund management, accounts receivable management, debt collection, factoring, credit risk consultation and credit rating, and other products and services approved by the government. SINOSURE also introduces its SINOSURE Online, a multi-function e-commerce platform, and the E-Plan, an online insuring platform particularly for small and medium-sized enterprises (SMEs), through which policyholders are able to get fast and convenient service.

Chapter Review

1. Why do host countries restrict foreign investments?
2. What are the different types of foreign inward investment restrictions maintained by many countries?
3. What are the investment facilitation and promotion measures usually taken by host countries? What shall be considered in making such measures?
4. Briefly summarize the history of Chinese opening-up policy in foreign investment.
5. Name the main progresses made by China in its Foreign Investment Law (2018).
6. What are the measures promoting outward investment?
7. Name China's outward investment promotion measures.

Key Terms

China Export and Credit Insurance Corporation (SINOSURE)	中国出口信用保险公司
foreign direct investment (FDI)	外国直接投资
Overseas Private Investment Corporation (OPIC)	海外私营投资公司

Further Readings

1. UNCTAD, *World Investment Report 2020: International Production Beyond the Pandemic*, 2020, available at https://unctad.org/webflyer/world-investment-report-2020.

2. UNCTAD, *World Investment Report 2021: Investing in Sustainable Recovery*, 2021, available at https://unctad.org/webflyer/world-investment-report-2021.

3. UNCTAD, *World Investment Report 2022: International Tax Reforms and Sustainable Investment*, 2022, available at https://unctad.org/webflyer/world-investment-report-2022.

4. http://www.mofcom.gov.cn.

5. https://unctad.org.

Chapter 2
Bilateral and Regional Investment Treaties

Study Guide

Bilateral, regional and sectoral investment treaties constitute the main body of international investment law. In Chapter 2, both the historical development of international investment treaties and the contents of these treaties will be discussed. The substantive issues in most investment treaties include the market access of foreign direct investment, treatment of investors, performance requirements, expropriation and compensation, repatriation of profits and other issues. Different standard provisions regarding these issues together with their reforms will be discussed in this Chapter.

The procedural matter in the investment treaties usually include the provisions on dispute settlement, which will also be analyzed in the Chapter. Cases and materials of international investment treaty provisions are given for the students to better understand the duties imposed by these treaties to the host states.

From the very beginning, the development of international investment law deviates from the normal path of other branches of international economic law. Unlike international trade law and international monetary and finance law that multilateral rules play a major role, multilateral investment rules are scarce, and the main body of international investment law is composed by over three thousands of inconsistent bilateral, regional and sectoral provisions. The study of bilateral and regional investment treaties is significant in understanding the *status quo* of international investment law tendency of development.

1 Development of Bilateral and Regional Investment Treaties

1.1 Development of international investment law

The evolvement of international investment law is triggered by three factors. Firstly, to alleviate or reduce the political risk in foreign direct investment, it is necessary to have international cooperation to provide an orderly structure for international investment scheme. The existence of political risk is a unique feature of foreign direct investment, which is different from trade flows. World trade law governs trade relations between exporting states and importing states, while international investment law deals with the relationship between a sovereign state and a private investor. Thus, it is inevitable for the FDI to involve the host state as a sovereign actor. In attracting the FDI, the host state and investors have largely converging interests initially, but the situation changes once an investment has been made. If the host state changes its investment regulations and policies, modifies the original investment contract or terms, or even expropriates or nationalizes the investment without compensation, the investor has no option to withdraw his investment or reinvest it elsewhere, and it will definitely suffer financial loss. Such risk is called political risk, which not only increases the cost of investment for investors and consumers, but also prevents the flow of foreign investment completely. The existence of political risk is a reason that requires legal intervention through well-established international rules.

Secondly, most of the investments flow from the developed countries to developing countries, thus the investors from developed countries worry that the legal systems of many host states are less open and do not provide sufficient protection to their investors and investments. Lobbied by the investors, the capital exporting countries launch negotiation with the capital importing countries on the basis that the national legal systems of the developing countries often fail to provide a sufficiently stable and predictable legal framework that protects property and effectively restricts the arbitrariness of the executive and legislator.

Thirdly, in case of disputes, the investors have to resort to the domestic courts in the host state for remedies. However, they think the court system in the host states lacks independence and efficiency, and sometimes it may also prevent the investors from enforcing their rights against the government. The investors and capital importing countries believe that it is necessary to have an unbiased international legal instrument to solve the disputes between the investors and host states.

1.2 Concept of foreign direct investment and its difference with portfolio investment

Customarily, international investment law only disciplines FDI, while transboundary portfolio investment is not within its domain. The reason that lies behind this is that portfolio investment is attended by ordinary commercial risks which shall be borne by the investors themselves and there is no political risk embedded in the investment. Thus, customary international law protects FDI with the purpose of reducing the political risks through diplomatic protection and state responsibility, which is far from enough to establish a comprehensive and coherent international legal system for the world.

Since foreign portfolio investment and FDI are differently treated by customary international law, it is necessary to differentiate FDI from portfolio investment. Conceptually, FDI involves the transfer of tangible or intangible assets from one country to another for the purpose of their use in that country to generate wealth under the total or partial control of the owner of the assets. Portfolio investment, on the other hand, can be made on stock exchanges virtually anywhere in the world, which does not involve control of assets or management.

Hence, it is generally believed that the distinguishing element between FDI and portfolio investment is the notion of "direct control". In portfolio investment, there is a separation between, on the one hand, management and control of the company and, on the other, the share of ownership in it.

In a narrow sense, FDI just refers to building new facility, and a lasting management interest in an enterprise operating in an economy other than that of the investor. But in modern BITs, FDI is usually defined broadly, and it includes contribution of physical assets and establishment of new plants, mergers and acquisition, contractual rights and administrative rights such as environmental licenses and planning permissions, transfer of intellectual property. This is because the capital-exporting state tends to adopt the strategy of defining the foreign investment broadly so as to provide protection to as many types of investment as possible. It includes not only physical assets, but also intangible assets.

But the enlargement of the definition of investment is not without limit. There are a number of disputes brought by investors from capital exporting states with an attempt to associate their costs in preparing for the making of the investment to be treated as FDI. For example, in *Mihaly v. Sri Lanka*, the investor brought a dispute against the host state and alleged that the costs involved in tendering for a project and negotiation should be considered as investment if the negotiations failed for improper reasons after an expectation as to their success has been created. The investor argued that its reasonable and legitimate expectations of acquiring the project constituted rights which should be protected through expansive interpretations of treaty provisions. If new rights had been effectively created by treaties for foreign investors, the meaning of investments for the purpose of those treaties should be correspondingly enlarged. This argument, however, was not supported by the tribunal.[①]

---

① See Mihaly International Corporation *v.* Democratic Socialist Republic of Sri Lanka, ICSID Case No. ARB/00/2.

1.3 Sources of international investment law

The international legal framework consists of international treaties, customary international law, general principles of law relating to investment. They provide rules for market access of FDI, treatment of investors, protection of investors and investments, and settlement of disputes between foreign investors and host states, among other issues.

1.3.1 Treaties

There are over 3,000 bilateral, regional and sectoral investment treaties that contain substantive standards for the protection of foreign investors against undue government interference. These treaties typically grant national treatment, most-favored-nation treatment, fair and equitable treatment, and full protection and security to the investors, and they prohibit direct and indirect expropriations without compensation, and contain the consent of host states to investor-state arbitration. Apart from bilateral and regional treaties, there are also several multilateral treaties such as the conventions establishing the ICSID and Multilateral Investment Guarantee Agency (MIGA), and a multilateral treaty named Agreement on Trade-Related Investment Measures (TRIMs) specifically targeting at investment performance requirement. These multilateral treaties provide instruments for insurance against political risk, regulate state's behavior in managing investments and provide facility for settlement of investment disputes.

1.3.2 Customary international law

Customary international law developed on state's responsibility to aliens also forms a part of international investment law, and it is argued that customs such as state's permanent sovereignty over natural resources could be developed as customary international investment law by General Assembly through its resolutions. Even though the custom has not transferred into a binding rule in treaties, it shall be obeyed by all countries.

1.3.3 General principles

General principles of law such as good faith, equity of law and non-discrimination are also recognized in international investment law, and many investment regulations are developed based on such principles. Thus, they are also a part of the sources of international investment law.

1.3.4 Judicial decisions

According to Vienna Convention on the Law of Treaties (1969), judicial decisions are a subsidiary source in interpreting international treaties, so judicial decisions relating to investment made by the Court of Justice could be regarded as a subsidiary source of international investment. Considering most of investment disputes are settled through investor-state dispute settlement mechanism, it shall be noted that the arbitration decisions are not considered as precedents in the realm of international investment law so as to become the source of international investment law, as they are frequently criticized for their inconsistence with each other and lack of certainty and foreseeability.

1.4 History of international investment law

The history of international investment law can be divided into two periods bluntly: the colonial period and post-colonial period, and the latter can be further divided into four sub-periods.①

1.4.1 Investment law in the colonial period

In the 18th and 19th centuries when investments flew from the big marine powers to their overseas colonial territories, investments did not need protection as the colonial legal systems were integrated into the colonial areas. And the imperial system gave sufficient protection for the investments which went into the colonies. The investments and investors from the imperial state were protected by the imperial parliament and imperial courts, even they were in the colonies, that is, the host states. During this period, the investors required even higher standard of treatment than the nationals of the colonies. For example, to ensure its citizens were sufficiently protected in other countries, North America argued that aliens should be treated in accordance with some external standard, such as the international minimum treatment standard, which was higher than the national treatment standard.②

In colonial period, the imperial state used force or economic coercion to settle investment disputes occurred in the colonies. The use of overt or covert force to coerce the settlement of disputes continued even after the World War II and into the post-colonial period.

But it is not to say that international investment law did not develop for alien protection and treatment in the colonial period. The customary international law emerged to protect property against unlawful expropriation, and clarified standards of treatment of

① See M. Sornarajah, *The International Law on Foreign Investment*, 3rd ed., Cambridge University Press, 2010, p. 19.
② See M. Sornarajah, *The International Law on Foreign Investment*, 3rd ed., Cambridge University Press, 2010, p. 21.

aliens as regard to their life, security, and property more generally.

Besides, the predecessor of investment treaties, namely, the friendship, commerce, and navigation treaties (FCN) also came into shape. Although these treaties were general and concise, bearing little likeness as compared to modern BITs, they contained provisions protecting investors against expropriation, requiring fair and equitable treatment and full protection and security over investment. Unlike modern BITs, their primary purpose was to establish closer commercial and political relations between the contracting parties.

1.4.2 Investment law in the era of infancy: 1945 through mid-1960s

The end of colonialism marked an increased demand of international investment rules, hence they developed quickly after the World War II. The rebuilding of world economy required fast-speed flow of FDI. The end of trade protectionism and beggar-thy-neighbor policy after the War provided a welcomed surrounding for the development of international investment law. Hence, the investment treaties developed quickly in the post-colonial period.

1945 through mid-1960s is the period that international investment law is in its early period of infancy. In the first half of the 20th century, customary international law was the primary source of international legal rules governing foreign investment. The emergence of a number of major investment disputes between foreign investors and their host countries after 1945 showed the significant limitations of protection afforded under customary international law and through the system of home state diplomatic protection, and triggered a move towards international investment treaty making.①

The first bilateral investment treaty in modern sense was concluded in 1959 between the Federal Republic of Germany and Pakistan. The treaty followed the investment provisions in FCN concluded by a number of countries in the inter-war years and following World War II. From that time on, BITs gradually became the main instrument to govern investment relationships among countries of different levels of economic development.

Besides, there were also efforts to establish multilateral rules on investment protection in this period, exemplified as the proposed investment chapter in the Havana Charter that purported to establish the International Trade Organization in 1948, even though it failed eventually.

---

① See M. Sornarajah, *The International Law on Foreign Investment*, 3rd ed., Cambridge University Press, 2010, p. 22.

1.4.3 Investment law in the era of dichotomy: period between mid-1960s and 1980s

The second period in the post-colonial times began in mid-1960s. In 1965, there was a landmark event in the history of international investment law. The Convention on the Settlement of Investment Disputes between States and Nationals of Other States (ICSID Convention) was concluded and a multilateral framework containing procedural rules for conducting arbitrations between host states and foreign investors was established a year later. This was a milestone of international investment law, as it provided a specialized facility to solve investment disputes between investors and host states. In addition, the Convention Establishing the Multilateral Investment Guarantee Agency (MIGA Convention) which was finalized in 1985 constituted a second successful incidence of genuine multilateralism in the investment context. It created a multilateral insurance framework for foreign investment projects against political risk and risk from wars.

Apart from the efforts to establish multilateral treaties, bilateral and regional treaties containing substantive rules on international investment protection began to flourish. From the mid-1960s to the late 1980s, international investment treaties, mainly in form of BITs, expanded in number and substance. The main signatories of BITs during this period were developed countries from Europe and those developing countries—including in Africa, Asia and Latin America—that considered FDI an important contribution to their economic development strategies. Specifically, Netherlands developed a comprehensive network of investment treaties which were famous for its Dutch Golden Standard of investment protection. In terms of substance, the main development in BITs was the increasing inclusion of ISDS provisions. The earliest known example of ISDS is the bilateral investment treaty between Indonesia and the Netherlands signed in 1968. The BITs adopted by the United Kingdom was also well-known for its concise treaty terms.

1.4.4 Investment law in era of proliferation: period between 1990 and 2007

Encouraged by the successive conclusion of hundreds of bilateral investment treaties after the end of the Cold War, as well as the success of the ICSID and MIGA Conventions, capital-exporting countries continued to make efforts to draft multilateral rules concerning the treatment of foreign investment to reduce the inconsistency among different bilateral treaties. It included endeavors in the various negotiation rounds of the GATT, and later the WTO, as well as a major project named Multilateral Investment Agreement at the end of the 1990s initiated by the OECD. Even though the content of this multilateral draft convention closely resembled the content of the treaties already in existence, the negotiation failed to reach a consensus among OECD members. Similarly, consistent efforts to launch negotiations of multilateral investment rules within the WTO in the new millennium produced almost no results.

The universe of BITs expanded rapidly in the 1990s, with almost three new agreements signed per week on average. Therefore, the number of BITs multiplied by five throughout the next decade to reach 2,067 by end of 2000 while only 381 BITs existed at the end of the 1980s. Most countries, both developed and developing, considered adoption of BITs or international investment agreements in the regime as a "must" in the global competition for foreign investment. Emerging economies such as China and India, with enormous potential as both recipients and source of FDI, rapidly expanded their treaty networks. Brazil was exceptional, as it signed several IIAs but never ratified them.

1.4.5 Investment law in the era of reorientation: reform of IIAs after 2008

One of the key characteristics in this period is the shift from BITs to regional international investment agreements (IIAs). Traditional BITs are specialized treaties covering investment, while more and more investment rules are made through IIAs covering a number of areas such as trade in merchandized goods, investment, transboundary service, intellectual property, government procurement, technical barriers, etc. It is more efficient for the trade delegates to negotiate investment rules with other issues relating to trade. Furthermore, trade benefits generated in merchandized goods will attract the less developed countries to accept more aggressive investment rules proposed by developed countries.

The other outstanding feature of investment rules during this period is the re-orientation of IIAs. The international investment agreements (IIAs) rush of the 1990s gradually slows down in the new century. Many countries refine treaty contents. The biggest capital exporting countries and districts such as the US and EU become the biggest capital importing countries as well. This has changed their attitude toward the function of investment treaties. Their increased exposure to investor-state dispute settlement (ISDS) cases has reminded them the offensiveness of investment treaties. And other factors such as the global financial crisis, a paradigm shift towards sustainable development and important changes at regional levels mark the beginnings of a concerted move towards IIA reform.

Governments have entered into a phase of assessing the costs and benefits of IIAs and reflecting on their future objectives and strategies as regards these treaties. Mounting criticism from civil society that the investment treaties have disregarded the environmental and labor interests plays a role as well. As a result, several countries have embarked on a path of IIA reform by revising their BIT models with a view to concluding "new generation" IIAs and renegotiating their existing BITs. The US and EU are in the lead. Developing countries such as India also engage in the BITs reform to protect its national and ethnic interest. Hence, the BITs and IIAs need to provide more regulatory space to the host states in providing public good such as safety, health and good environment to their citizens, and shall restrain the arbitration panel's discretion on treaty interpretation toward investor protection.

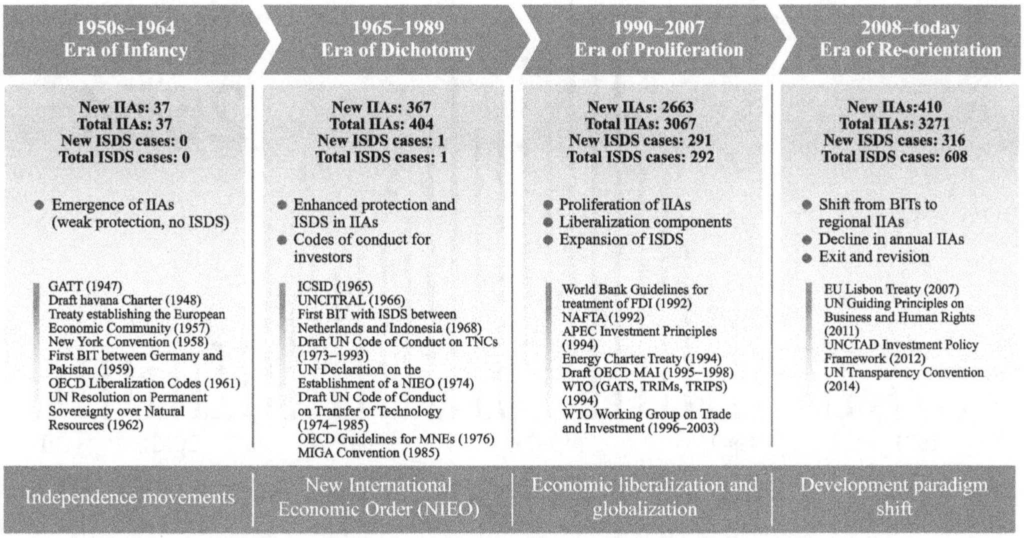

Figure III-1 Development of Investment Treaties in Post-colonial Era①

In 2019, 22 new IIAs were signed. The new treaties included 16 BITs and six treaties with investment provisions (TIPs). The most active economies in concluding IIAs were Australia, Brazil and the United Arab Emirates, each with three new IIAs. With these new IIAs, the size of the IIA universe rose to 3,284 (2,895 BITs and 389 treaties with investment provisions). By the end of the year, at least 2,654 IIAs were in force. The COVID-19 pandemic in 2019 is slowing down the pace of IIA negotiations. Several rounds of negotiations of BITs and TIPs scheduled for 2020 have been cancelled or postponed. Some of the policy responses to the health crisis and its economic fallout

① Source: UNCTAD, *World Investment Report 2016—Investor Nationality: Policy Challenges*, 2016.

could be challenged by foreign investors through arbitration proceedings under IIAs. This highlights the need to safeguard sufficient regulatory space in IIAs to protect public health and to minimize the risk of investor-state dispute settlement (ISDS) proceedings.

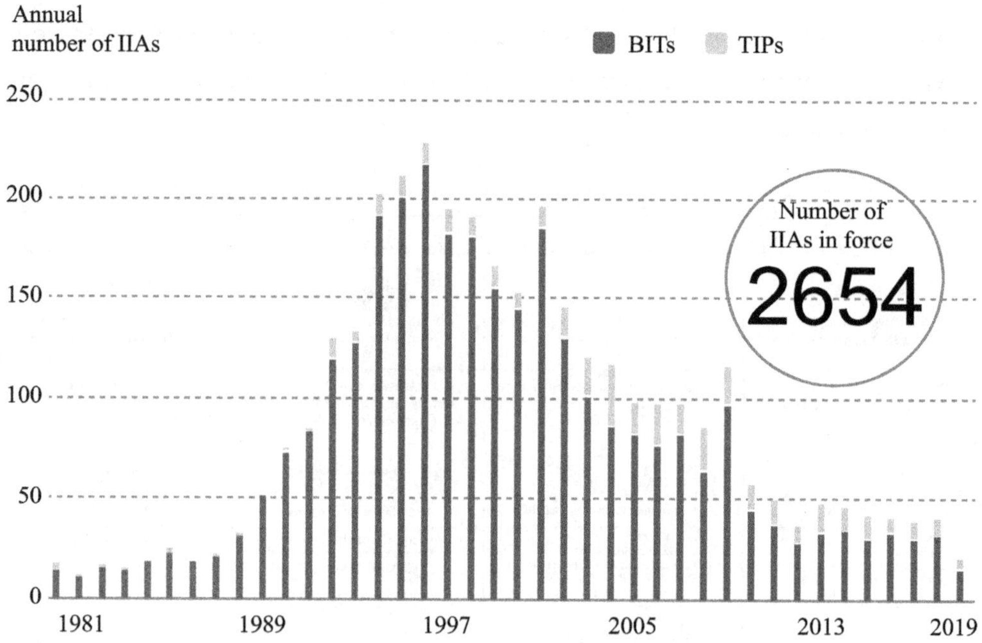

Figure III-2 Number of IIA Signed (1980–2019)[①]

1.5 Features of international investment treaties

The development of international investment law has revealed its unique features to the academics. Firstly, international investment law is highly fragmented. Unlike international trade law which is mainly characterized as multilateral in nature, international investment law is composed of hundreds of treaties, most of which are bilateral or sectoral in nature. By the end of 2016, there have been 3,324 international investment treaties, which include BITs and other regional or sectoral investment treaties. Both of the developed countries and developing countries have incentives to sign BITs, as the former need to ensure that investments that flow into states which have political and other risks are protected by rules, and the latter need to compete with each other for attracting

① Source: UNCTAD, *World Investment Report 2020: International Production Beyond the Pandemic*, 2020.

investments by easing their political risks. The outer shell of bilateral investment treaties looks similar, but the contents of the treaties vary so greatly.

Secondly, the international treaties keep evolving from one generation to next generation. They are reoriented from time to time for better protection of overseas investors or offering more regulatory power to the host state, resulting in the old generation IIAs being taken place by the new generation ones. The developed countries as the capital exporting states mainly lead the evolution of the treaties.

Thirdly, the IIAs are made between unequal partners. They are usually agreed between a capital exporting developed state and a developing state who is keen to attract capital from the capital exporting state. Hence, the contents of the treaties are mainly influenced by the capital exporting countries. That is also the reason why investment treaties, adopted by different countries, nevertheless share common features.

Fourthly, the development of modern investment treaties is positive to the rule-making of international society. Unlike the coercion used in the colonial or War period, BITs are voluntarily signed at least, and there is no element of overt coercion involved in their rule-making.

2 Substantive Issues in Bilateral and Regional Investment Treaties

The old generation BITs are usually concise, while the modern IIAs have rich contents. They include both substantive and procedural issues. The substantive issues mainly include statement of purpose, scope of treaty application, market access of investment, standard of treatment, performance requirement, expropriation and nationalization, repatriation of profits, etc. The procedural issues consist of provisions of transparency and dispute settlement. The following section will discuss substantive provisions in these treaties at first.

2.1 Statement of purpose of the treaties

Every bilateral investment treaty begins with a declaration as to the purpose of the treaty. Most treaties state that their mandate is to promote the reciprocal encouragement and protection of investments. This actually disguises the important fact that investment flow that is contemplated is in reality a one-way flow from the developed state to the developing state. Although the purpose of statement is not treaty text itself, it sheds light on interpretation of a specific treaty term, as the Vienna Convention on the Law of Treaties states that the preamble to a treaty indicates the context of the agreement and treaty interpretation shall also refer to the purpose of treaty. As most of the statement of purpose states that the treaty is for the protection of investment, various tribunals intend to interpret the treaty terms in a way that is beneficial to the investors, even this is against the original intentions of treaty maker. Therefore, an increasing number of countries include specific language in the preamble to their treaties aiming at making clear that the objective of investment promotion and protection must not be pursued at the expense of other key public policy goals, such as the protection of health, safety, and the environment.

2.2 Scope of application of IIAs

In order for an investor to benefit from the substantive and procedural rights of an investment treaty, the treaty in question has to be applicable *ratione materiae*, *ratione personae*, and *ratione temporis*. That is, the treaty must have subject matter jurisdiction, personal jurisdiction and temporal jurisdiction over the specific investor and investment. This requires that a covered investment has been made by a covered investor and that the state's measure that interferes with the investment in question is subject to the treaty in time. The definition of investment, investor, and the specifications of the temporal component, therefore, determine the scope of application of the obligations states incur under their investment treaties.

In terms of investment, there is no uniform definition of it. Most of treaties define investment broadly, and may give a non-exhaustive list of rights and interests that are covered as investment. Meanwhile, they may declare that portfolio investments, investments below a certain value, or for investments in certain economic sectors are not subject to treaty protection. For instance, the following definition of investment extracted from Article 8.1 of CETA explains its coverage of investment in the treaty. The provision includes a general defining paragraph and nine specific illustrations of investments, illustrating the usual forms of investment that are acknowledged by the EU and Canada.

"Investment means every kind of asset that an investor owns or controls, directly or indirectly, that has the characteristics of an investment, which includes a certain duration and other characteristics such as the commitment of capital or other resources, the expectation of gain or profit, or the assumption of risk. Forms that an investment may take include:

(a) an enterprise;

(b) shares, stocks and other forms of equity participation in an enterprise;

(c) bonds, debentures and other debt instruments of an enterprise;

(d) a loan to an enterprise;

(e) any other kind of interest in an enterprise;

(f) an interest arising from:

(i) a concession conferred pursuant to the law of a Party or under a contract, including to search for, cultivate, extract or exploit natural resources,

(ii) a turnkey, construction, production or revenue-sharing contract; or

(iii) other similar contracts;

(g) intellectual property rights;

(h) other moveable property, tangible or intangible, or immovable property and related rights;

(i) claims to money or claims to performance under a contract.

[...]

Returns that are invested shall be treated as investments. Any alteration of the form in which assets are invested or reinvested does not affect their qualification as investment..."

Similarly, as regard to the personal coverage of investment treaties, there is no uniform approach of defining investors in every single treaty. Yet the scope of investors who are covered is generally wide. Definition of investor regularly encompasses natural persons and legal entities that have the nationality of the other contracting state, that is, the nationality of the state where the investment is not located.

Concerning legal entities, their nationality is usually determined in view of their place of incorporation or based on their principal place of business. In rare case, the nationality of their controlling shareholder may be determinant. The acknowledged legal entities usually include corporations, partnerships, sole proprietorships and other organization forms acknowledged by contracting parties, but branches or representative offices are usually excluded.

Frequently, the treaties also accord protection to investors whose investment is not effectuated directly in the host country, but structured by means of one or several subsidiaries. For example, investor defined in CETA means "a Party, a natural person or an enterprise of a Party, other than a branch or a representative office, that seeks to make, is making or has made an investment in the territory of the other Party". For the purposes of this definition, an enterprise of a Party is: (a) an enterprise that is constituted or organized under the laws of that Party and has substantial business activities in the territory of that Party; or (b) an enterprise that is constituted or organized under the laws of that Party and is directly or indirectly owned or controlled by a natural person of that Party or by an enterprise mentioned under item (a).

Apparently, CETA refers to the place of incorporation in identifying the nationality of legal entities, and requires that the enterprises shall have substantial business activities in that country.

Temporal coverage of IIAs causes less ambiguities compared to the scope of investments. BITs usually keep in force for a considerable long period of time, sometimes as long as 30 years. In addition, after a possible termination of the BIT, some treaties protect the covered investment for an additional period of time before the new BIT is adopted. Most BITs protect both investments that have been made prior to and after the entry into force of the treaty in question. And treaties apply to those disputes crystalized after the treaties become effective, unless it is stipulated otherwise. That is, the investment protected could be formed before or after the treaties take effect, while the specific dispute calling for protection shall arise after the treaties take effect.

2.3 Market access of investment

The market access decides which industry and sector, to what extent, and on what condition that foreign investors will be admitted to invest in the host state. Such requirements and conditions are usually recorded in a list or schedule in the host state's foreign investment law. Pre-entry national treatment and provisions relating to prohibited market access restriction in IIAs will also illustrate a state's promise of market access to foreign investors.

2.3.1 Pre-entry national treatment

The provision of pre-entry national treatment appears as a discipline on alien's standard of treatment. Actually it is also a provision regarding to the extent of market access in the host country.

National treatment can be afforded on a post-entry basis or pre-entry basis. Post-entry national treatment means that the investors will be accorded national treatment only after it enters into the host country, while pre-entry national treatment means national treatment shall be afforded at the stage of entry, so it entitles the foreign investor to a right of entry and establishment in the host state if such right is given to the nationals of the host state.

A typical pre-entry entry national treatment reads as Article 9.4 of TPP, stipulating that, "each Party shall accord to investors of another Party treatment no less favorable than that it accords, in like circumstances, to its own investors with respect to the establishment, acquisition, expansion, management, conduct, operation, and sale or other disposition of investments in its territory". The equal treatment to aliens has been given on the stage of establishment and acquisition of investments, which are typically pre-entry national treatment.

The NAFTA is the first IIA incorporating the pre-entry national treatment. When the pre-entry national treatment was negotiated among the US, Canada and Mexico, it was a great challenge to Mexico, as Mexico had no previous experience in adopting an agreement with pre-entry national treatment. To remove the uncertainty which might be caused by such requirement, Mexico incorporated all the sectors from which it excluded foreign investment under Mexican Foreign Investment Law as sectors that were exempted from the obligation of national treatment, even though some exemptions are subject to the phase-out requirement during a given period.

Once pre-entry national treatment is adopted, the use of a negative list of sectors is a common practice to let the states remove those sectors that they would wish to offer extra protection. Thus, for example, the Canada-Thailand Bilateral Investment Treaty contains in its appendix the Thai investment laws, which list the sectors into which foreign investment is not permitted and the sectors into which foreign investment is permitted in partnership with its nationals. Where states have investment codes with such negative lists, it is sensible to include that list of sectors as industries that are not subject to national treatment.

The first IIA with pre-entry national treatment signed by China is RCEP. Provided by Article 10.3, national treatment is given with respect to the establishment and acquisition apart from expansion, operation, management, conduct, sale or disposition of investments.

2.3.2 Negative list and positive list

Another provision relevant to market access is the positive list and negative list in market access. They are schedules showing what industries and what sectors will be offered market access of the host state. All investment chapters of free trade agreements (FTAs) include schedules wherein parties make their market access commitments to which the substantive commitments in the investment chapter apply. There are two main approaches for listing market access commitments in a FTA, namely through the use of a positive list or a negative list of commitments.

The positive list is a GATS-style approach, whereby members list those sectors which they are prepared to subject to the FTA investment chapter commitments such as market access, national treatment and MFN treatment. The old generation BITs and FTAs usually adopt a positive list approach to scheduling commitments on investment, such as the Thailand-Australia FTA and the Japan-Singapore Economic Partnership Agreement.

In contrast, under the negative list approach to scheduling FTA investment chapter commitments, all measures affecting investment in all sectors of the economy are required to be in conformity with the FTA investment chapter unless otherwise specified in a list of reservations to the FTA. More and more modern FTA investment chapters, especially in the FTAs signed by the US and countries influenced by it, have adopted the negative list approach to scheduling commitments, including Australia-US FTA, Canada-Chile FTA, Republic of Korea-Singapore and Central America-Dominican-US FTA.

The negative list in US FTAs normally consists of two annexes. Under Annex I, contracting states list those nonconforming measures that they do not agree to make any more nonconforming or restrictive. This is often referred to as a standstill commitment. Some FTA investment chapters, such as those in Republic of Korea-Singapore FTA, Canada-Chile FTA, and Japan-Singapore EPA, are also subject measures listed in Annex I to a ratchet mechanism, whereby any future amendment to a measure in that Annex that brings it into greater conformity with the FTA automatically becomes an international commitment or binding. The effect is that the measure cannot then be returned to its original nonconforming state without being in breach of the FTA. Standstill clause and ratchet mechanism help to accelerate the liberalization of investment market access.

In Annex II, states list those sectors with nonconforming measures they may wish to maintain or make more restrictive in the future. Annex II can also be used by a state to list those sectors in which a state desires the flexibility to introduce new measures which may not conform to their FTA commitments.

2.3.3 Prohibitive market access restrictions

The market access provision in CETA is different from other FTAs in that it includes a provision which is similar to Article 17 of GATS. Article 16 prohibits the WTO members from taking or maintaining measures that would limit the market access of transboundary service, which is copied by the investment chapter of CETA:

“A Party shall not adopt or maintain with respect to market access through establishment by an investor of the other Party, on the basis of its entire territory or on the basis of the territory of a national, provincial, territorial, regional or local level of government, a measure that:

(a) imposes limitations on:

(i) the number of enterprises that may carry out a specific economic activity whether in the form of numerical quotas, monopolies, exclusive suppliers or the requirement of an economic needs test;

(ii) the total value of transactions or assets in the form of numerical quotas or the requirement of an economic needs test;

(iii) the total number of operations or the total quantity of output expressed in terms of designated numerical units in the form of quotas or the requirement of an economic needs test;

(iv) the participation of foreign capital in terms of maximum percentage limit on foreign shareholding or the total value of individual or aggregate foreign investment; or

(v) the total number of natural persons that may be employed in a particular sector or that an enterprise may employ and who are necessary for, and directly related to, the performance of economic activity in the form of numerical quotas or the requirement of an economic needs test; or

(b) restricts or requires specific types of legal entity or joint venture through which an enterprise may carry out an economic activity."

This provision reflects a new trend of IIAs signed by the EU, which bears more likeness with the multilateral agreements of GATS.

2.4 Standard of treatment

There are a variety of standards of treatment provided for in bilateral investment treaties. They would usually contain one article on treatment standards but that article would identify several different standards of treatment. These include national treatment, a fair and equitable standard of treatment, an international minimum standard of treatment and full protection and security.

2.4.1 National treatment

National treatment, especially pre-entry national treatment decides the extent of market access in the host state. It also has implications on the standard of treatment that a foreign investor enjoys in the host state. In FTAs and BITs signed by the developed countries, the national treatment clause may have both post-entry element and pre-entry element. National treatment ensures that foreign investors would participate in a level playing field and compete fairly with the domestic investors. Thus, such provision is significant in the BITs or in the investment chapter of the FTAs.

First, it offers equivalent treatment to investors if states reserve many of their economic sectors and privileges to their nationals. Second, it entitles the foreign investor to a right of entry and establishment in the host state. Third, it provides a basis for the argument that performance requirements such as export quotas or local purchase requirements should not be imposed upon the foreign investor. Fourth, it requires no other performance requirement if such requirements are not imposed on nationals.①

However, many countries exempt government procurement and special sectors that they wish to protect from their commitments of national treatment. The following dispute concerns a Canadian corporation invested in the US challenging the host state's government procurement measure.

Case III-1

ADF Group Inc. v. United States②

A Canadian company which had contracted for the supply of steel girders to be used in the construction of a highway in the United States, argued that the use of domestic material policy mandated by statute was a violation of the national treatment standard. ADF proposed that some of the work on the fabrication of the steel girders produced in the United States be done in Canada. The Virginia Department of Trade ruled that such fabrication would not be in compliance with the buy America provisions and could not therefore be permitted. The main contract had a buy America clause which would be violated, and the federal government would not reimburse the state government for the costs of the highway if the provision was violated. A waiver of the provision was refused on the ground that there were local providers of steel fabrication within the United States. As a result, ADF had to incur greater costs

① See M. Sornarajah, *The International Law on Foreign Investment*, 3rd ed., Cambridge University Press, 2010, p. 202–203.

② Source: ADF Group Inc. *v.* United States of America, ICSID Case No. ARB (AF)/00/1.

by subcontracting the fabrication of the steel. It fulfilled its contractual obligations but brought NAFTA proceedings against the United States on the ground that there were violations of NAFTA standards on national and fair and equitable standards of treatment. But the tribunal found that there was no violation of the national treatment standard, as all that the regulations required—a requirement that applied just as much to US as to foreign operators—was that the steel that was to be used in government projects should be fabricated in the United States. On the argument that the requirements were performance requirements as to local content, the tribunal held that, if so, the exception relating to procurements by a state party applied to excuse the state from liability.

Discussions:

1. Were steel girders fabricated in the US more preferentially treated than those fabricated in Canada in the case?

2. Did the US nationals receive better treatment than Canadian investors in this dispute?

3. Why did the tribunal conclude that the Buy America Policy were equally applied to both domestic and foreign investors?

4. Could ADF bring the dispute to ICSID relied on national treatment clause in chapter of trade in merchandized goods of the NAFTA?

2.4.2 Most-favored-nation treatment

In the provision regarding the standard of treatment, there would be references to the most-favored-nation standard of treatment (MFN) as well as national treatment.

MFN clauses, routinely included in traditional IIAs, aim to prevent less favorable treatment of investors from the signatory state *vis-à-vis* comparable investors from any third country. That is, this provision purports to get rid of nationality-based discrimination and aims to ensure a level playing field between investors with different foreign nationalities.

Unfortunately, unlike the MFN clause in the multilateral trade agreement, the application of MFN treatment in IIAs is distorted to some extent. In actual ISDS practice, investors have relatively infrequently alleged that they have been discriminated against by virtue of the host states' more favorable application of domestic measures to investors of third states. Instead, investors have most often invoked the MFN clause to access more investor-friendly provisions in IIAs concluded by the host state with third countries.

In particular, investors have frequently relied on the MFN clause to avoid dispute resolution requirements imposed by the applicable IIAs. Several tribunals have allowed this circumvention in cases involving broadly drafted MFN clauses. In those cases, the tribunal acknowledged that the claimant was able to point to an IIA signed by the host state in which disadvantageous pre-arbitration requirements were absent. That is, the investors can avoid the application of pre-arbitration requirements such as a waiting period before the arbitration in the treaty that apply to them or exhaustion of local remedies. In other cases, investors have invoked the MFN clause to benefit from higher protection standards or enjoy more substantive rights than the ones found in the base treaty.

Thus, illustrated by the following dispute *Siemens v. Argentina*, the application of MFN clauses results in investors' "cherry picking" or treaty shopping of the most advantageous clauses from different treaties concluded by the host state, thereby potentially undermining individual treaty bargains and sidelining the base treaty. As shown by the following Figure III-3, the modern IIAs have engaged in the reform of MFN treatment clause and provide at least five solutions to reduce the negative consequence of treaty shopping through MFN provision.

A first option is to specify that the MFN clause does not allow for the importation of substantive or ISDS-related elements contained in older treaties, while leaving procedural issues silent. The second option is to specify that MFN treatment does not apply to ISDS provisions found in other IIAs, existing or future. The third option is to specify that the MFN clause does not apply to substantive obligations undertaken in both existing and future IIAs. Fourthly, treaty parties can carve out from the MFN obligation certain sectors or industries or certain policy measures through a general carve-out (applicable to both parties) or through country-specific reservations. The fifth mechanism to limit the abuse of MFN treatment is to require that such treatment shall be given only in like circumstance. The last option is to delete the MFN clause completely in IIAs.

It is also argued that the denial of benefit provision in IIAs has the capability of limiting the treaty shopping potentially. A typical denial of benefit provision confines the benefits of the treaty or the protection of the host state only to investments approved by the state parties. For example, as given by Article 14.14 of USMCA, a Party may deny the benefits of this Chapter to an investor of another Party that is an enterprise of that other Party and to investments of that investor if the enterprise: (a) is owned or controlled by a person of a non-Party or of the denying Party; and (b) has no substantial business activities in the territory of any Party other than the denying Party. Theoretically, if an investor relies on MFN clause to stop the most preferential treaty, the host state would deny the benefit to the investor. However, it is difficult to invoke the denial of benefit provision as the tribunals usually require that the denial of benefit must be announced when the investors enter into the host state, and there are other conditions for such provision to apply.

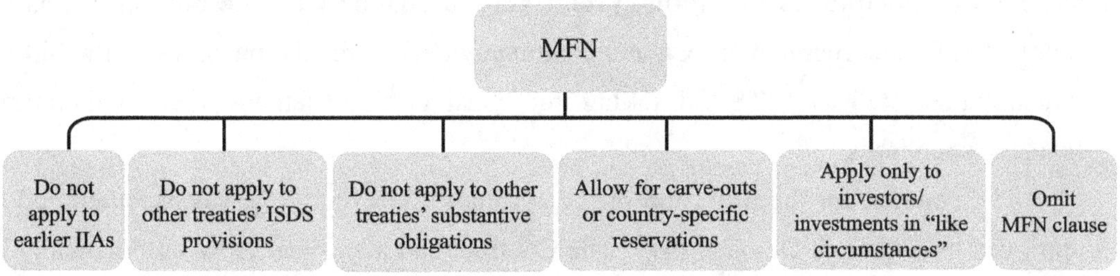

Figure III-3 Reforms of MFN Clause in IIAs①

Among these six solutions, some IIAs have adopted a hybrid approach in reshaping the MFN clause. For example, as shown by Article 8.7 of CETA, it is emphasized that procedural matters in ISDS or investment courts shall not be included in the coverage of MFN treatment, and treatment also does not extend to other IIAs' substantive treatment. Such reform approach is more ambitious than that found in the IIAs ratified by the US.

It is given by Article 8.7 of CETA:

"Each Party shall accord to an investor of the other Party and to a covered investment, treatment no less favorable than the treatment it accords in like situations, to investors of a third country and to their investments with respect to the establishment, acquisition, expansion, conduct, operation, management, maintenance, use, enjoyment and sale or disposal of their investments in its territory.

"For greater certainty, the 'treatment' referred to in paragraphs 1 and 2 does not include procedures for the resolution of investment disputes between investors and states provided for in other international investment treaties and other trade agreements. Substantive obligations in other international investment treaties and other trade agreements do not in themselves constitute 'treatment', and thus cannot give rise to a breach of this Article, absent measures adopted or maintained by a Party pursuant to those obligations."

① Source: UNCTAD, *World Investment Report 2015: Reforming International Investment Governance*, 2015.

Case III-2

Siemens v. Argentina[①]

This case is one of the more than 40 arbitrations against Argentina related to measures taken during its financial crisis in 2001–2002. In 1996, Argentina called for bids to provide an integrated immigration control system, personal identification system and electoral information system. In accordance with the bidding terms, Siemens A.G. incorporated an Argentine company (SITS) for the purposes of the bid. Argentina selected the SITS bid, taking into consideration Siemens' credentials and financial soundness.

The contract for the provision of the system ("the Contract") was executed and approved by decree in October 1998. The Contract had a six-year term, automatically renewable for two further three-year terms, with parties agreeing to give notice of intent not to renew only if the purpose of the Contract had been fully met.

In March 2000, the government set up a special commission under the Ministry of the Interior ("the Commission") to review the Contract. Following negotiations, Siemens reached agreement with the Commission on a proposal in November 2000. The government gave Siemens a Contract Restatement Proposal in the renegotiated terms. Also in November 2000, the Argentine Congress approved an emergency law to address the financial crisis that, *inter alia*, empowered the President to renegotiate public sector contracts. Siemens did not object to the government's proposal to include the Contract under the provisions of the 2000 Emergency Law, allegedly hoping that this step would speed up approval of the Contract Restatement Proposal. In a meeting in December 2000, the President of Argentina promised Siemens to issue the decree approving the Contract Restatement Proposal by the end of the month; however, in March 2001, the Minister of the Interior claimed to have been unaware of the Contract Restatement Proposal. In early May 2001, SITS received a new Draft Proposal from the government, differing from the Contract Restatement Proposal. Siemens was later informed that the new proposal was not negotiable. Two weeks later, the Contract was terminated by decree under the terms of the 2000 Emergency Law. Siemens filed an administrative appeal, which was rejected by another decree. In May 2002, Siemens

① Source: Emilio Agustín Maffezini *v*. Kingdom of Spain, ICSID Case No. ARB/97/7.

filed its request for arbitration at ICSID.

This case is notable in several respects. For one, it concludes that an investor can use a BIT's most-favored-nation (MFN) clause to get access to a more favorable dispute resolution clause in another BIT to which the host state is party.

Siemens sought to use the MFN clause in the BIT to avoid the treaty's requirement that disputes be submitted to local courts for 18 months before investors can resort to arbitration. Siemens claimed that the BIT's MFN clause entitled it to import a more favorable dispute resolution clause from the Chile-Argentina BIT, which did not require recourse to local courts first. Argentina filed a preliminary objection to jurisdiction, *inter alia*, objecting to Siemens' use of the MFN clause in this way.

The Tribunal held that access to the special dispute settlement mechanism provided under the BIT was part of the treatment of foreign investors and investments protected under the BIT's MFN clause. The Tribunal referred to the much-cited case of *Maffezini v. Spain*, where the investor was likewise allowed to use an MFN clause to access a more favorable dispute settlement clause in another Spanish BIT. The *Siemens* Tribunal noted that the MFN clause at issue in *Maffezini v. Spain* referred to "all matters subject to this Agreement", while the MFN clause in the BIT applicable to the Siemens dispute (the Germany-Argentina BIT) referred only to "treatment". The *Siemens* Tribunal concurred with the *Maffezini* Tribunal's finding that the formulation used in the Germany-Argentina BIT was a narrower formulation of the MFN obligation, but held that the term "treatment" and the phrase "activities related to the investments" were still sufficiently wide to include dispute settlement. The Tribunal, in fact, held that the term "treatment" was so general that its application could not be limited except as specifically agreed upon by the parties. The Tribunal concurred with the *Maffezini* Tribunal that an MFN clause may not override public policy considerations judged by the BIT's parties as essential, but held that the public policy considerations adduced by Argentina were not applicable. The Tribunal thus dismissed Argentina's preliminary objections to jurisdiction.

Discussions:

1. Did the Tribunal deem special dispute settlement mechanism provided under the BIT was part of the treatment in MFN clause?

2. How did the Germany-Argentina BIT require in its ISDS provisions, and how

did the Chile-Argentina BIT require in its ISDS provisions?

3.Did the Tribunal allow SITS to stop for Chile-Argentina BIT to avoid the requirement of recourse to local courts first?

2.4.3 Minimum standard of treatment

Apart from the national treatment and MFN treatment, most of IIAs include minimum standard of treatment. Minimum standard of treatment has a close relationship with national treatment since its emergence. In the colonial period, the capital-exporting states, argued that it was not sufficient for the host state to provide national treatment to aliens, as its domestic protection to property was far from adequate and developed. Hence, they argued that the investors should be treated in accordance with certain external standard such as the international minimum standard. Then the minimum standard of treatment came into being. The purpose of this treatment is to offer utmost protection to the foreign investors beyond the national treatment. The recognition of it will permit international scrutiny of the treatment of the foreign investor by the host state. Since its emergency, the minimum standard of treatment has been resisted by the developing countries. To defeat such external standard, many Latin American countries and other capital-importing countries argued for the national standard of treatment of aliens instead.

The minimum standard of treatment has experienced new development in the 21st century, which began to limit the high level of investment protection standard in the field of international investment law. The treatment is also relevant to fair and equitable treatment. In IIAs ratified by the US such as NAFTA, the US has insisted on that the minimum standard of treatment shall be confined to the rules given in customary international law, and fair and equitable treatment provides no higher standard of treatment than minimum standard of treatment.

2.4.4 Fair and equitable treatment

In most IIAs signed by European countries, fair and equitable treatment is usually included. This phrase consists of two abstract and subjective terms—fair and equitable. Thus, the standard is vague and is open to different interpretations, and its application causes much anxiety among the host states. It was once thought by investors and tribunals that this standard was a higher standard than the international minimum standard, especially in European BITs. In disputes based on NAFTA, the tribunal also accorded a wide interpretation to the standard. As some of the disputes were against the US and Canada, this later resulted in the NAFTA Commission issuing an interpretative note declaring that the fair and equitable standard was no more than the international minimum standard of customary international law.

In practice, the fair and equitable treatment standard has been expanded to include notions of transparency and due process, not to denial of justice, non-discrimination, and legitimate expectations of foreign investors. Among all these formula, one ambiguity caused by the standard is the overlapping of such standard with the national treatment and MFN treatment. Another particularly challenging issue arising through arbitral practice is the use of the fair and equitable standard to protect investors' legitimate expectations. It may be argued by the investors that they legitimately expect that their investments are subject to the laws and polices applicable when they entered into the host states, hence any change to the laws shall not apply to them. Given the potentially far-reaching application of the concept of "legitimate expectations", there is a concern that the fair and equitable clause can restrict countries' ability to change investment-related policies or introduce new policies—including those for the public good—if they have a negative impact on individual foreign investors.

In some disputes, the tribunal limited the application of fair and equitable treatment. For example, the case *S.D. Myers v. Canada* involved Canadian export prohibitions of hazardous waste material for disposal in the United States. S.D. Myers, a US company which alone carried out such waste disposal by exporting the waste to its plants in Ohio, argued that the prohibition was discriminatory and violated both national treatment and the fair and equitable standard of treatment. The claimant ascribed the prohibition to the Canadian interest in promoting the Canadian waste disposal industry. The Tribunal found a violation of both the national treatment standard and the fair and equitable treatment standard. However, it limited violations of the fair and equitable standard to situations in which there was arbitrary treatment that was unacceptable from an international perspective.

To clarify the fair and equitable treatment, the new generation IIAs have reformed the fair and equitable standard by limiting its scope and application. A first option is to qualify the fair and equitable standard by reference to the minimum standard of treatment of aliens under customary international law (MST/CIL), which was adopted by the NAFTA Commission, and appeared in most FTAs signed by the US.

A second option is to clarify the fair and equitable standard with an open-ended list of state obligations. The formulation may be a positive list, specifying what the standard includes. For example, the standard includes state's obligation not to deny justice in criminal, civil or administrative adjudicatory proceedings. The clarification could also be a negative list, explaining what the standard does not include. For example, the fair and equitable treatment in TPP stipulates that the mere fact that a Party takes or fails to take an action that may be inconsistent with an investor's expectations does not constitute a breach of this Article, even if there is loss or damage to the covered investment as a result. And the mere fact that a subsidy or grant has not been issued, renewed or maintained, or has been modified or reduced, by a Party, does not constitute a breach of this Article, even if there is loss or damage to the covered investment as a result.

A third option is to clarify or replace the general fair and equitable clause with an exhaustive, that is, a "closed" list of more specific obligations. The third option differs with the second one in that the list here is exhaustive, while the list in the second option is illustrative and open.

A fourth option is to reduce the fair and equitable treatment (FET) to a softer commitment, that is, by referring to FET in the preamble but not in the main treaty text. For example, the Turkey-United Arab Emirates BIT (2005) adopts such method to reduce its negative effects.

The last option that some countries have implemented in some of their IIAs is omitting the fair and equitable clause altogether. The typical treaties are Bangladesh-Uzbekistan BIT (2000) and Australia-Singapore FTA (2003).

It shall be noted that many modern IIAs narrow down the fair and equitable treatment through inclusion of both a negative list and a positive list. In TPP, fair and equitable treatment clause has been interpreted to include obligation of not to deny justice and due process, but does not equal host state's action against investor's expectation or suspension of a subsidy or grant. The text is given below.

"1. Each Party shall accord to covered investments treatment in accordance with applicable customary international law principles, including fair and equitable treatment and full protection and security.

2. For greater certainty, paragraph 1 prescribes the customary international law minimum standard of treatment of aliens as the standard of treatment to be afforded to covered investments. The concepts of 'fair and equitable treatment' and 'full protection and security' do not require treatment in addition to or beyond that which is required by that standard, and do not create additional substantive rights. The obligations in paragraph

1 provides:

(a) 'fair and equitable treatment' includes the obligation not to deny justice in criminal, civil or administrative adjudicatory proceedings in accordance with the principle of due process embodied in the principal legal systems of the world; and

(b) 'full protection and security' requires each Party to provide the level of police protection required under customary international law.

3. A determination that there has been a breach of another provision of this Agreement, or of a separate international agreement, does not establish that there has been a breach of this Article.

4. For greater certainty, the mere fact that a Party takes or fails to take an action that may be inconsistent with an investor's expectations does not constitute a breach of this Article, even if there is loss or damage to the covered investment as a result.

5. For greater certainty, the mere fact that a subsidy or grant has not been issued, renewed or maintained, or has been modified or reduced, by a Party, does not constitute a breach of this Article, even if there is loss or damage to the covered investment as a result."

The fair and equitable treatment in RCEP is strongly influenced by the US-style fair and equitable treatment provision that corelates the treatment with the minimum standard of treatment in customary law as shown below.

"1. Each Party shall accord to covered investments fair and equitable treatment and full protection and security, in accordance with the customary international law minimum standard of treatment of aliens.

2. For greater certainty:

(a) fair and equitable treatment requires each Party not to deny justice in any legal or administrative proceedings;

(b) full protection and security requires each Party to take such measures as may be reasonably necessary to ensure the physical protection and security of the covered investment; and

(c) the concepts of fair and equitable treatment and full protection and security do not require treatment to be accorded to covered investments in addition to or beyond that which is required under the customary international law minimum standard of treatment of aliens, and do not create additional substantive rights.

3. A determination that there has been a breach of another provision of this Agreement, or of a separate international agreement, does not establish that there has been a breach of this

Article."[①]

2.4.5 Full protection and security

Finally, the treatment provision encompasses the provision of full protection and security to the foreign investment. It has been held in arbitral awards that a state shall not use its force to harm the foreign investor's property or that the state should give protection from violence against the interests of the foreign investor if such violence could be reasonably anticipated. The provision is likely to be invoked by the investors when their investments are damaged by forces.

Again, there has been a tendency to expand the scope of the provision well beyond its meaning in customary international law to include a wider notion that the clause mandates the maintenance of conditions of stability for the investment.

2.5 Performance requirements

Performance requirements refer to measures imposed by host state on investors or investments after the investments are made. These measures are imposed by host states to ensure foreign investments would generate real and continuous benefits to the host states. Such performance requirements usually require the foreign investor to export a certain percentage of its production abroad, buy or use local products and services in the manufacturing process, and employ certain number of local employees. From the point of view of developing countries, the imposition of such requirements enhances the value of the foreign investment and ensures that they will truly contribute to the economy of the host state.

Typical performance requirements include export performances, local content requirements, and requirements on employment of local personnel. The export performance ensures that more foreign exchange is earned for the host state than profits made for the foreign investor through sales on the local market. It is argued, for example, if the investor makes an investment valuing USD 1 million, the inflow of foreign currency is USD 1 million. If the investor earns USD 1 million later in total, and repatriates its investment and profits back to its home state, there will be USD 2 million outflow of foreign exchange from the host state. Hence, the host state argues that the export performance will ensure that there will be real inflow of foreign exchange for the host country. Another reason for

---

① RCEP, Article 10.5.

the export requirement is that the host state can preserve the market for local entrepreneurs.

The adoption of local content requirements ensures that local products are utilized in the manufacture of products made by the foreign investor and not imported from abroad. Such requirements are adopted to protect the upstream and downstream industries of the host country.

The employment of local personnel also ensures one of the presumed advantages of the foreign investment, that is, it will raise the employment rate of the host state. Performance requirements benefit the host state in one way or another, but they raise the costs of manufacture and operation of the investment and are firmly rejected by the investors.

The Agreement on Trade-Related Investment Measures (TRIMs) was adopted in Uruguay Round of multilateral trade negotiation of WTO to restrict the host state's utilization of performance requirements. However, as the Agreement is presumed to be a trade agreement instead of an investment agreement, it prohibits only trade-related performance requirements, which influences export or import directly. Various IIAs concluded by the developed countries address the issue of performance requirements and seek to prohibit them altogether. Besides, the provision of national treatment will also require that these restrictions be done away with as they are not imposed on nationals. In the investment chapter of CETA, prohibited performance requirements include export performance, import substitution requirements, local employment, transfer of technology, etc. The host state cannot impose the most trade-related performance requirements as mandatory requirements as conditions for their entry, acquisition, expansion, conduct, operation and management. It cannot use them as a favorable condition to receive an advantage in the host market as well. The treaty text of prohibited performance requirements in CETA is given below.

"A Party shall not impose, or enforce the following requirements, or enforce a commitment or undertaking, in connection with the establishment, acquisition, expansion, conduct, operation, and management of any investments in its territory to:

(a) export a given level or percentage of a good or service;

(b) achieve a given level or percentage of domestic content;

(c) purchase, use or accord a preference to a good produced or service provided in its territory, or to purchase a good or service from natural persons or enterprises in its territory;

(d) relate the volume or value of imports to the volume or value of exports or to the amount of foreign exchange inflows associated with that investment;

(e) restrict sales of a good or service in its territory that the investment produces or provides by relating those sales to the volume or value of its exports or foreign exchange earnings;

(f) transfer technology, a production process or other proprietary knowledge to a natural person or enterprise in its territory; or

(g) supply exclusively from the territory of the Party a good produced or a service provided by the investment to a specific regional or world market.

"A Party shall not condition the receipt or continued receipt of an advantage, in connection with the establishment, acquisition, expansion, management, conduct or operation of any investments in its territory, on compliance with any of the following requirements:

(a) to achieve a given level or percentage of domestic content;

(b) to purchase, use or accord a preference to a good produced in its territory, or to purchase a good from a producer in its territory;

(c) to relate the volume or value of imports to the volume or value of exports or to the amount of foreign exchange inflows associated with that investment; or

(d) to restrict sales of a good or service in its territory that the investment produces or provides by relating those sales to the volume or value of its exports or foreign exchange earnings."①

The performance requirement provision in RCEP appears to be similar to its counterpart in CETA. However, the former introduces a new type of performance requirement which is absent in the CETA. No party shall impose or enforce, as a condition for establishment, acquisition, expansion, management, conduct, operation, or sale or other disposition of an investment in its territory of an investor of any other Party to adopt a given rate or amount of royalty under a license contract, in regard to any license contract in existence at the time the requirement is imposed or enforced, or any future license contract freely entered into between the investor and a person in its territory, provided that the requirement is imposed or enforced in a manner that constitutes direct interference with that license contract by an exercise of non-judicial governmental authority of a Party. For greater certainty, this subparagraph does not apply when the license contract is concluded between the investor and a Party. And it is acknowledged by the RCEP that its prohibition

---

① CETA, Article 8.5.

of performance requirement will not prevent a Party from conditioning the receipt or continued receipt of an advantage, in connection with an investment in its territory of an investor of any other Party, on compliance with a requirement to locate production, supply a service, train or employ workers, construct or expand particular facilities, or carry out research and development, in its territory.①

2.6 Repatriation of profits

Repatriation of profits is the most ostensible objective of FDI, which is necessary for the foreign investors, who may have to pay for loans, buy equipment and machinery and pay for services. Many of the treaties contain absolute statements protecting investors' right of repatriation. But this is unrealistic in most host states, as countries usually adopt currency controls to solve their exchange shortfalls problem. Absolute repatriation of profits in such countries might result in further exchange shortage and devastating their financial condition. One way to keep the policy space in case of foreign exchange shortage is to include exception provisions in IIAs. For example, some UK treaties provide that the right of repatriation of profits may be restricted in exceptional economic or financial circumstances. And in case of foreign-exchange difficulties, the treaties might also require that the repatriation of a percentage of the profits might be subject to a restriction of certain percentage, which is usually 20%.② Exceptions are also made in relation to delays occurring due to reporting requirements or seizures of assets that may be made by courts to satisfy debts.

Even though exceptions are given in IIAs, there may still be disputes regarding to the application of the exceptions, as the terms of exceptional economic or financial circumstance and foreign-exchange difficulties are obscure. The Argentinian financial crisis resulted in a number of investment disputes, which raised issues as to whether these crises gave rise to situations of necessity justifying the suspension of the right of repatriation and other interventions.

2.7 Confiscation, expropriation and nationalization

The provision in relation to expropriation and nationalization is the most indispensable

① See RCEP, Article 10.6.

② See M. Sornarajah, *The International Law on Foreign Investment*, 3rd ed., Cambridge University Press, 2010, p. 230–232.

provision in IIAs, as taking investors' property without compensation poses the greatest threat to foreign investment. Capital-exporting states have sought to circumscribe the right of a state to expropriate or nationalize foreign property by regarding at least certain types of taking of alien property as unlawful. It is now generally accepted that a state shall not nationalize foreign-owned property, subject to exceptions for public purpose and being applied in a manner of non-discrimination and full or fair compensation is provided.

IIAs may also prohibit a state from confiscating a foreign investor's property. A distinction must be made among these three terms. Confiscation is the capricious taking of property by the ruler or the ruling coterie of the state for personal gain. Nationalization refers to across-the-board takings that are designed to end or diminish foreign investment in the whole economy or in sectors of the economy. When the colonial states obtained independence, these new governments nationalized almost all foreign property in their domain, which were called nationalization. In modern law, it is best to refer to takings by states as expropriation, and expropriation in most IIAs is restricted to takings for public purpose.

A typical nationalization and expropriation provision in IIAs signed by the US and other countries influenced by the US usually state that Party shall not expropriate or nationalize a covered investment either directly or indirectly through measures equivalent to expropriation or nationalization (expropriation), except: (a) for a public purpose; (b) in a non-discriminatory manner; (c) on payment of prompt, adequate and effective compensation and in accordance with due process of law. The amount of compensation shall be equivalent to the fair market value of the expropriated investment immediately before the expropriation took place (the date of expropriation), and it shall be paid without delay and fully realizable and freely transferable.

The core of expropriation provision in US IIAs requires that the taking must be against prompt, adequate and effective compensation. This requirement is also called Hull Formula, which is subsequently accepted by many other developed countries and developing countries that signed with the US. Latin American countries have collectively insisted on Calvo Doctrine, which deemed expropriation lawful and appropriate compensation will be adequate, and the host state should be the sole arbiter of the amount of compensation. This latter standard is a flexible standard that would permit a state to take into account factors such as the profits made by the foreign investor, the duration of the period during which the profits were made, and similar factors, in assessing the compensation.

The new IIAs signed tend to be more specific in the compensation terms. For example, the expropriation provision in RCEP not only includes the conditions for a lawful expropriation, is but also with details regarding how compensation shall be decided and paid. Hereunder is the treaty terms found in Article 10.13 of the RCEP.

"1. No Party shall expropriate or nationalize a covered investment either directly or through measures equivalent to expropriation or nationalization (hereinafter referred to as "expropriation" in this Chapter), except:

(a) for a public purpose;

(b) in a non-discriminatory manner;

(c) on payment of compensation in accordance with paragraphs 2 and 3; and (d) in accordance with due process of law.

2. The compensation referred to in subparagraph 1(c) shall:

(a) be paid without delay;①

(b) be equivalent to the fair market value of the expropriated investment at the time when the expropriation was publicly announced,② or when the expropriation occurred, whichever is earlier (hereinafter referred to as the "date of expropriation" in this Chapter);③

(c) not reflect any change in value occurring because the intended expropriation had become known earlier; and

(d) be effectively realizable and freely transferable.

3. In the event of delay, the compensation shall include an appropriate interest in accordance with the expropriating Party's laws, regulations, and policies provided that such laws, regulations, and policies are applied on a non-discriminatory basis.

4. This Article does not apply to the issuance of compulsory licenses granted in

---

① The RCEP Parties understand that there may be legal and administrative processes that need to be observed before payment can be made.

② For the Philippines, the time when the expropriation was announced for the purpose of calculating the fair market value of the expropriated investment refers to the date of filing of the Petition for Expropriation.

③ For Australia, Brunei Darussalam, the Republic of Korea, Malaysia, New Zealand, and Singapore, the date of expropriation for the purpose of calculating the fair market value of the expropriated investment means the date immediately before the expropriation occurs. For Cambodia, Lao People's Democratic Republic, Myanmar, and Vietnam, the date of expropriation for the purpose of calculating the fair market value of the expropriated investment means the date when the expropriation decision is issued by the competent authority. For Thailand, the date of expropriation for the purpose of calculating the fair market value of the expropriated investment means the date when the expropriation occurs.

relation to intellectual property rights, or to the revocation, limitation, or creation of intellectual property rights, to the extent that such issuance, revocation, limitation, or creation is consistent with Chapter 11 (Intellectual Property) and the TRIPS Agreement.①

5. Notwithstanding paragraphs 1 through 3, any measure of expropriation relating to land shall be as defined in the existing laws and regulations of the expropriating Party, and shall be, for the purposes of and on payment of compensation, in accordance with the aforesaid laws and regulations. Such compensation shall be subject to any subsequent amendments to the aforesaid laws and regulations relating to the amount of compensation where such amendments follow the general trends in the market value of the land."

Judged from the arbitral awards, tribunals express their different attitude toward the amount of compensation, resulting in inconsistent decisions. Some tribunals support a full compensation to investors. In *Anglo-American Oil Company v. Iran*, Judge Carneiro argued that full compensation for expropriated property must be made, as such a rule is a prerequisite of international cooperation in the economic and financial fields.② His view is based on the grounds that the flow of much-needed capital would be reduced if the norm of full compensation were not recognized, and not based on any examination of precedents.

In *Libyan American Oil Co. (LIAMCO) v. Libya*, a US company named LIAMCO had entered into a number of concessions with Libya in 1955. After the nationalizations imposed by the then-new Qaddafi regime, LIAMCO initiated arbitration proceedings under its Concession Agreements, requesting as its primary remedy the reinstatement of its concessions and as an alternative, damages in the amount of USD 207,652,667 plus interest. That amount consisted of the following three components: (a) Physical plant and equipment — USD 13,882,667; (b) Concession 20 — USD 186,270,000 (lost profits); and (c) Concession 17 — USD 7,500,000 (lost profits).③

Initially, the sole arbitrator ruled that he could not award restitution, stating among other things that "it is impossible to compel a state to make restitution; this would constitute in fact an intolerable interference in the internal sovereignty of states". As to LIAMCO's alternate claim for damages, turning first to the physical property, the arbitrator said that "there is no difficulty also that the indemnity should include as a minimum the

① For greater certainty, the RCEP Parties recognize that, for the purposes of this Article, the revocation of intellectual property rights includes the cancellation or nullification of such rights, and the limitation of intellectual property rights includes exceptions to such rights.

② See Anglo-Iranian Oil Co. (United Kingdom *v.* Iran), Judgment, I.C.J. Reports 1952, para. 93.

③ See Libyan American Oil Co. ("LIAMCO") *v.* Libya, 17 I.L.M. 3 (1978), 4 Y.B. COM. ARB. 177 (1979).

damnum emergency, e.g., the value of the nationalized corporeal property, including all assets, installations, and various expenses incurred". For these assets and expenses, the arbitrator awarded LIAMCO the full amount of its claim.

With respect to the two concessions, the arbitrator first undertook a full conceptual analysis of the recoverability of lost profits. He found that (a) most municipal law systems permit lost profits as part of the damages for breach of contract; (b) both Libyan law and Islamic law also allow the recovery of lost profits; and (c) classical international law allows the recovery of lost profits for both wrongful taking of property and lawful nationalizations. He noted, however, that the recent evolution of international law indicated there was no constant and uniform rule for the compensation of lost profits for nationalizations, at least not all future profits.

Turning next to the specific claims of quantum, as for Concession 20, the arbitrator considered that to award lost profits for all future concession reserves would be an "extreme" position. In lieu of this "extreme", the arbitrator held that "it would be reasonable and just to adopt the formula of 'equitable compensation' as a measure for the estimation of damages..."[①] Relying on this compensation formula, the arbitrator awarded LIAMCO only USD 66 million (out of its USD 186 million claim) for its rights in Concession 20.

The situation for Concession 17 was different. Unlike Concession 20, no oil had ever been produced from that field, but LIAMCO argued that the increase in the price of oil would have rendered the field economic, such that LIAMCO should be compensated USD 7.5 million for its lost opportunity. But the arbitrator awarded nothing on this claim, reasoning that such profits were not "certain and direct", were doubtful, and were probably not realizable.

The risk of direct expropriation has decreased after 1970s. However, the expropriation clause in IIAs not only applies to direct expropriation, but also applies to indirect expropriation, which is also called creeping expropriation. That is, the investor's ownership rights have been slowly eroded or hampered by host state's regulatory measures. In 21st century, over 40% of ISDS disputes related to the indirect expropriation, which also triggered the reform of such provision in the new generation IIAs. Investors have used provisions on indirect expropriation to challenge general non-discriminatory regulations that have had a negative effect on their investments (e.g., a ban or the

① Libyan American Oil Co. ("LIAMCO") *v.* Libya, 17 I.L.M. 3 (1978), 4 Y.B. COM. ARB. 177 (1979).

imposition of restrictions on a certain economic activity on environmental or public health grounds). This raises the question of the proper borderline between expropriation (for which compensation must be paid) and legitimate public policymaking (for which no compensation is due).①

The US IIAs, among other investment treaties, define the indirect expropriation as any measure or series of measures the effect of which would be tantamount to expropriation or nationalization. Normally, they do not include a direct taking of physical assets, but could take the following forms: (a) forced sales of property; (b) forced sales of shares in an investment through a corporate vehicle; (c) indigenization measures; (d) taking over management control of the investment; (e) inducing others to take over the property physically; (f) failure to provide protection when there is interference with the property of the foreign investor; (g) administrative decisions which cancel licenses and permits necessary for the foreign business to function within the state; (h) exorbitant taxation; (i) expulsion of the foreign investor contrary to international law; and (j) acts of harassment such as the freezing of bank accounts or promoting strikes, lockouts and labor shortages.

The draft of indirect expropriation clause in modern IIAs usually limits the application of indirect expropriation clause by establishing criteria for indirect expropriation through a positive list or making a negative list to explain what does not constitute indirect expropriation. There are also a few IIAs that omit or explicitly exclude indirect expropriation. The Figure III-4 hereunder illustrates the reforms that various IIAs have embarked on.

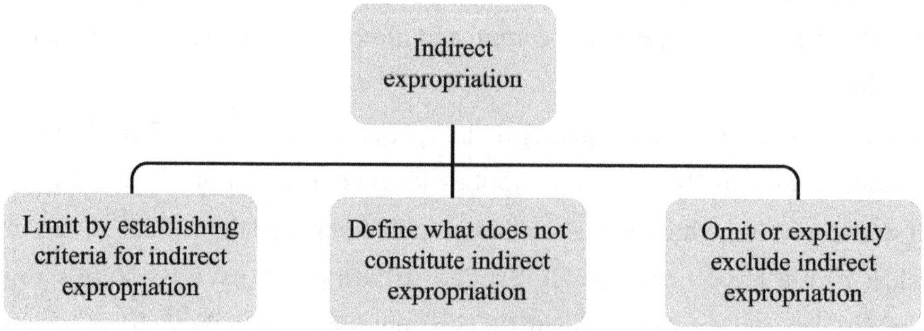

Figure III-4 Reform of Indirect Expropriation Provision②

① See M. Sornarajah, *The International Law on Foreign Investment*, 3rd ed., Cambridge University Press, 2010, p. 419–423.

② Source: UNCTAD, *World Investment Report 2015: Reforming International Investment Governance*, 2015.

Case III-3

S.D. Myers v. Canada[①]

This dispute involved Canadian order of export prohibitions of hazardous waste material for disposal in the United States. S.D. Myers (SDMI), a US company which alone carried out PCB waste disposal by exporting the waste to its plants in Ohio, and were more competitive than its Canadian competitors. As export of waste would cause damage to environment, the Minister of the Environment is recorded by Hansard stated that the handling of PCBs should be done in Canada by Canadians in 1995. On 16 November 1995 the Minister of the Environment signed an Interim Order that closed the border and had the effect of banning the export of PCBs from Canada. On 26 February 1995, by means of an Order in Council of the Governor General amending the PCB Waste Export Regulations, Canada turned the Interim Order into a Final Order banning the commercial export of PCB waste for disposal. This Order was in the following terms.

SDMI brought a dispute to the ICSID and claimed that the Interim Order and the Final Order were "tantamount" to an expropriation and violated Article 1110 of the NAFTA.

The Tribunal did not support the investor. The Tribunal accepted that, in legal theory, rights other than property rights may be "expropriated" and that international law makes it appropriate for tribunals to examine the purpose and effect of governmental measures. The Interim Order and the Final Order were regulatory acts that imposed restrictions on SDMI. The general body of precedent usually did not treat regulatory action as amounting to expropriation. Regulatory conduct by public authorities was unlikely to be the subject of legitimate complaint under Article 1110 of the NAFTA, although the Tribunal did not rule out that possibility.

An expropriation usually amounts to a lasting removal of the ability of an owner to make use of its economic rights although it may be that, in some contexts and circumstances, it would be appropriate to view a deprivation as amounting to an expropriation, even if it were partial or temporary.

In this case the closure of the border was temporary. SDMI's venture into the

---

① Source: S.D. Myers Inc. *v.* Government of Canada, 40 I.L.M. 1408 (2001).

Canadian market was postponed for approximately 18 months. Mr. Dana Myers testified that this delay had the effect of eliminating SDMI's competitive advantage. This may have significance in assessing the compensation to be awarded in relation to Canada's violation of Articles 1102 and 1105, but it did not support the proposition on the facts of this case that the measure should be characterized as an expropriation within the terms of Article 1110.

SDMI relied on the use of the word "tantamount" in Article 1110(1) to extend the meaning of the expression "tantamount to expropriation" beyond the customary scope of the term "expropriation" under international law. The primary meaning of the word "tantamount" given by the Oxford English Dictionary is "equivalent". Both words require a tribunal to look at the substance of what has occurred and not only at form. A tribunal should not be deterred by technical or facial considerations from reaching a conclusion that an expropriation or conduct tantamount to an expropriation has occurred. It must look at the real interests involved and the purpose and effect of the government measure.

The Tribunal agreed with the conclusion in the Interim Award of the *Pope & Talbot* Arbitral Tribunal that something that was "equivalent" to something else cannot logically encompass more. In common with the *Pope & Talbot* Tribunal, this Tribunal considered that the drafters of the NAFTA intended the word "tantamount" to embrace the concept of so-called "creeping expropriation", rather than to expand the internationally accepted scope of the term expropriation.

In this case, the Interim Order and the Final Order were designed to, and did, curb SDMI's initiative, but only for a time. Canada realized no benefit from the measure. The evidence did not support a transfer of property or benefit directly to others. An opportunity was delayed. The Tribunal concluded that this was not an "expropriation" case.

Discussions:

1. Did the Tribunal agree creeping expropriation has a broader coverage than expropriation?

2. How did the Tribunal interpret expropriation or indirect expropriation?

3. Did the Tribunal opine that in the case, Canada have engaged in expropriation? Please explain.

2.8 Umbrella clause

An umbrella clause, frequently included in traditional IIAs, requires a host state to respect any obligation that it has assumed with regard to a specific investment (e.g., obligations undertaken in an investment contract or concession agreement). The clause thus brings these contractual obligations under the "umbrella" of the IIA, meaning that their breach becomes a violation of the IIA, incurring state's obligation in international law.

Umbrella clauses have proven problematic in application, both with respect to the scope of the obligation undertaken and with respect to the potential for parallel dispute settlement proceedings, as investors may initiate two disputes, one based on the contract and one based on the treaty.

Countries wishing to avoid the potentially far-reaching legal consequences of an umbrella clause can clarify its meaning or reduce its scope. For instance, states can clarify that the clause covers only "written obligations" and that the obligations must be "entered into" with respect to specific investments. They can also indicate that the umbrella clause applies only to conduct that constitutes an exercise of sovereign powers by a government, that is, not an ordinary commercial breach of contract by the state. Another option is to exclude the applicability of the IIA dispute settlement mechanism to claims arising out of the umbrella clause. Finally, an increasing number of treaties omit the umbrella clause.

Contrary views are fostered in regard to the function and effect of umbrella clauses in investment treaties. Some tribunals support a broad application of umbrella clauses which allows foreign investors to use investment treaty arbitration in order to seek relief for any breach of an investment-related promise by the host state, regardless of the nature of the obligation and the nature of the breach. It applies to commercial as well as sovereign conduct of host states.

The opposite opinion attributes a narrower function to umbrella clauses and restricts their operation to breaches of investor-state contracts resulting from sovereign acts of the host state. This approach views of umbrella clauses essentially restate the customary international law and clarifies that rights of an investor under an investor-state contract can be integrated into the expropriation clause of investment treaties and accordingly require compensation if they are taken.

3 Procedural Matters and Exceptions in Bilateral and Regional Investment Treaties

3.1 Investment dispute settlement mechanism

Traditional investment dispute settlement mechanisms created by customary international law include diplomatic protection, administrative or judicial remedies in in the host country, conciliation and state arbitration. Investor-state arbitration is a comparative modern device that provides for the resolution of investor disputes between the investor and host state in a neutral forum. These approaches will be discussed in detail in Part VI.

A foreign investor, justifiably in many instances, will not have confidence in the impartiality of local tribunals and courts in settling any disputes that may arise between him and the host state. Commercial arbitration, in a neutral state before a neutral tribunal, has traditionally been seen as the best method of securing impartial justice for him. Where an international treaty backs him up by establishing the investor-state arbitration named investor-state dispute settlement mechanism (ISDS) and creating an obligation on the host state to submit to arbitral proceedings brought against it by the foreign investor, a major step could be said to have been taken towards investment protection.[①]

Nowadays, ISDS is common in the IIAs. There are several different types of clauses providing for such device and creating different obligations as to such arbitration. At the lowest level, the clauses merely direct the parties to arbitration as a way of resolving disputes arising out of foreign investment transactions. In these treaties, investor to state arbitration is only mentioned as a method of settlement of the dispute without creating an obligation on the part of the host state to accept the compulsory jurisdiction of arbitration. At the highest level, the treaties entitle the foreign investor unilaterally to initiate proceedings before an ICSID tribunal.

In some treaties, there is a period during which conciliation of the dispute should be attempted prior to arbitration or pre-arbitration conditions just as exhaustion of local remedies must be met before the arbitration. Most dispute-settlement provisions

① See M. Sornarajah, *The International Law on Foreign Investment*, 3rd ed., Cambridge University Press, 2010, p. 217.

in investment treaties refer to ICSID arbitration or United Nations Commission on International Trade Law (UNCITRAL) arbitration rules. They are also the most frequently used facilities in investment dispute settlement. Generally, over 60% of investment disputes have been brought to the ICSID and 30% of disputes have been solved by ad hoc arbitration based on UNCITRAL rules.

Exhaustion of local remedies is regarded as a burdensome pre-arbitration requirement. Some of the arbitration provisions themselves recognize the local remedies rule, which requires the prior exhaustion of all administrative and judicial remedies provided for by the law of the host state before resorting to international remedies. For example, the UK-Jamaica treaty permits submission of disputes to ICSID arbitration only if "agreement cannot be reached through pursuit of local remedies in accordance with international law".[①] Some are less stringent on the investor, imposing a time limit and permitting the international arbitration after the time limit has expired.

3.2 Exceptions

Traditional IIAs typically do not contain express public policy exceptions, while an increasing number of new treaties do include them. For instance, the new model treaties of Canada and the United States contain many exceptions, indicating that foreign investment protection is not the only objective of the treaties and that such protection would not be granted at any cost. The result of this change would introduce many defenses to liability of the host state for violation of the treaty standards.

Investors may bring claims against public interest measures that have a negative effect on an investment's profitability. The general exception clause in modern IIAs would read similarly to the general exception in GATT that protects the public interest.

These provisions aim at balancing investment protection with other public policy objectives and at reducing states' exposure to investor challenges of such measures. Public policy exceptions can also have an important signaling effect towards the general public, indicating an agreement's compatibility with sustainable development and public policy considerations. The formulation of such exception is often modelled on Article 20 of the GATT and Article 14 of the GATS, which provide more regulatory space to protect non-economic values, while they avoid the abuse of such provision by the host state by

---

① See M. Sornarajah, *The International Law on Foreign Investment*, 3rd ed., Cambridge University Press, 2010, p. 220.

requiring their measures to pass a necessity threshold and meet a good faith and non-discrimination test as part of the clause's chapeau.

There would also be a national security exception clause as well. A national security exception enables a state to introduce emergency measures when its essential security interests are threatened or for the maintenance of international peace and security, even if these measures contradict substantive IIA obligations. Such measures may include the freezing of assets, other types of sanctions, or discriminatory treatment of investors of certain nationalities (or of foreign investors in general). In the pre-establishment context, such measures may include refusal of access to specific projects or transactions in industries considered as strategically important (such as manufacturing of arms, telecommunications, transportation, energy or water supply).

Chapter Review

1. Who signed the first BIT?
2. What is the full name of ICSID, and why is it significant?
3. What is the difference between international trade law and international investment law?
4. What are the sources of international investment law?
5. In the late 1990s and new century, why were BITs taken place by IIAs?
6. Why do states reform their IIA contents in the new century?
7. Explain the four stages of IIA development in the post-colonial era.
8. Explain the features of development of IIAs.
9. How does COVID-19 affect the IIAs?
10. Can you name the multilateral investment treaties with binding force?
11. What are the main components embodied by IIAs?
12. What does investment mean in a modern IIA?
13. Which terms will determine the subject matter and personal jurisdiction of an IIA?
14. State the difference between positive list and negative list in market access provisions.
15. State briefly pre-entry national treatment and post-entry national treatment.
16. Discuss the relationship between the minimum standard treatment and fair and equitable treatment.
17. How do investors use MFN treatment in investment disputes?
18. Compare the fair and equitable treatment in TPP and RCEP.
19. What does umbrella clause mean?

20. What does indirect expropriation or creeping expropriation mean?
21. What is the Hull Formula? How is Calvo Doctrine different with Hull Formula?
22. What are the most frequently used facilities in investor-state disputes?
23. What does exhaustion of local remedies mean?
24. What kind of public policy is usually protected by the general exception clause of an IIA?
25. What is the national security exception clause in an IIA, and how is it drafted usually?

Key Terms

bilateral investment treaties	双边投资协定
Calvo Doctrine	卡尔沃主义
confiscation	没收
exhaustion of local remedies	穷尽当地救济
export performance	出口实绩要求
expropriation	征收
fair and equitable treatment	公平公正待遇
friendship, commerce, and navigation treaties (FCN)	友好通商航海条约
full protection and security	充分保护与安全
Hull Formula	赫尔准则
indirect expropriation	间接征收
International Centre for Settlement of Investment Disputes (ICSID)	解决投资争端的国际中心
international investment agreements	国际投资协议
investor-state dispute settlement (ISDS)	投资者与国家间争端解决机制
local contents	当地成分要求
local employment	当地雇佣要求
minimum standard of treatment	最低标准待遇
nationalization	国有化
negative list	负面清单
performance requirement	履行要求
positive list	正面清单
post-entry national treatment	准入后国民待遇

pre-entry national treatment	准入前国民待遇
ratione materiae	属事管辖
ratione personae	属人管辖
ratione temporis	属时管辖
Regional Comprehensive Economic Partnership (RCEP)	《区域全面经济伙伴关系协定》
repatriation of profits	利润汇回（本国）
umbrella clause	保护伞条款
Vienna Convention on the Law of Treaties	《维也纳条约法公约》

Further Readings

1. Collins, David, *An Introduction to International Investment Law*, 2nd ed., Cambridge University Press, 2022.

2. Miles, Kate, *The Origins of International Investment Law: Empire, Environment and the Safeguarding of Capital*, Cambridge University Press, 2013.

3. Salacuse, Jeswald W., *The Law of Investment Treaties*, 3rd ed., Oxford University Press, 2021.

4. Schefer, Krista N., *International Investment Law: Texts, Cases and Materials*, 3rd ed., Edward Elgar Publishing, 2020.

5. Sornarajah, M., *The International Law on Foreign Investment*, 5th ed., Cambridge University Press, 2021.

Chapter 3
Multilateral Investment Treaties

Study Guide

In Chapter 3, knowledge about multilateral investment treaties and attempts and efforts taken to establish multilateral investment agreements is given.

This Chapter first introduces two specificized agencies in the World Bank Group, which are Multilateral Investment Guarantee Agency (MIGA) and International Centre for Settlement of Investment Disputes (ICSID). These two agencies exert profound influence on international investment law, even though their coverage of international investment law is limit.

Several covered agreements of the WTO also relate to the investment. They are Agreement on Trade-Related Investment Measures (TRIMs), GATS and TRIPS. Chapter 3 discusses the investment provisions given by these agreements together with the draft of the Code of Conduct on Multinational Corporations and the draft of Multilateral Investment Agreement.

The capital importing countries always have attempts to adopt a comprehensive multilateral investment treaty to take place of the fragmented and inconsistent BITs. However, those attempts are rigorously resisted and frustrated by the newly independent countries and NGOs. The treaties and conventions with multilateral nature only relate to limited and specific areas of foreign investments such as insurance and guarantee to political risks, settlement of investment disputes and trade-related performance requirements. This Chapter introduces several binding conventions reached in the field of international investment law and several unsuccessful attempts that purported to conclude a comprehensive investment treaty.

1 Specialized Investment Organizations under the World Bank—MIGA and ICSID

The Multilateral Investment Guarantee Agency (MIGA) is an international institution that promotes investment in developing countries by offering political and economic risk insurance. In September 1985, the World Bank endorsed the idea of creating a multilateral agency to provide political risk insurance, thereafter MIGA was established in April 1988. As a member of the World Bank Group, MIGA is headquartered in Washington D.C. By promoting foreign direct investment into developing countries, the agency aims to support economic growth, reduce poverty, and improve people's lives.

The Agency started out with USD 1 billion worth of capital among its initial 29 member states. These nations included Bahrain, Bangladesh, Barbados, Canada, Chile, Cyprus, Denmark, Ecuador, Egypt, Germany, Grenada, Indonesia, Jamaica, Japan, Jordan, Kuwait, Lesotho, Malawi, Netherlands, Nigeria, Pakistan, Samoa, Saudi Arabia, Senegal, Sweden, Switzerland, The Republic of Korea, United Kingdom, and the United States.

In 1991, the number of members of MIGA topped 100. Eight years later, guarantees issued by the Agency reached a total of USD 1.3 billion, topping the USD 1 billion dollar mark for the first time ever. The Agency also provided guarantees worth USD 1.2 billion in 2009 to support the economies in Europe and Central Asia following the global financial crisis. As of March 2020, MIGA had 181 member governments, among which 156 are developing countries and another 25 are industrialized countries.

MIGA offers a variety of services in order to encourage foreign direct investment. These include risk insurance against foreign exchange restrictions, an outbreak of conflicts or wars, imposed spending limits, and related restrictions on company assets.

In addition to providing political risk insurance to corporations that want to invest in developing countries, MIGA offers advisory services to developing country governments. The organization advises on the policies and procedures these governments should follow and the best ways these countries can attract foreign investment. Other services by MIGA include licensing arrangements, franchising, and technology support.

Among the World Bank Group, there is another agency that provides facilities in the area of investment—the International Centre for Settlement of Investment Disputes (ICSID). In the mid-1960s the Convention on the Settlement of Investment Disputes between States and Nationals of Other States was concluded. This multilateral treaty created the International Centre for Settlement of Investment Disputes (ICSID) and established a procedural framework for the settlement of investment disputes between foreign investors and states through binding arbitration.

The agency is the smallest World Bank Group institution, formed in 1966 to provide facilities for mediation for disputes between countries and private foreign investors. It is one of the few global dispute settlement mechanisms allowing a private entity be a party to a dispute against a country. The agency contains procedural rules for conducting arbitrations between host states and foreign investors.

Recourse to arbitration under the ICSID Convention is, however, entirely voluntary. Namely, the ratification of the ICSID Convention does not per se entail the signatory's acceptance of the Center's jurisdiction for investment disputes. Instead, the host state and the investors have to consent separately to ICSID arbitration. Originally drafted in order to offer a forum for contractual arbitration between foreign investors and host states, consent to ICSID arbitration nowadays is most often contained in BITs under which host states extend a standing offer to covered investors that they can accept by initiating arbitration under the Convention. The Convention only provides procedural rules for ISDS, without stipulating the applicable law to the arbitrating parties, and it does not impose direct obligations relating to the treatment of foreign investors that could have been perceived as limiting the sovereignty of host states.

One of the special features and advantages of ICSID arbitration are the finality of ICSID awards and the automatic recognition in the Convention's members. Unlike awards in international commercial arbitration, ICSID awards are subject only to Convention-specific annulment proceedings.

Recourse to ICSID arbitration, therefore, enables foreign investors to settle disputes with host states in an independent forum, aiming at depoliticizing the settlement of investment disputes. The mechanism is particularly salient in promoting and protecting investments in countries with an underdeveloped, politically biased, corrupt or inefficient court system.

2 Investment Provisions Adopted by the WTO

The first attempt to reach a multilateral treaty relating to investments occurred after the World War II. The Havana Charter of 1948 purported to establish the International Trade Organization (ITO), containing provisions on investment. If the Havana Charter ever entered into force, the provisions on investments would be the first multilateral investment rules binding all its members. However, when the chapter of trade in merchandized goods was taken out and transformed into the GATT 1947, the investment rules were left out.

Articles 11 and 12 of the Havana Charter dealt with investment. Article 11 stated that no member shall take unreasonable or unjustifiable action against investment, and it shall assure just and equitable treatment of foreign investors. Article 12 provided members with the right to take appropriate safeguards against foreign investment and to determine whether and to what extent and upon what terms it will allow future foreign investment. This is the first part of Article 12, and this part reflects requirements of developing countries on the regulation of FDIs that enter into their countries. But, the second part of Article 12 contains the genesis of the developed-country position. It stated that members undertake to provide reasonable opportunities for investments acceptable to them and adequate security for existing and future investments, and to give due regard to the desirability of avoiding discrimination as between foreign investment. It suggested that the host states shall give reasonable market access to foreign investors, and shall be refrained from taking discriminatory and discretional measures on investors.

In several decades, the major efforts of GATT negotiation concentrated on reduction of tariff and removal of non-tariff barriers. It was not until the Uruguay Round that definite efforts were made to introduce measures relating to investment into international trade. The covered agreements regulating investment in the WTO include the Trade-Related Investment Measures (TRIMs), the General Agreement on Trade in Services (GATS), and the Agreement on Trade-Related Aspects of Intellectual Property Rights (TRIPS). Other instruments deal with investments indirectly. For example, the Agreement on Government Procurement requires that there be no discrimination in sourcing materials for purchase by the host government as between foreign investors and local manufacturers. But, the more significant instruments are TRIMs and GATS.

The TRIMs was concluded in Uruguay Round, and it deals directly with foreign investment. It is, however, not a comprehensive document covering every aspects of investment, as it deals only with certain types of performance requirement, without stipulation on market access and treatment of investors. Even on the issue of performance requirement, the Agreement sets disciplines on measures related to investments which cause trade-restrictive and distorting effects, thus cautiously establishing a link between foreign investment and international trade in goods.[①]

The main aim of TRIMs is to prohibit the use of performance requirements that directly affect the import or export of its members. Prohibited measures include the purchase or use by an enterprise of products of domestic origin or from any domestic source, whether specified in terms of particular products, in terms of volume or value of products, or in terms of a proportion of volume or value of its local production; or that an

---

① See M. Sornarajah, *The International Law on Foreign Investment*, 3rd ed., Cambridge University Press, 2010, p. 266.

enterprise's purchases or use of imported products be limited to an amount related to the volume or value of local products that it exports.

Furthermore, it is forbidden that the Members limit the importation by an enterprise of products used in or related to its local production, generally or to an amount related to the volume or value of local production that it exports, or the importation by an enterprise of products used in or related to its local production by restricting its access to foreign exchange to an amount related to the foreign exchange inflows attributable to the enterprise. In *Indonesia–Autos*, the Panel found that the tax and tariff benefits contingent on meeting local requirements under the Indonesian car program constituted "advantages" within the meaning of the chapeau of paragraph 1 of the Illustrative List of TRIMs, and as a result were inconsistent with Article 2.1 of the TRIMs Agreement.

Finally, the TRIMs prohibits the Members from taking any measures to restrict the exportation or sale for export by an enterprise of products, whether specified in terms of particular products, in terms of volume or value of products, or in terms of a proportion of volume or value of its local production.

Other provisions, such as MFN treatment or national treatment, also help to restrain the boundary of a Member's performance requirement measures. In *EC–Bananas III*, the Panel found that the allocation of import licenses to a particular category of operators was inconsistent with Article 3.4 of GATT 1994, as well as Article 2 of the TRIMs Agreement.

The GATS is a specific agreement that deals with services. It also bears a close relationship with investments. Of the four modes of supply that are covered by GATS, one is the provision of services through commercial presence in the territory of a member. This "commercial presence" could be created through the establishment of a juridical person or through a branch or office for the supply of services within the territory of a member, which are exactly the most obvious forms of foreign direct investment. Thus, GATS provides some provisions for foreign investment in the services sector.

GATS adopts a bottom-up approach requiring the commitments in the services sector to be listed in each member's schedule.[①] The schedules contain sector-specific disciplines on market access and national treatment. It also includes a general obligation of MFN treatment. Any commitments made in a Member's schedule on commercial presence bind their related measures on investments.

---

① See M. Sornarajah, *The International Law on Foreign Investment*, 3rd ed., Cambridge University Press, 2010, p. 264.

The Agreement on Trade-Related Aspects of Intellectual Property Rights (TRIPS) deals with standards of protection of intellectual property. Investment treaties do create international obligations, which protect intellectual property as investment, suggesting that TRIPS may have relevance to investment as well. However, TRIPS is largely intended to address the problem of piracy, and, to that extent, it is not aimed at investment protection.

The link between TRIPS and investment treaties is obscure. Under the TRIPS regime, the case for compulsory licensing could be made out, but under a strong investment treaty regime, compulsory licensing would amount to a taking of property. Even it is for public purpose, compulsory licensing does not conform to the IIAs if the host state fails to afford full compensation as required by the investment treaties. To avoid such potential conflict, the investment treaties usually make exceptions for TRIPS.

In Doha Round, investment has once been included as a negotiated issue. However, due to the conflicts and divergency on the negotiation of the agriculture issue among the Members, the investment was taken out from the negotiation agenda.

3 Other Attempts to Establish a Multilateral Investment Treaties

There are also other attempts initiated by developed countries or developing countries to establish a multilateral investment treaty on FDI, although they failed, they are nevertheless worthy of studying.

3.1 UNCTC's Code of Conduct on Multinational Corporations

The draft of Code of Conduct on Multinational Corporations (CCMC) was prompted by a serious scandal of transnational corporations (TNCs). In 1972, Jack Anderson, an investigative reporter in the United States, asserted that the International Telephone and Telegraph Company (ITT) had plotted with the United States Central Intelligence Agency in 1970 to block the election of Salvador Allende, who had threatened to nationalize ITT's 60% share of the national phone company in Chile. These allegations prompted the United States Senate Foreign Relations Committee to establish the Subcommittee on Multinational Corporations, which held highly publicized hearings critical of TNCs in the developing world under Senator Frank Church from 1973 to 1976. On another front, critics accused the Swiss giant Nestlé of dressing its sales personnel to look like doctors and nurses to discourage breastfeeding of babies and to substitute what the sales people claimed to be medically superior baby formula. At the United Nations, Philippe de Seynes, United Nations Under-Secretary-General, crafted a resolution in 1972 calling for the formation of a Group of Eminent Persons to study the impact of multinational corporations on economic development and international relations. The goal was to create a focal point within the United Nations to develop the institutions needed for a new international economic order.① The Group's hearings and report led to the establishment of the United Nations Commission on TNCs and the United Nations Centre on Transnational Corporations (UNCTC) in New York in 1974. For almost two decades, from 1975 to 1992, the UNCTC struggled over the Code. By 1992, the draft Code of Conduct on Multinational Corporations was finalized.

The Code significantly understated the importance of these TNCs. The Group of 77 developing countries, supported by the socialist bloc, demanded a legally binding international instrument of rules to govern the activities of TNCs. The representatives of the developed market economies insisted on a voluntary code of principles. The debate represented a clash between those who believed in government-directed development and those who preferred the primacy of the market mechanism.②

The preamble to the conduct on multinational corporations states that the object of the CCMC is to maximize the contributions of transnational corporations to economic development and growth and to minimize the negative effects of the activities of these corporations. Typical provisions in the Code include Articles 7, 12, 16 and 21.

Article 7 restates the principle of sovereignty by requiring that transnational corporations shall respect the national sovereignty of the host countries and the right of each state to exercise permanent sovereignty over its natural resources. They seek to spell out the fact that the foreign corporation which operates in the territory of the host state should recognize the sovereignty of the host state. They require foreign corporations to accept and abide by the laws of the host state and ensure that they do not act in any way that is inconsistent with the economic objectives of the host state. In Article 12, an obligation is created to renegotiate contracts where the contractual equilibrium which existed at the time of the contract has been altered by a fundamental change of

① See Theodore H. Moran, *The United Nations and Transnational Corporations: A Review and a Perspective*, 18 Transnational Corporations 91, 92 (2009).

② See Theodore H. Moran, *The United Nations and Transnational Corporations: A Review and a Perspective*, 18 Transnational Corporations 91, 92 (2009).

circumstances.[①]

Article 16 imposes a duty on transnational corporations not to interfere in the domestic politics of the host state. Nor should transnational corporations attempt to persuade their home states to intervene on their behalf in a manner inconsistent with the latter's obligations under the Charter of the United Nations and the Declaration on Friendly Relations Between States.

The inspiration for these articles is the fear on the part of developing states that transnational corporations will use their economic power to influence domestic politics. There is also the fear that they will induce their home states to interfere with the internal politics of host states.

Article 21 requires TNCs to abstain from corrupt practices. The draft of CCMC creates a definite duty on the part of multinational corporations to refrain from making payments to public officials as a consideration for the performance of their duties and also requires a register to be kept of payments made to officials. And other duties imposed by CCMC are related to transfer of technology, restrictive business practices, labor relations, transfer pricing, consumer protection, environmental protection, and information disclosure.

The draft of CCMC mainly imposes duties on TNCs to avoid their negative impacts on host states, although it also requires the host state to protect the investment and provide non-discriminatory and fair treatment to foreign investments. Compared with the rights that it empowered on the TNCs, the CCMC clearly pays more attention to their duties and obligations, and it was rejected by the TNCs.

3.2 Multilateral Agreement on Investment

Unlike the CCMC, there are also some codes favoring developed countries, including the Multilateral Agreement on Investment (MAI) attempted by the Organisation for Economic Co-operation and Development (OECD).

As hostility to multinational corporations ended, and with the new states resulting from the break-up of the Soviet Union embracing free market notions, the competition for foreign investment among developing countries increased. The ascendancy of neo-liberalism speeded the process of the liberalization of trade regimes, resulting in the

① See M. Sornarajah, *The International Law on Foreign Investment*, 3rd ed., Cambridge University Press, 2010, p. 244.

formation of the WTO. The OECD, just a few years later, embarked upon the framing of a binding Multilateral Agreement on Investment (MAI).

The MAI soon became the focus of protests. They were generated largely by human rights and environmental groups. It was seen as driving a wedge between the rich and the poor not only on a global scale but also within the developed states themselves. The protesters had organized themselves so effectively that they were able to exert sufficient pressure on their governments to pull out of the negotiations of the MAI.①

While authorizing the negotiations, the OECD Ministerial Council aimed to reach a broad multilateral framework for international investment with high standards for the liberalization of investment regimes and investment protection and with effective dispute-settlement procedures. Negotiated in the same period, the draft of MAI is similar in most respects to the investment chapter of NAFTA. The negotiation was initially kept in secrecy, which caused much unease to the public, especially to the NGOs. The draft of the Agreement was leaked in March 1997, causing a turmoil in the civil society in the developed countries. They protested the further negotiation on the draft before their governments.

Compared with other investment treaties, the provisions in MAI are advanced. The right of establishment contained in the MAI is at the heart of the liberalization of investment flows. The provision on national treatment applies to both the pre-entry phase as well as to the post-entry phase.

There are standstill provisions permitting existing sectoral reservations from national and most-favored-nation treatment and rollback provisions, though their eventual elimination is required. National treatment after entry is also an important feature of the MAI. This would pose problems for a large number of developing states, as developing countries also operate large sectors of their economies through state corporations which are monopolies.

The MAI prohibits export requirements, domestic content requirements, domestic purchase requirements, the tying of imports to the value of exports, requirements relating to the transfer of technology, territorial exclusivity in export, the compulsory location of research and development activities, the entry of investment through joint ventures and a requirement to hire local personnel.

---

① See M. Sornarajah, *The International Law on Foreign Investment*, 3rd ed., Cambridge University Press, 2010, p. 241.

The dispute-resolution provisions of the MAI are more extensive than those commonly used in investment treaties, even more comprehensive than NAFTA. They provide for both state-to-state and investor-to-state arbitration.

The MAI failed shortly after the leakage of its draft. It failed for a variety of reasons. There have been various assessments of the causes of its failure. The role of the NGOs is regarded by some as the reason for its failure. Others regard the MAI as not being strong enough, so that the multinational business community did not give it its wholehearted support. But it was also criticized if it were any stronger, the MAI would have proved unacceptable to more states. The seeds of the failure of the MAI lay in the fact that there was insufficient agreement within the developed world on the norms of investment protection.

Chapter Review

1. What is the political risk? How is it different from the commercial risk?
2. Why is MIGA established? What are the functions of MIGA?
3. What is the significance of ICSID? What facilities does it provide for its members?
4. Does ICSID rules apply to its members voluntarily?
5. Does ICSID consist of rules for treaty interpretation?
6. How does Havana Charter of ITO relate to foreign direct investment?
7. What are the basic rules of TRIMs on performance requirements? Does it cover all types of performance requirements?
8. How is GATS relevant to foreign direct investment?
9. What is the conflict between investment treaties and TRIPS?
10. In what situation was Code of Conduct on Multinational Corporations negotiated? What were the purposes of the negotiation?
11. What does MAI refer to? State briefly its basic provisions.
12. Why did the negotiation of MAI fail? Why did NGOs protest the negotiation of MAI?

Key Terms

Agreement on Trade-Related Investment Measures (TRIMS)	《与贸易有关的投资措施协议》
Code of Conduct on Multinational Corporations (CCMC)	《跨国公司行动守则》

Multilateral Agreement on Investment (MAI)	《多边投资协定》
Multilateral Investment Guarantee Agency (MIGA)	多边投资担保机构

Further Readings

1. Waelde, T. W., *International Law of Foreign Investment: Towards Regulation by Multilateral Treaties*, University of Dundee, Centre for Energy, Petroleum & Mineral Law & Policy, 2000.

2. Yahaya, Shamsu, *Multilateral Investment Treaties: Is the Energy Charter Treaty an Effective Instrument for Protecting International Investments?*, GRIN Verlag, 2010.

3. Yu, Eden Siu-hung & Chi-chur Chao, *Trade-related Investment Measures: Theory and Applications*, Imperial College Press, 2014.

Part IV International Monetary and Financial Law

Chapter 1 International Monetary Law

Study Guide
This Chapter is about the international legal disciplines on monetary law. First, the Chapter explains the difference between money and currency, and state's monetary sovereignty. Next, the Chapter discusses the establishment of European Monetary Union and International Monetary Fund to help students understand why states need to cooperate on monetary matters and how regional and multilateral cooperation on monetary matters works. Their institutional structure, functions, membership and members' subscription and duties are explained as well. Finally, the weakness and power of such regional and multilateral monetary unions are discussed to give students more information about the significance and deficiency of current international monetary law.

1 Introduction to Monetary Law

International monetary law includes both public international law and private international law. Public international law focuses on the issue and regulation of money by the state, that is, state's sovereign power on monetary issue. Private law, on the other hand, concerns the notion of payment and the function of money as a means of payment. The public law on issuance and regulation of money is mainly discussed hereunder.

1.1 Definition and types of money and currency

Before studying international monetary law, students must understand the meaning of money and currency. The concept of money varies in different contexts. The economic definition of money is typically functional, based upon its four basic functions commonly accepted as medium of exchange, means of payment, unit of account, and store of value. Though sometimes the notions of money and currency are used indistinctly, the concept of money is broader than that of currency. Currency is a more formal term, defined as a medium of exchange for goods and services. It is usually in form of paper or coins, issued by the government and generally accepted at its face value as a method of payment. Most countries issue their own currencies. Switzerland's official currency is the Swiss franc, and Japan's is the yen. States can control the issue of currency within their territory, but the creation of money is not exclusively the monopoly of the state. For example, digital money such as bitcoin has value of store and can be used as a payment tool, though it is not issued by a sovereign state. It nevertheless performs the functions of money. Countries may accept other currency as legal tender in addition to their own currencies. For example, Costa Rica, El Salvador, and Ecuador accept US dollars.

Currency is often used interchangeable with money. It can be classified into different types: fiat currency, asset backed currency, commodity backed currency and digital currency. Some types have been very old, and have exited the market, and new type of currency is also forming and entering the market. Fiat currency is, at its core, money that is worth what the government and free market determine it is worth. The term "fiat currency" stands for a currency declared by the government as legal tender. Thus, it has value because of a law or government regulation and not an intrinsic value, even though it is not backed by reserves. Fiat currency is based on faith. Today every country uses fiat currency, because the value can be controlled through monetary policies. The most negotiable fiat currencies include the US dollar, British sterling, and Euro.

Asset backed currency means currency backed up by assets. Asset backed currency is units of value that are pegged to real world assets, such as gold, silver, diamonds, company shares and real estate. They represent a large subcategory of security tokens and allow users to hold ownership rights over a physical and tangible asset in a digital form. Usually, an asset backed currency is made of a precious metal. Sometimes, an asset backed currency can be exchanged for a given quantity of the asset, like the American dollar was exchangeable for gold prior to the 1930s.

Commodity backed currency means currency backed up by merchandized goods. Commodity backed currencies are largely a relic of history. Commodities like tobacco were used to guarantee the value of currency.

Digital currency is a modern currency, which gets their value through scarcity imposed on them by the need to solve difficult equations. For example, bitcoins need to be mined by computers that solve mathematical problems. Digital currencies tend to be anonymous by design, and can only be spent by using computers to handle the transaction.

As each state has its sovereignty to issue its own currency, when they trade with each other, exchange rate among different currencies must be determined. The exchange rate is the current value of any currency in exchange for another currency. This rate fluctuates constantly in response to economic and political events. The fluctuations create the market for currency trading.

1.2 State's monetary sovereignty

The power to issue currency is a sovereign power, one of the attributes of sovereignty as classically defined. Although the notion of monetary sovereignty is not expressly recognized in the Charter of the United Nations, nor in the Articles of Agreement of the International Monetary Fund, nor in other key instruments of international law, this power is recognized by customary international laws and general principles. In 1929, the Permanent Court of International Justice stated that it is indeed a generally accepted principle that a state is entitled to regulate its own currency.[①]

Generally, the state sovereignty over the state's currency includes the exclusive power to issue and regulate money. Specifically, it has been argued in the legal literature that monetary sovereignty includes the power to issue the currency, to define the monetary unit and the notes and coins in multiples of that unit, to require that payments in such notes and coins must be accepted as legal tender, to decide whether or not the currency should be based on gold or silver, to depreciate and appreciate the value of the currency, to impose exchange controls, and to take other measures affecting the monetary system or monetary relations.[②] Zimmermann views monetary sovereignty in two ways. One

---

① See Rosa M. Lastra, *International Financial and Monetary Law*, 2nd ed., Oxford University Press, 2015, para. 1.36.

② See Rosa M. Lastra, *International Financial and Monetary Law*, 2nd ed., Oxford University Press, 2015, para. 1.51.

from the perspective of the supreme and irreducible authority of independent states and the other from the perspective of the various sovereign powers (or attributes) that can be exercised by different levels of governance (notion of cooperative sovereignty). According to this view, in a monetary union like European Monetary Union (EMU), what has been transferred from the national to the supranational level is the exercise of some sovereign powers or state competences, but not monetary sovereignty per se.①

Like state's sovereignty over trade regulation and investment admission, the monopoly power enjoyed by the state with regard to the issuance and regulation of money within its territory has been eroded or limited by a number of factors in recent years. Some of those limitations are consensual or agreed by the states as a voluntary surrender of monetary sovereignty, and others have not been agreed by the states, but are the result of globalization, the revolution of information technology, and of economic and financial developments in the past few decades.

At a regional level, the most obvious example of consensual limitations of monetary sovereignty is the establishment of EMU in 1999. The adoption of a single currency, the euro, and the creation of the European System of Central Banks with responsibility to formulate and implement the monetary policy of the Community have been described as the most profound limitation to monetary sovereignty ever to be agreed by sovereign states. Member states participating in EMU agreed to transfer most parts of their sovereign rights over the monetary issue to the European Union. Although it is a limited surrender, a non-exclusive transfer of sovereign powers, it has changed our view of monetary sovereignty. The members of the Euro zone retain their national sovereignty in those domains where no other consensual limitation has been agreed.② Member states participating in EMU have given up their national currencies. The Union will exercise the Members' power that they have surrendered. The Union's exclusive competence in monetary policy is exercised by the European System of Central Banks, which is composed by the European Central Bank and the central banks of 27 members of EU.

At the international level, the most relevant example of consensual limitations to the monetary sovereignty of states is the Articles of Agreement of the International Monetary

---

① See Claus D. Zimmermann, *The Concept of Monetary Sovereignty Revisited*, 24 European Journal of International Law 797, 797 (2013).

② See Rosa M. Lastra, *International Financial and Monetary Law*, 2nd ed., Oxford University Press, 2015, para. 1.59.

Fund. These limitations were greater with the par value regime under the original Articles of Agreement than they are nowadays. IMF members reaffirmed some of the attributes of their monetary sovereignty with regard to the conduct of exchange rate policy. However, IMF members must still comply with the obligations under Article 4 and Article 8 of the IMF Articles of Agreement, where the jurisdiction (regulatory powers) of the Fund applies.①

2 European Monetary Union

The history of European monetary cooperation is linked to the history of international monetary cooperation. The Bretton Woods par value regime provided an anchor for international monetary stability until its demise in the early 1970s. After its demise, the European Community had to find an alternative to promote the regional monetary cooperation. It is no coincidence that the real momentum for monetary integration came after the international anchor ceased to exist.

In the 1950s and 1960s, it is the Marshall Plan that contributed to the establishment of the European Payments Union (EPU) in 1950, which was the first multilateral system of European payments. The EPU was a mechanism for settling payments amongst 17 West European Countries: Austria, Belgium, Denmark, France, Federal Republic of Germany, Greece, Holland, Iceland, Ireland, Italy, Luxembourg, Norway, Portugal, Sweden, Switzerland, Turkey, and the United Kingdom. The EPU was a clearing union which encouraged movement towards full currency convertibility. After the creation of the Organization for European Economic Cooperation (OEEC), the Bank for International Settlements operated the EPU as an agent for the OEEC. By 1958, member currencies became *de facto* fully convertible, that is, transferable between each other, and they became *de jure* convertible in 1961 on formal acceptance of Article 8 of the IMF Articles of Agreement.② In 1958, the Monetary Committee with advisory status was established under Article 105(2) of the EEC Treaty. In 1964, the Committee of Governors of the

① See Rosa M. Lastra, *International Financial and Monetary Law*, 2nd ed., Oxford University Press, 2015, para. 1.64.

② See Rosa M. Lastra, *International Financial and Monetary Law*, 2nd ed., Oxford University Press, 2015, para. 6.09.

Central Banks of the Member States was established in order to promote cooperation between the central banks of the member states. The European Monetary Cooperation Fund (EMCF) was established in 1973 to promote the narrowing of the margins of fluctuation between the currencies of the member states. The EMCF provided for the administration and settlement of claims resulting from interventions in the foreign exchange market. The Fund was entrusted with three interrelated tasks: the promotion of the proper functioning of the progressive narrowing of the margins of fluctuation of the Community currencies against each other, the conduct of interventions in Community currencies on the exchange markets, and the carrying out of settlements between central banks leading to a concerted policy on reserves.[①]

The cooperation among the EC member states over monetary issues started to boost in respect of membership and authorities during the 1960s and 1970s. However, in the early 1970s, although the Werner Plan was accepted by its member states, the member states lacked the political and economic willingness of monetary integration. On 15 August 1971, US President Nixon announced that the United States would no longer fulfill its obligation to deliver gold for US dollars at the parity which had been established in 1944 and applied since the IMF began operations. This has become a turning point in this loss of momentum, thus signifying the end of par value regime, while initiating the plan for European Monetary Union.

On 7 July 1978, the European Council met in Bremen and issued a communique, stating that it aimed to establish the European Monetary System (EMS). This institutional arrangement was to foster a closer monetary policy cooperation so as to attain a stable monetary zone in Europe. The European Monetary System was set up in 1979, aiming to establish a zone of monetary stability in Europe. It was intended to coordinate the exchange rate policies and establish the European Monetary Union. The member states of the EMS managed their exchange rates together. The band for exchange rate fluctuations was expanded to a maximum of 15% more or less. In order to keep the market exchange rate within the band, central banks were permitted to intervene in the forex market. The Maastricht Treaty aimed to closely coordinate the monetary, fiscal and exchange rate policies and meanwhile it laid the foundation for the adoption of a single European currency, the euro.

---

① See Rosa M. Lastra, *International Financial and Monetary Law*, 2nd ed., Oxford University Press, 2015, paras. 6.14–6.28.

Despite the weak legal value of this Resolution, the EMS became the primary arrangement of monetary cooperation in the EC from its inception to the advent of European Monetary Union. The EMS was a creature of the Franco-German alliance, an alliance which has often been regarded as the engine of European integration.

The EMS had three fundamental objectives: to stabilize the exchange rates in order to rectify the existing instability, to reduce inflation, and to prepare for eventual European monetary unification through cooperation.

The EMS consisted of two main elements. First, it was the establishment of the European Currency Unit (ECU) as a basket of currencies. The share of each of the participating currencies in the basket was determined by the percentage of their state's contribution to the gross national product (GNP) of the Community. The value of the composite currency derived from the addition of all the currency elements. The ECU was not legal tender but it served as unit of account in Community affairs, as a means of payment between the monetary authorities in the Community, and as a store of value (reserves at the central banks).①

The second element of the EMS was to set up the Exchange Rate and Intervention Mechanism (ERM). The ERM was considered as a system of fixed whereas adjustable exchange rate. It was a parity grid of bilateral exchange rates, imposing limitations on the fluctuation in currency prices between pre-set floors and ceilings. The currencies could fluctuate against each other within an utmost domain of plus or minus 2.25% (or 6% for currencies when they just participated in the ERM). It was the central banks' job to intervene so as to maintain their currencies within the established fluctuation band. The central bank of each participant had an obligation to deposit with the European Monetary Cooperation Fund (EMCF) 20% of its US dollars and gold holdings in renewable swaps of three months' duration. In return, the EMCF issued ECUs to the participant. The ERM set for each one of the participating currencies a central exchange rate against the ECU. That, in turn, gave them central cross-rates against one another.②

In December 1989, the Strasbourg European Council called for an intergovernmental conference that would identify what amendments needed to be made to the Treaty on

① See Rosa M. Lastra, *International Financial and Monetary Law*, 2nd ed., Oxford University Press, 2015, paras. 6.34–6.35.

② See Rosa M. Lastra, *International Financial and Monetary Law*, 2nd ed., Oxford University Press, 2015, para. 6.36.

European Union in order to attain economic and monetary union. The work of this intergovernmental conference and the one on political union (both launched at the Rome European Council in December 1990) led to the Treaty on European Union (the so-called Maastricht Treaty), which was formally adopted by the Heads of State and Government at the Maastricht European Council in December 1991 and signed on 7 February 1992.

The EEC Treaty first introduced the notion of the monetary union by the 1986 Single European Act, via the adoption of a new Article 102A. Nowadays, the concept of monetary union is enshrined in EU law since the 1992 Maastricht Treaty on European Union came into force. It has also been confirmed in Article 119(2)(3) of the Lisbon Treaty on the Functioning of the European Union. Monetary Union has three components: (a) an integrated Community monetary system; (b) an institutional structure, with a European Central Bank at its center; (c) a single currency, the euro, replacing present national currencies in all the participating member states.[①]

On 1 January 1999, 11 of the 15 European countries adopted the euro as their common currency. These countries are Austria, Belgium, Finland, France, Germany, Ireland, Italy, Luxembourg, Netherlands, Portugal, and Spain. First, the exchange rates of 11 members of the European Union were locked to each other at irrevocably fixed rates, and then the 11 domestic currencies will be replaced by one single currency, the euro. This was a major step towards the establishment of the European Monetary Union (EMU) and the European Central Bank (ECB). Greece joined the euro group in 2001. Denmark, Sweden, and the United Kingdom have not adopted the euro. Each national currency of the euro countries was irrevocably fixed to the euro at a conversion rate as of 1 January 1999. The European Central Bank (ECB), with its headquarters in Frankfurt, Germany, maintains the monetary policy of the members of the euro 12 groups. The national central banks of these countries, along with the ECB, form the European System of Central Banks. The major benefits from euro adoption are reduced transaction costs and elimination of exchange rate uncertainty. European companies have been able to save millions of dollars since exchange rate uncertainty was removed.

Since its establishment, scholars have been discussing the shortcomings of EMU, especially after the European range monetary crisis in the early 1990s that severely threatened the EMU-project. Firstly, EMU is criticized by lack of a central lender of

① See Rosa M. Lastra, *International Financial and Monetary Law*, 2nd ed., Oxford University Press, 2015, paras. 6.41–6.42, 6.96.

last resort. The ECB has not been granted power by the Maastricht Treaty to serve this function. This stands in sharp contrast with modern central banks, which exercise lender of last resort responsibilities to guarantee the liquidity and functioning of the payments system. In the face of a liquidity crisis, the absence of a lender of last resort may undermine the existence of EMU.①

Secondly, the EMU is void of a central power to supervise the financial systems, including the commercial banks of Euroland. Although the Maastricht Treaty entitles the ECB to some supervisory functions, they are mainly the task of the union members. This situation predicts that in the future a pan-European financial crisis may not be settled in an efficient manner, thus jeopardizing the stability of the whole Eurosystem.

Thirdly, the ECB lacks democratic control and accountability. The ECB will be subject to political attacks and controversies that damage the legitimacy of EMU and erode popular support for the euro. The role of the European Parliament in monitoring the ECB is unclear at this point as well. Should major economic problems arise within a single member of EMU, populist political movements may use them to attack EMU and the ECB.②

Fourthly, the policy directives for the ECB are inconsistent, unclear, and badly designed. Although the ECB is to carry out domestic monetary policy within Euroland, according to the Maastricht Treaty, exchange rate policy for EMU is set by the Council of the European Union, that is by the council of finance ministers of EMU. This will result in political discussion, tensions and political pressure on the monetary policy of the ECB.

Fifthly, the absence of central coordination of fiscal policies within EMU in combination with unduly strict criteria for domestic debt and deficits, as set out in the Maastricht rules, and the Stability Pact implies that EMU will not be able to respond to asymmetric shocks and disturbances in a satisfactory way.

And lastly, Europe is too large a geographical area to form a well-functioning monetary union.③ Nevertheless, the EMU is still a remarkable regional cooperative mechanism for integration of monetary policies among sovereign states.

---

① See Michael D. Bordo & Lars Jonung, *The Future of EMU: What Does the History of Monetary Unions Tell Us?*, NBER Working Paper No. w7365, 15 December 1999, p. 2–4.

② See Michael D. Bordo & Lars Jonung, *The Future of EMU: What Does the History of Monetary Unions Tell Us?*, NBER Working Paper No. w7365, 15 December 1999, p. 2–4.

③ See Michael D. Bordo & Lars Jonung, *The Future of EMU: What Does the History of Monetary Unions Tell Us?*, NBER Working Paper No. w7365, 15 December 1999, p. 2–4.

3 International Monetary Fund

3.1 Development of IMF

There is no formal intergovernmental monetary institution until the establishment of Bretton Woods. With the development of the International Monetary Fund (IMF) and the World Bank (International Bank for Reconstruction and Development, IBRD), international monetary and banking governance emerge and function well to keep a relative long period of international monetary stability. Originally, the Bretton Woods institution adopts the par value regime, meaning that the value of currency was defined in terms of gold or, alternatively, in terms of the US dollar of 1 July 1944, which had a fixed gold value.

It is acknowledged that the members can adopt exchange rate arrangements to their choice by the Second Amendment of the IMF Articles of Agreement of 1 April 1978. Such rights include: (a) the maintenance by a member of a value for its currency in terms of the special drawing right or another denominator, other than gold, selected by the member, or (b) cooperative arrangements by which members maintain the value of their currencies in relation to the value of the currency or currencies of other members, or (c) other exchange arrangements of a member's choice.

However, the members also bear responsibilities: (a) to endeavor to direct their economic and financial policies toward the objective of fostering orderly economic growth with reasonable price stability, with due regard to its circumstances; (b) to seek to promote stability by fostering orderly underlying economic and financial conditions and a monetary system that does not tend to produce erratic disruptions; and, crucially, (c) to avoid manipulating exchange rates or the international monetary system in order to prevent effective balance of payments adjustment or to gain an unfair competitive advantage over other members.

Second Amendment of the IMF Articles of Agreement draws a line between state's power and obligations, deciding state's surrender of monetary sovereignty. Objectively speaking, the IMF is crucial in fostering a fundamental stabilization function to fragile global economies in areas of financial and technical assistance in early years, and developing requisite legal and supervisory infrastructure within fledging member countries.

But due to the bureaucracy of IMF in terms of management, the IMF failed to foresee the breakout of financial crisis of East Southern Asia in 1997 and the global financial crisis in 2008.

3.2 The role and purpose of IMF

The functions of IMF and Members' rights and duties are set in its Articles of Agreement. The IMF mandate is to maintain the good order of this predictable and stable international monetary system, by enforcing rules about adjustment in international monetary relations and by providing temporary resources to deal with short-term balance of payments problems. The IMF Articles of Agreement provides for its functions and Members' rights and obligations. It is to maintain the good order of the foreseeable and stable international monetary system. IMF shall enforce rules to adjust international monetary relations and offer temporary resources to settle the short-term balance of payment problems. As defined by Article 1 of the Articles of Agreement, the objectives of the IMF are to guide all its policies and decisions:

(a) To promote international monetary cooperation through a permanent institution which provides the machinery for consultation and collaboration on international monetary problems.

(b) To facilitate the expansion and balanced growth of international trade, and to contribute thereby to the promotion and maintenance of high levels of employment and real income and to the development of productive resources of all members as primary objectives of economic policy.

(c) To promote exchange rate stability, to maintain orderly exchange arrangements among members, and to avoid competitive exchange depreciation.

(d) To assist in the establishment of a multilateral system of payments in respect of current transactions between members and in the elimination of foreign exchange restrictions which hamper the growth of world trade.

(e) To give confidence to members by making the Fund's resources available to them under adequate safeguards, thus providing them with the opportunity to correct maladjustments in their balance of payments without resorting to measures destructive of national or international prosperity.

(f) In accordance with the above, to shorten the duration and lessen the degree of disequilibrium in the international balances of payments of members.

3.3. Institutional issues of IMF

The membership of IMF can be divided into two types. The original members are the countries represented at the Bretton Woods conference, whose governments accepted membership before 31 December 1945. As the IMF's membership is open to all sovereign states, thus subsequent membership can be obtained through the accession process. By June of 2021, there are 190 members in total in IMF.

The institutional structure of the IMF mainly includes Board of Governors, the Executive Board, and the Managing Director. The organizational structure of IMF is similar with the structure of a company. The Board of Governors functions as the shareholders' meeting in a company, and the Executive Board and Managing Director act as board of director and chairman of the board.

The IMF is accountable to its member country governments. At the top of its organizational structure is the Board of Governors, consisting of one governor and one alternate governor from each member country, usually the top officials from the central bank or finance ministry. The Board of Governors meets once a year at the IMF-World Bank Annual Meetings. On 2 October 1974, the Board of Governors established the Interim Committee of the Board of Governors on the International Monetary System, which was later renamed as the International Monetary and Financial Committee or IMFC, and the Joint Ministerial Committee of the Board of Governors of the Bank and the Fund on the Transfer of Real Resources to Developing Countries, renamed as the IMF-World Bank Development Committee.

24 of the governors serve on the IMFC, which represent the entire membership and supported by IMF staff. They advise the IMF's Executive Board on the supervision and management of the international monetary and financial system. The day-to-day work of the IMF is also overseen by its 24-member Executive Board. The Executive Board approves the loans that the members apply for. It selects the Managing Director, who serves as Chairman of the Executive Board and as head of the staff of the IMF, and is assisted by four Deputy Managing Directors.

3.4 Quotas and subscriptions

Unlike the WTO that operates on a one-country-one-vote basis, the IMF functions on a weighted voting system: the larger a country's quota in the IMF, the more votes it has, thus the distribution of quota decides a state's voting power on IMF matters. On joining the IMF, each member is assigned a quota, which determines its subscription to the capital and voting rights in IMF. The quota is expressed in special drawing rights (SDRs). The subscription of each member is equal to its quota and has to be paid in full to the IMF. An amount not exceeding 25% of the quota needs to be paid in SDR by members in reserve assets and the rest can be paid in the member's own currency. The first 25% segment is known as the reserve asset portion. The remainder is the non-reserve asset portion.

The quotas form a pool of money. In case of payment difficulties or emergency, the IMF can use the money to provide financing for its members. This does not mean that members can require as much finance as needed to solve the balance of payment problem. The amount of financing depends on a member's allocation, which is proportional to its quota.

The allocation of decision power of the IMF is very different from the WTO. For general matters, the decision of the IMF requires 30% of the voting power, and for special matters, it requires a majority voting by 85%. Country with over 75% or even 85% of votes such as the United States has a *de facto* veto power. The quotas can be adjusted according to Article 3, Section 2(a) of the IMF Articles of Agreement. But the adjustment procedure is usually tenuous and demanding, as it requires a majority of 85% of the total voting to approve the adjustment. Hence, the adjustment is difficult to be carried out.

During the adjustment procedure, two main issues would be addressed in a general review: the size of a possible overall increase and the distribution of the increase among the members. There have been 15 general reviews of quotas in the history of the IMF so far, and the latest adjustment of quotas took place in January 2015. With the adjustment of quotas in 2015, a 6% shift of quota shares from over-represented to under-represented member countries. As a result, China becomes the third largest member of the IMF, and Brazil, India and Russia also rise to top ten in the IMF.

3.5 Financial affairs of IMF

The IMF operates its financial functions through three separate accounting entities: the General Department, the SDR Department, and the Administered Accounts. These accounting entities are not organizational units. The division between the General Department and the SDR Department (Articles 16 and 21 of the IMF Articles of Agreement) is an accounting division. The financial functions of the IMF are discharged by the Finance Department (known as the Treasurer's Department until 2003), which is an organizational unit of the Fund.

3.5.1 Creation of SDR

The creation of the SDR is attributed to the increasing concerns about liquidity in the international monetary system. It was created through the First Amendment to the IMF Articles of Agreement, and took effect on 28 July 1969. The SDR is an international reserve asset in order to supplement the official reserves of the member countries. Due to the limitations of gold and dollars as the sole means of settling international accounts at that time, SDRs boost international liquidity by supplementing the standard reserve currencies. A SDR is essentially an artificial currency instrument used by the IMF, and is built from a basket of important national currencies. The IMF uses SDRs for internal accounting purposes. SDRs are allocated by the IMF to its member countries and are backed by the full faith and credit of the member countries' governments. The makeup of the SDR is re-evaluated every five years. For example, the currency makeup of the SDR in 2016 was represented by the following Table IV-1.

Table IV-1 Currency Makeup of the SDR in 2016①

Currency	Weights Determined in the 2015 Review	Fixed Number of Units of Currency for a Five-Year Period Starting 1 October 2016
US Dollar	41.73	0.58252
Euro	30.93	0.38671
Chinese Yuan	10.92	1.0174
Japanese Yen	8.33	11.900
Pound Sterling	8.09	0.085946

3.5.2 Obligations set by the IMF's articles

Since 1969, the primary sources of international liquidity have been gold, foreign exchange reserves, and allocations of SDRs by the IMF. The Articles of Agreement impose upon members a set of obligations of varying nature. The Fund's regulatory powers comprise both Article 8, Section 2 and Article 4. Article 4 refers to the obligations regarding exchange arrangements, which forms the basis of the exercise of surveillance by the Fund. Article 8 imposes some general obligations upon member countries with regard

① Source: https://www.investopedia.com/terms/s/sdr.asp.

to avoiding restrictions in current international transactions.

According to Article 8, Section 2, the jurisdiction of the Fund extends only to payments and transfers for current international transactions, not to capital transactions. That is, the regulation of capital movements is left to the Members.

Article 8, Section 2 of the IMF Articles of Agreement imposes an obligation upon members to avoid restrictions on current payments and transfers. That is, the members shall give unrestricted access to foreign exchange to conduct trade in goods and services. This obligation is often referred to as an obligation to maintain current account convertibility. Article 8, Section 2 reads as follows:

"(a) Subject to the provisions of Article VII Section 3(b) ['scarce currency' provisions] and Article XIV Section 2 [transitional arrangements], no member shall, without the approval of the Fund, impose restrictions on the making of payments and transfers for current international transactions.

(b) Exchange contracts which involve the currency of any member and which are contrary to the exchange control regulations of that member maintained or imposed consistently with this Agreement shall be unenforceable in the territories of any member. In addition, members may, by mutual accord, cooperate in measures for the purpose of making the exchange control regulations of either member more effective, provided that such measures and regulations are consistent with this Agreement."

In accordance with the IMF Articles of Agreement, members can set restrictions on capital movements without the Fund's approval. Article 4, Section 3 allows members to exercise controls of capital transfers as necessary to regulate international capital movements. The Fund's jurisdiction over capital movements has been expanded, thus requiring an amendment of the Articles of Agreement to endow the IMF with an explicit mandate on this issue. However, the "institutional view" states that member's rights to regulate international capital movements are not unlimited, and points that the Fund's legal framework for surveillance has long recognized the importance of capital flows and policies to manage them.

3.5.3 IMF's surveillance and financial assistance to its members

The main functions performed by the IMF in relation to its members are surveillance (IMF Articles of Agreement, Art 4), financial assistance (Art 5, s 3), and technical assistance [Art 5, s 2(b)].

Article 4, Section 3(a) confers upon the IMF a clear role in this regard. The Fund shall oversee the international monetary system in order to ensure its effective operation, and shall oversee the compliance of each member with its obligations under Section 1 of this Article.

Article 4, Section 3(b) further states: the Fund shall exercise firm surveillance over the exchange rate policies of members, and shall adopt specific principles for the guidance of all members with respect to those policies.

The Fund carries out surveillance mainly through its so-called "Article IV consultations" with each individual member country. In addition to this bilateral surveillance, there is also multilateral surveillance, with the publication by the Fund of a World Economic Outlook Report and a Global Financial Stability Report twice a year. Another form of surveillance is regional surveillance, under which the IMF also examines development in regional areas, such as the European Union and the euro area.

IMF provides financial assistance to members experiencing temporary balance of payments problems. However, the financial assistance is generally conditional on the adoption and implementation of adjustment policies. IMF financing is typically available through stand-by arrangements (or extended arrangements). Though these arrangements are not technically nor legally loans, however, they are the functional equivalent of loans.

All members are in principle eligible to use the Fund's general resources in proportion to their quota. A member is entitled to purchase the currencies of other members in exchange for an equivalent amount of its own currency, subject to the four conditions established in Article 5, Section 3(b). These four conditions are: (a) the use must be consistent with the Articles of Agreement; (b) the member makes a declaration (representation) of balance of payments need; (c) the proposed purchase does not raise the Fund's holdings of the member's currency above 200% of the member's quota; and (d) the member has not been declared ineligible to use those resources. The third and fourth requirements can be waived.

Conditionality refers to the policies and procedures developed by the Fund to govern the access to and the use of its resources by member countries. Since these resources exist for the benefit of the entire membership and are finite, their use needs are to be temporary and consistent with the purposes of the Fund.

Conditionality can be defined as the link between the approval or continuation of the Fund's financing and the implementation of specified elements of economic policy by the country receiving the financing, that is, the link between the adjustment effort by the country and the financing by the Fund.

Andreas Lowenfeld suggested that the regime of conditionality of the International Monetary Fund in the use of its resources is changing the traditional boundaries between the domestic jurisdiction of the states and the international community, which also affects the monetary sovereignty of a state. Lowenfeld pointed to the ever increasing level of examination of a large variety of domestic policies in the IMF program of structural reform, ranging from national budgets, taxes, interest rates, and exchange rates to subsidies, wage policies, competition law, corporate governance, and even accounting practice and legal reform. These domestic policies are subject to scrutiny, negotiation, and commitment. The eagerness to get or maintain the IMF (conditional) financial assistance may lead the legitimate political institutions in the country to design the economic reform program without a full analysis of its potentially negative social implications. He suggested that in some cases the jurisdictional barrier between the international organization and the sovereign states has been overstepped or breached, and that a new understanding regarding the relationship between the IMF (and other international agencies) and the countries that need financial assistance is needed.①

Chapter Review

1. What does currency mean? How is it different from money?
2. What are the functions of money?
3. What are the different types of currencies?
4. Explain state's sovereignty over monetary matters.
5. What are the factors which erode state's sovereignty in making and enforcing monetary policy?
6. Give some examples that states give up their monetary sovereignty for regional or international cooperation over monetary matters.
7. Do you think the conditionality of the International Monetary Fund in providing the loans also erodes a state's monetary sovereignty?
8. How is EMU established? Introduce the development of harmonized monetary union in EU briefly.
9. Why is the development the EMU relevant with the demise of par value regime?

---

① See Andreas F. Lowenfeld, *The International Monetary System and the Erosion of Sovereignty: Essay in Honor of Cynthia Lichtenstein*, 25 Boston College International and Comparative Law Review 117, 117–120 (2002).

10. State briefly the three fundamental objectives and two elements of EMS.
11. What are the shortcomings of EMU?
12. What does par value regime mean?
13. State briefly the purpose and aim of IMF.
14. What does SDR mean? And what is the currency makeup of a SDR?
15. How is the subscription to the capital and voting rights in IMF decided?
16. What are IMF's power over its members' currency issue?
17. Does IMF have authority over members' capital movement?
18. Do states have obligation to maintain current account convertibility? Which article of IMF Articles of Agreement requires state shall maintain currency account convertibility?
19. On what condition can a member purchase the currencies of other members in exchange for an equivalent amount of its own currency?
20. What does conditionality of Fund mean? How does it affect a state's currency sovereignty?

Key Terms

currency sovereignty	货币主权
European Central Bank (ECB)	欧洲中央银行
European Currency Unit (ECU)	欧洲货币单位
European Monetary Union (EMU)	欧洲货币联盟
International Monetary Fund (IMF)	国际货币基金组织
special drawing rights (SDRs)	特别提款权

Further Readings

1. Herrmann, Christoph & Corinna Dornacher, *International and European Monetary Law: An Introduction*, Springer, 2017.

2. Lastra, Rosa M., *International Financial and Monetary Law*, 2nd ed., Oxford University Press, 2015.

3. Taylor, John B., *Reform of the International Monetary System: Why and How?*, MIT Press, 2019.

Chapter 2
International Finance and Banking Law

Study Guide

International finance and banking law includes rules of corporate finance and the international principles of bank supervision. Chapter 2 discusses different methods of international finance such as international business loans, syndicate loan, and project finance. Further, the Chapter shows how the Basel Committee was established, and its most recent development of policies and suggestions to enhance government and banks' capability of preventing and dealing with the financial crisis, such as Basel Concordat, Basel I, Basel II and Basel III.

International finance and banking law includes the international rules for corporate finance and the international principles of bank supervision and the evolving work and influence of the Basel Committee on bank regulation. The former provides more facilities to the public and private institutions and enterprises in financing their projects, and the latter reduces the credit risks and operation risks inherent in a state's banking industry. International rules and disciplines on central banks, however, are not included in this Chapter as they are mostly relevant to monetary and currency issues, and have been analyzed in Chapter 1.

1 International Finance

1.1 International commercial loans

Corporations need additional capital for various reasons such as starting or expanding business, purchasing or refinancing equipment or restructuring its balance sheet. A business loan provides probably the most flexible solution to meet the financial needs. A loan is an agreement in which a lender gives money to a borrower, and the borrower agrees to repay the money with interest, at some time in the future.

International commercial loans can be defined as a loan borrowed by domestic entities from financial institution, enterprises, individuals or other economic organizations in other territories, or from foreign-funded financial institutions within the debtor's territory in the form of loans contracted for repayment in foreign currencies. The loan may be used for export credits, international financial leasing, compensation trade repaid of foreign exchange. Foreign exchange deposits of institutions and individuals outside the debtor's territory, project financing, trade financing with a maturity of more than 90 days, and foreign exchange loans in other forms are taken as international commercial loans.

When acquiring international commercial loan, the most significant issue is to sign an international commercial loan contract. As most of such agreements are drafted based on the standard contract in common law countries, the key articles on the agreement usually include purpose of loan, commitment amount and period, interest rate, term of loan, pre-payment, payment and post-payment, conditions precedent, representation and warranty, covenants, events of default, and governing law and jurisdiction.

Among these terms and articles, conditions precedent refers to the requirements that should be met before a loan facility is executed by the creditor or before the loan is withdrawn by the debtor. The general conditions apply to all loans covered by the agreement and the specific conditions apply to specific loans that they refer to.

Representation and warranty list the facts provided by the debtor regarding to its legal, financial and business situations and other promises warranted by the debtor. If the statements given are found untrue, the party making the statement shall be liable for his or her misrepresentation. Legal warranty usually includes a debtor's warranty to his legal capacity, authorized power, legality and enforceability of the loan. Commercial warranty includes statement to the debtor's financial and business conditions.

Covenants are the most important provisions in a loan agreement, which reflect the promises made by the borrower regarding to the execution and performance of the agreement. Covenants consist of various provisions such as negative pledge, *pari passu*, financial covenants, uses of loans, restriction to equity disposal or maintenance of equity, and merger and acquisition.

Event of default happens when the borrower fails to make payment according to the agreement. When the borrower breaches the contract terms such as covenants, representation and warranty, it will also amount to an event of default. Event of default includes not only actual default, but also anticipatory repudiation. Besides, bankruptcy and bankrupt declaration also indicate an event of default.

1.2 Syndicate loans

Syndicate loan means a group of banks making a loan jointly to a single borrower.

It is a very efficient financing mechanism through which surplus liquidity from the financial markets can be mobilized to support significantly larger financing requirements of borrowers. A syndicate loan is typically provided by a consortium of at least two or more financial institutions to appropriate borrowers under a common set of financing terms governed by the same loan facility documentation. An agent bank will intermediate between the borrower and the financial institutions during the tenure of the loan.

Syndication offers several benefits. First, it allows banks to diversify and expand their lending to broader geographic areas and industries. Second, syndication allows banks that are constrained by their capital-asset ratios to participate in loans to larger borrowers. Despite these benefits, loan syndication could pose additional risks for the banking system, if the originating or lead banks withhold information about the borrower from participating banks, misleading them into making loans that are riskier than they thought.

Generally, the financing quantum must be of a significant amount to warrant such an arrangement and to facilitate cost savings through economies of scale. Such financing can be sourced from local, regional or international financial markets depending on the features of the underlying financing. The participating lenders may also originate from different geographical domiciles. This mode of financing is widely applicable to support purposes such as working capital, general corporate and treasury funding, investments, acquisitions and project financing requirements, and is relevant to different industry sectors. The financing can be raised through term loan, revolving credit or other structures to suit the borrower's requirements.

Most loan syndications take the form of a direct-lender relationship, which means the leading bank loans to the borrower directly, then sells part of loan to other participatory banks. This indicates that the lead lender is the agent for the other lenders in the origination and administration of the loan, and the other lending banks are signatories to the loan agreement. The leading bank is the only lender to the borrower, and the management of the loan is responsible by the leading bank.

For most loan syndications, a lead financial institution or leading bank is used to coordinate the transaction. As an agent, the leading bank is also often responsible for the initial transaction, fees, compliance reports, repayments throughout the duration of the loan, loan monitoring, and overall reporting for all lending parties.

A third party or additional specialists may be used throughout various points of the loan syndication or repayment process to assist with various aspects of reporting and monitoring. Due to the vast reporting and coordination required to complete and maintain the loan processing, a syndicate loan often requires high fees, which can be as high as 10% of the loan principal.

For example, Company ABC is interested in purchasing an abandoned airport and converting it into a large development, consisting of a sports stadium, multiple apartment complexes, and a mall. It is looking for a loan in the size of USD 1 billion. ABC heads to J.P. Morgan to discuss obtaining a loan, which J.P. Morgan agrees to, but because the loan is such a large size and greater than J.P. Morgan's risk tolerance, the bank decides to form a loan syndicate to provide the loan for Company ABC.

J.P. Morgan acts as the lead agent on the syndicated loan, bringing together other banks to participate. It contracts with Bank of America, Credit Suisse, Citibank, and Wells Fargo to participate in the loan. J.P. Morgan contributes USD 300 million to the loan, and the remaining USD 700 million is shared between the remaining members of the syndicate. Bank of America lends out USD 200 million, Credit Suisse USD 100 million, Citibank USD 250 million, and Wells Fargo USD 150 million. As the lead bank on the loan syndicate, J.P. Morgan also organizes the terms, covenants, and other details needed for the loan. Once the process is complete, Company ABC receives the USD 1 billion loan through the loan syndicate.

1.3 Project finance

Project finance is the financing of long-term infrastructure, industrial projects, and public services using a non-recourse or limited recourse financial structure. The debt and equity used to finance the project are paid back from the cash flow generated by the project. It is a loan structure that relies primarily on the project's cash flow for repayment, with the project's assets, rights, and interests held as secondary collateral. Project finance is especially attractive to the private sector because companies can fund major projects off-balance sheet.

Project finance loans are usually used for the construction and operation of one or a set of large projects, including construction projects, reconstruction projects, expansion projects, and projects that are already in operation, or refinancing existing project loans. Specific projects generally include infrastructure projects and energy projects.

The borrower is usually a special purpose vehicle (SPV) especially established for the construction, management and operation of the project. The SPV's sole activity is carrying out the project by subcontracting most aspects through construction and operations contracts. Because there is no revenue generated during the construction phase of new-build projects, debt service only occurs during the operation phase. For this reason, parties take significant risks during the construction phase. The sole revenue stream during this phase is generally under an offtake agreement or power purchase agreement. The task of the SPV is to implement the project by subcontracting most issues through construction and operation contracts. Debt service could only happen during the operation phase owing to no revenue generated during the construction phase of newly-built projects. Hence, the parties will take huge risks during the construction phase, when the only revenue stream is generally under an offtake agreement or power purchase agreement. Because there is limited or no recourse to the project's sponsors, company shareholders are typically liable up to the extent of their shareholdings. The project remains off-balance sheet for the sponsors and the government. The source of the repayment fund is mainly from the sales income, subsidy income or other income generated by the project, and funds obtained from refinancing.

2 International Banking Supervision

2.1 Bank risks in international finance

Banks engaged in international finance usually face credit risk and operational risk. Disciplines on international banking regulation and supervision are to reduce banks' exposure to excessive credit risk and operational risk.

2.1.1 Credit risk

Credit risk, also called default risk, refers to the risk arising from the possibility that a bond issuer will default, by failing to repay principal and interest in a timely manner. Credit risk accounts for the bulk of most banks' risk-taking activities and hence their regulatory capital requirements. The standardized approach used by the majority of banks around the world, involving in non-Basel Committee jurisdictions includes improving banks' granularity and risk sensitivity, and reducing mechanistic reliance on credit ratings.

2.1.2 Operational risk

A bank will face some jeopardies and uncertainties when it intends to do its day-to-day business activities within a given field or industry. This is referred to as operational risk, a type of business risk which can be caused by breakdowns in internal procedures, people and systems. On the contrary, there is systemic risk, attributed to external forces, such as political or economic events, or inherent to the entire market or market segment.

The financial crisis highlighted two main shortcomings with the existing operational risk framework. First, capital requirements for operational risk proved insufficient to cover operational risk losses incurred by some banks. Second, the nature of these losses—covering events such as misconduct, and inadequate systems and controls—highlighted the difficulty associated with using internal models to estimate capital requirements for operational risk.

The Basel Committee has streamlined the operational risk framework. The Advanced Measurement Approaches (AMA) for calculating operational risk capital requirements (which are based on banks' internal models) and the existing three standardized approaches are replaced with a single risk-sensitive standardized approach to be used by all banks.

The new standardized approach for operational risk determines a bank's operational risk capital requirements based on two components. One is a measure of a bank's income, and the other is a measure of a bank's historical losses. Conceptually, it assumes that operational risk increases at an increasing rate with a bank's income; and banks which have experienced greater operational risk losses historically are assumed to be more likely to experience operational risk losses in the future.

2.2 Basel Committee and Basel Accords

Unlike international monetary law that is dominated by hard law, international banking law evidences a proliferation and revival of soft law, focusing on self-discipline of the banking industry. This is attributed to the Basel system, which is the legal framework where the Basel Committee on Banking Supervision (BCBS) regulates banks of its members according to the core regulatory principle of capital adequacy ratio.

2.2.1 Basel Committee

The Basel Committee was established in a meeting held in September 1974, consisting of ten developed countries with an aim to manage bank collapses prior to the meeting. Since then, the Basel Committee has developed a set of principles, standards, and recommendations and coordinated regulatory standards of banks in its members through the so-called Basel Capital Accord. The Basel Committee is the primary global standard-setter for the prudential regulation of banks and provides a forum for cooperation on banking supervisory matters. Its mandate is to strengthen the regulation, supervision and practices of banks worldwide with the purpose of enhancing financial stability.

Basel Capital Accord is also known as the Basel Accord, which is a set of policy agreements on the supervision of banks. The Basel Accord offers recommendations on banking laws and regulations to financial institutions to encourage the management of capital and the ability to handle losses. Since its establishment, Basel Accord has been revised from time to time, adapting to the fast-changing needs of bank supervision and prevention and overcome of financial crisis.

2.2.2 Basel Concordat

In September 1975, Basel Committee published its first document Principles for the Supervision of Banks' Foreign Establishments, which gave two suggestions to its members. First, it suggests that overseas establishments of any bank should not avoid regulation; second, it defines regulatory responsibilities of the home and host countries of the banks. The Basel Committee's Concordat established the responsibilities of home and host supervisors and was later amended in light of the Banco Ambrosiano and Bank of Credit and Commerce International episodes. The revised Basel Concordat defines the specific regulatory responsibilities and powers of the home and host countries as well as those of branches and subsidiaries of banks and joint venture banks such as solvency, liquidity, foreign exchange activities and positions.

2.2.3 Basel I

In July 1988, the Basel Committee published the Agreements on Unifying Capital Measurement and Capital Standards, which was also called Basel I. The Accord aims to achieve international convergence in the measurement of capital adequacy of banks and to establish minimum capital standards. Basel I focuses on unexpected losses of financial institutions such as the one that Bank Herstatt experienced by establishing minimum capital requirements. The Accord established five tiers of capital adequacy risks—0%, 10%, 20%, 50% and 100%—that measure the extent to which a bank can be hurt by a financial loss. For example, a bank with 0% of its risk-weighted assets can be considered as having Tier 1 capital. According to Basel I, the BCBS suggests that institutions acting on an international level operate on an 8% risk weight, which is also called fixed minimum capital requirements.

2.2.4 Basel II

Basel II, published in 2004, expands beyond the credit risk focus of its predecessor. Adding supervisory review and market discipline to the minimum credit requirements, the Basel Committee thus established the so-called three pillars of the accords. Pillar 1 requires the banks to determine the minimum capital requirements for credit, operational and market risk. Pillar 2 mandates that banks should establish a supervisory review process where supervisors should evaluate how well banks are assessing their capital requirements based on the risks they are having, and intervene where necessary. Pillar 3 encourages market discipline by developing a set of disclosure requirement, i.e., to disclose key information to the peers.

With the global financial crisis that took hold in the late 2000s, the third edition of the Basel Accords appeared in 2009. Basel III revised the previous accords by focusing on strengthening individual financial institutions to prevent widespread shocks from happening. Such strengthening is encouraged through techniques such as bank leverage and liquidity.

2.2.5 Basel III

Basel III is a comprehensive set of reform measures based on Basel II, created to strengthen the regulation, supervision and risk of the banking sector. The new standards are presumed to markedly reduce banks' incentive to take excessive risks, lower the likelihood and severity of future crisis, and enable banks to withstand stresses of a magnitude associated with the recent financial crisis.

The Basel Committee has been dedicated to optimizing Basel III since its publication. In order to regain trust and credibility in calculating risk-weighted assets (RWAs) and to better the comparability of banks' capital ratios, a reform has been carried out in 2017 through boosting vitality and risk sensitivity of the standardized approaches for credit risk, credit valuation adjustment (CVA) risk and operational risk. Further, it constrains banks' use of the internal model approaches, by placing limits on certain inputs used to calculate capital requirements under the internal ratings-based (IRB) approach for credit risk and by removing the use of the internal model approaches for CVA risk and operational risk. Moreover, it introduces a leverage ratio buffer to further limit the leverage of global systemically important banks (G-SIBs), and it replaces the existing Basel II output floor with a more robust risk-sensitive floor based on the Committee's revised Basel III standardized approaches.

Even though the Basel Accord is not compulsory, to ensure visibility of the implementation of reforms, the Basel Committee has been regularly publishing information about members' adoption of Basel III to keep all stakeholders and the markets informed, and to maintain peer pressure where necessary.

Chapter Review

1. What are the main issues covered by international finance and banking law?
2. What is the meaning of international commercial loan agreement? What are the main articles included in an international commercial loan agreement?
3. What is the meaning of syndicate loan? What are the benefits of such finance?
4. What does direct-lender relationship mean? What are the responsibilities of leading bank in such relationship?
5. What does project finance mean? How is the finance paid back?
6. When and how was Basel Committee established?
7. Briefly explain Basel Concordat.
8. How does Basel I classify the adequacy risks?
9. What have been added in Basel II based on Basel I?
10. Can you summarize the major improvements made by Basel III?

Key Terms

Basel Accords	巴塞尔协议
Basel Committee on Banking Supervision (BCBS)	巴塞尔银行监管委员会
credit risk	信贷风险
operation risk	运营风险
project finance	项目融资
risk-weighted assets (RWAs)	风险评级资产
syndicate loan	辛迪加贷款，银团贷款

Further Readings

1. Bamford, Colin, *Principles of International Financial Law*, 3rd ed., Oxford University Press, 2020.

2. Campbell, Mark, & Christoph Weaver, *Syndicated Lending: Practice and Documentation*, 7th ed., Harriman House, 2019.

3. Chey, Hyoung-kyu, *International Harmonization of Financial Regulation?: The Politics of Global Diffusion of the Basel Capital Accord*, Routledge, 2013.

Part V International Taxation Law

Study Guide
This Part explains different tax jurisdiction such as resident jurisdiction and source jurisdiction, and explains the factors causing double jurisdiction.   It further discusses states' unilateral measures of avoiding double taxation such as tax credit, tax allowance, and tax exemption.   To show how international society combats tax avoidance and double taxation, OECD and UN have both made Model Conventions to coincide states' tax policies and taxation methods. This Part explains the main contents of such Model Conventions to help students understand states' efforts of unifying their tax laws and coping with the problems of double taxation. Tax avoidance reduces a state's tax income and damages its tax sovereignty. The part also discusses how states take measures to reduce enterprises' possibilities of tax avoidance.

Imposing tax on a tax resident's income is within a state's sovereignty. However, both a state's tax law and a corporation's behavior can generate extraterritorial effects, either through double taxation or tax avoidance and tax evasion. This Part introduces resident jurisdiction and source jurisdiction, and explains the factors causing double jurisdiction and methods of reducing such unintended consequence. Motivated by profit maximization and tax minimization, corporations avoid or even evade taxes through tax planning, false profit statements, using tax havens, etc, which damage a state's interest. Several multilateral conventions and regional treaties have been made to reduce the possibility of double taxation or combating tax avoidance and evasion.

1 Tax Jurisdiction

Tax jurisdiction can be explained from different angles. In terms of power, it refers to as state government's authority to impose tax on its citizens and objects. From the perspective of tax area, a tax jurisdiction is a city, state, country, or other government that levies taxes within its limits. These taxes may be levied based upon residency, income received, or some other scheme within the physical limits of the jurisdiction. Each jurisdiction may have a different manner on which to base its taxes as well as its own manner for calculating taxes. Jurisdictions with limited or no taxes are considered tax havens.

1.1 Resident jurisdiction

A state may adopt resident jurisdiction, that is, the state claims tax on the income of a person who has tax residence within the territory of that state. Under a resident jurisdiction, income may be taxed under the tax law of a country because of a nexus between the country and the person earning the income, irrespective of the place where the income is earned. Tax residence is not equivalent to a person's nationality. The criteria for determining the tax residence usually include elements of permanent place of residence, habitual residence, and time of stay in the tax jurisdiction. While according to the criterion of nationality, a country charges with its residents, who realize income or own assets in that country, regardless that those residents live or do not live in their country.

For example, according to Article 4 of the Law on Lithuanian Personal Income Tax, Lithuanian resident means any natural person whose permanent place of residence is in Lithuania during the tax period, or any natural person whose place of personal, social or economic interests is in Lithuania rather than in a foreign country during the tax period, or any natural person who is present in Lithuania for a period or periods in the aggregate of 183 days or more during the tax period, or any natural person who is present in Lithuania for a period or periods in the aggregate of 280 days or more during successive tax periods and who has stayed in Lithuania for a period or periods in the aggregate of 90 days or more in any of such tax periods, or any natural person who is a citizen of the Republic of Lithuania but does not meet the abovementioned criteria, and who receives remuneration under an employment contract or a contract in its essence corresponding to an employment contract or whose costs of living in another country are covered from the state budget or municipal budgets of Lithuania.

Once a person is defined as a tax resident of a state, the state will require the taxpayer to pay taxes for all of his incomes, including those originating in the state of which the taxpayer is a resident, or those generated abroad.

When a state determines the tax residence for legal persons, place of incorporation, place of effective management, place of control are commonly used as standards, which are also criteria used to determine a company's nationality.

Many countries adopt the place of incorporation as the main standard deciding a company's tax jurisdiction. This standard is objective and easy to be identified. The US, Mexico, Canada and Sweden all adopt this standard. However, the disadvantages of such criterion is obvious. The taxpayer or investor can easily evade tax by structuring a company in a tax haven such as Cayman Islands and British Virgin Islands, while operating the company in its home country.

There are also some countries that adopt place of management or control as the criterion of tax residence for a company. The place of effective management usually refers to the place that the board of directors of the company is making decisions. The place of control, otherwise, means the place that the majority shareholders or controlling shareholders reside. It is adopted especially in the case that a company's veil is pierced for taxation purpose.

Other countries such as Japan adopt the place of general office as a company's tax residence. General office is the organizational branch in the company in charge of company's daily operation and management activities.

It shall be noted that the abovementioned criteria are not exclusive to each other. A country may adopt multiple criteria to expand its tax jurisdiction and avoid companies' tax evasion. For example, according to Chinese Income Tax Law, a tax resident company means a company incorporated in China according to Chinese law, or incorporated according to laws of foreign states (regions) but with its place of effective management in China.

1.2 Source jurisdiction

Source jurisdiction means a state has authority to impose tax on a person's income that originates in that country, rather than his global earnings. Under a source jurisdiction, income may be taxed under the tax law of a country because of a nexus between the country and the activities that generate the income, with no reference of the residence of the taxpayer. That is, in case of a resident jurisdiction, the taxpayer is usually the citizen or resident aliens obtaining permanent resident qualification in that country and the taxable income is that person's all earnings worldwide, including earning originating inside and outside his resident state. Under the source jurisdiction, the tax base is a person's income generating in the country, and the taxpayers are usually non-resident aliens who do not have resident identity in that country.

Most countries or jurisdictions adopt both the residence and source concepts in the tax system, such as the US and China. Some of the jurisdictions only adopt the source concept in the tax system such as Hong Kong SAR and Macao SAR. Tax residents are entitled to claim credit for tax paid on foreign income but non-tax residents are not entitled to do so. Some jurisdictions like the Cayman Islands and British Virgin Islands, do not impose income tax and their tax laws do not define residence for tax purposes. Companies that are incorporated in those jurisdictions have no residence for tax purposes. In case that the same income is taxed by a resident jurisdiction and a source jurisdiction, the source jurisdiction shall take precedence over the resident jurisdiction. In any bilateral double tax agreement, the tax right is allocated to the source country.

2 International Double Taxation

Modern international double taxation started to develop in the 1990s. Its features are determined by financial integration, globalization processes and international tax competition. This stage is characterized by a huge number of standards and rules for the avoidance of double taxation, which may be contained in international agreements and national legislation. Double taxation is often an unintended consequence of tax legislation. It is generally seen as a negative element of a tax system, and tax authorities attempt to avoid it whenever possible.

2.1 Causes of double taxation

International double taxation means the imposition of income tax by two or more countries on the same income during the same period of time. The advent of double taxation is due to the manner in which criteria are applied to the taxation of income or wealth. It is said that the root cause of double, multiple taxation is the contradictory tax laws. Double taxation occurs when two countries adopt resident tax jurisdiction and source jurisdiction respectively. One government applies taxes on income gained on the territory in question to the taxable individuals, and on the other hand, the state where the tax payer resides also imposes tax on the income. Even two countries both adopt resident jurisdiction, if they use different standards to determine the resident, double jurisdiction could still arise. The terms of "resident", "source of income" or "home" may have different interpretations from one state to another and it is possible that the same taxable individual, considered resident in two or more states or the same taxable object, be considered having the source in two or more states. And it might be case that the fiscal policy and the taxation systems from different states present particularities which leads to the double taxation or even to the cessation of the activities producing income as well.

Hence, inconsistent and contradictory tax laws, vague terms in taxation laws, both within the country and between countries, the application of different principles of taxation in interacting states (the principle of residency in one country, the principle of territoriality in another), taxation of the same income at the same time in different states that leads to double taxation will all cause double taxation.

The international double taxation may represent an excessive taxation for the taxpayer and an obstacle in the way of capital movement, of the cooperation between countries and the economic and financial increase, and it also constitutes a barrier in the way of the technical-scientific cooperation, of economic integration and trade enhancement, of the foreign investments of capital and of the external loans, of the development of other economic and financial affairs. Taking into account the multiple negative effects regarding the international commercial relationships created by the double taxation, at the state level there are proposed and applied varied solutions in order to decrease or eliminate this phenomenon.

Generally, the situations in which double taxation (economic or legal) appears, are determined by the fact that the governments of various states apply to taxes on income made in the territories concerned by subjects of taxation local and foreign, and on the other subject to taxes and the income from its own citizens abroad. Since double taxation affects the efficiency and competitiveness of exports of foreign goods, the removal of international double taxation is a necessity in order to ensure an economic development of relations at the international level.

2.2 Unilateral measures to avoid double taxation

The double taxation may be avoided either based upon some unilateral legislative measures, or by concluding bilateral or multilateral agreements between different countries. The avoidance of the double taxation by unilateral legislative measures is more difficult to be realized, as every country is interested to obtain fiscal income as large as possible. Measures available for resident states to reduce or even eliminate double taxation usually include tax exemption, tax credit, tax reduction and tax allowance.

2.2.1 Tax exemption

Among these measures, tax exemption and tax credit are more popular among states, as they also serve other purposes apart from avoiding double taxation. Tax exemption means that a state exempts residents' income or property originating in foreign states from tax. Most European countries, Australia and Latin American countries adopt tax exemption. Tax exemption includes full exemption and exemption with progression.

According to the full exemption approach, the income gained by the resident of a country in a foreign country and subject to the taxation in the respective country is deducted from the global taxable income which in the country of residence takes into account the totality of the income obtained by the tax payers.

For example, if a citizen gains in the country of residence (Country A) an annual income of USD 200,000, and in Country B (from its country of origin or of origin of the income) obtains an income of USD 50,000. The tax share in County A for the income obtained is of 25%, and the tax share in Country B for income obtained is of 20%. The tax share in Country A corresponding to the global income obtained in these two countries is of 30%. Considering Country A avoids double taxation by adopting the method of total exemption, the tax paid by the citizen in Country A will be 200,000×25% = USD 50,000, and the tax paid for the income obtained in Country B will be 50,000×20% = USD 10,000. The total tax paid by the citizen is of 50,000 + 10,000 = USD 60,000.

In the absence of such total exemption in Country A, the amount of the tax paid by the citizen in Country A would have been 250,000×30% = USD 75,000, and the amount of the tax paid in Country B is still of 50,000×20% = USD 10,000. Thus, the total amount of the tax would amount to 75,000+10,000 = USD 85,000. Tax saved by the citizen due to the total exemption is of 85,000-60,000 = USD 25,000.

In the context of the progression of the taxation, the income obtained abroad by the resident of a country is added to the taxable income achieved in the residence country, obtaining the global taxable income, depending on which the progressive related rate is determined or/and adequate progressive fix amount. In the abovementioned example, if the method of progressive exemption is used, the tax paid in County A by the citizen is 200,000×30% = USD 60,000, and the tax paid in Country B is 50,000×20% = USD 10,000. The total value of the tax in case of existence of the Convention on the avoidance of double taxation providing the use of the method of progressive avoidance shall be of 60,000+10,000 = USD 70,000. Taxed saved due to the progressive exemption is of

85,000 - 70,000 = USD 15,000.

2.2.2 Tax credit

Tax credit means that a resident shall pay tax in respect of all his income originating from foreign states, and the tax payable is applying the applicable tax rate to such income and then minus the amounts he has already paid for such income in foreign states, that is, the tax paid to the foreign country for the income obtained on its territory by the resident of other country shall be deducted directly from the total tax calculated in the residence country. A resident state could adopt tax credit or tax exemption to avoid double taxation, or adopt measures to avoid double taxation.

If full crediting is adopted, the tax paid abroad is deducted fully from the total tax calculated in the residence country, irrespective of its size. Still in the abovementioned case, in circumstance of full credits, the tax due in Country A before granting the credit is 250,000×30% = Euro 75,000. The credit given by Country A is equal to the tax paid in County B, which is 50,000×20% = Euro 10,000. Thus, the tax paid in Country A after granting the credit shall be 75,000 - 10,000 = Euro 65,000. The total value of the taxes paid by the taxpayer through the method of full crediting in Country A is 65,000+10,000 = Euro 75,000. Taxed saved is of USD 85,000 - 75,000 = USD 10,000.

2.2.3 Tax reduction

Tax reduction means that the taxpayer can sum up its taxes paid in foreign countries as the costs and deduct it from its total taxable income. Many countries adopt tax reduction as ancillary method of avoiding double taxation. For example, in US and Canada, tax reduction shall only apply in cases that tax credit is not applicable.

2.2.4 Tax allowance

Tax allowance means that the state applies a low tax rate to its residents when calculating its tax for foreign income. Belgium grants an 80% allowance to incomes from foreign states, while granting a 40% allowance to the business income of permanent trade companies established by its resident in foreign states.

Theoretically, tax exemption is most effective in avoiding double taxation. Tax reduction, tax credits, and tax allowance reduce the possibility of double taxation and relieve taxpayer's burden, but they cannot completely eliminate the phenomenon of double taxation.

2.3 Tax treaties

Progress had been made towards the elimination of double taxation through bilateral conventions or unilateral measures. One of these ways and modalities of preventing and eliminating the double taxation is the introduction, in bilateral or regional treaties, of some provisions meant to prevent the recurring taxation by two or more fiscal sovereignties.

2.3.1 Functions of tax treaties

A tax treaty is also referred to as a tax convention or double tax agreement. They prevent double taxation and fiscal evasion, and foster cooperation between Australia and other international tax authorities by enforcing their respective tax laws. Tax treaties are formal bilateral agreements between two jurisdictions. Australia has tax treaties with more than 40 jurisdictions.

Generally, tax treaties operate to reduce or eliminate double taxation caused by overlapping tax jurisdictions and provide a level of security about the tax rules that will apply to particular international transactions by allocating taxing rights between the jurisdictions over different categories of income, specifying rules to resolve dual claims in relation to the residential status of a taxpayer and the source of income, and providing an avenue to present a case for determination by the relevant taxation authorities where a taxpayer considers there has been taxation treatment contrary to the terms of a tax treaty.

2.3.2 The OECD Model Double Taxation Convention

The Organisation for Economic Co-operation and Development (OECD) adopted its first recommendation concerning double taxation on 25 February 1955 and offered applicable solutions in the bilateral relationships between countries. At that time, 70 bilateral general conventions had been signed between countries that are now members of the OECD. In 1963, the OECD published its Model Double Taxation Convention on Income and Capital [OECD Model (Convention)]. And the Model Convention was revised several times afterwards. The latest revision of the Model Convention is the 2017 OECD Model Tax Convention, which is the tenth edition of the full version of the OECD Model Tax Convention on Income and on Capital.

Since 1963, the OECD Model Convention has had wide repercussions on the negotiation, application, and interpretation of tax conventions. First, OECD member countries have largely conformed to the Model Convention when concluding or revising bilateral conventions. Second, the impact of the Model Convention has extended far beyond OECD area. It has been used as a basic document of reference in negotiations between member and non-member countries and even between non-member countries, as well as in the work of other worldwide or regional international organizations in the field of double taxation and related problems. Most notably, it has been used as the basis for the original drafting and the subsequent revision of the United Nations Model Double Taxation Convention between Developed and Developing Countries (UN Model), which reproduces a significant part of the provisions and commentaries of the OECD Model Convention. Third, the worldwide recognition of the provisions of the Model Convention and their incorporation into a majority of bilateral conventions have helped make the commentaries on the provisions of Model Convention a widely-accepted guide to the interpretation and application of the provisions of existing bilateral conventions.

The Convention applies to all persons who are residents of one or both of the contracting states. It deals with taxes on income and capital. For the purpose of eliminating double taxation, the Convention establishes two categories of rules. First, Articles 6 through 21 determine, with regard to different classes of income, the respective rights to tax of the State of source or situs and of the State of residence, and Article 22 does the same with regard to capital. In the case of a number of items of income and capital, an exclusive right to tax is conferred on one of the contracting states. The other contracting state is thereby prevented from taxing those items and double taxation is avoided. As a rule, this exclusive right to tax is conferred on the State of residence. In the case of other items of income and capital, the right to tax is not an exclusive one. As regards two classes of income (dividends and interest), although both States are given the right to tax, the amount of tax that may be imposed in the State of source is limited. Second, insofar as these provisions confer on the State of source or situs a full or limited right to tax, the State of residence must allow relief so as to avoid double taxation; this is the purpose of Articles 23A and 23B. The Convention leaves it to the contracting states to choose between two methods of relief, that is, the exemption method and the credit method.

Based on the OECD Model Convention, the recommended solutions suggest the member states to take into account the following factors:

(a) The taxation of the income made by the economic agent is to be done by the country on whose territory the income was obtained and in which those subjects have a stable exploitation headquarters.

(b) The income obtained under the form of interests to bonds, promissory notes or debentures, under the form of residuals from using the copyrights, patents, brands or trademarks, the secret procedures or formulae, etc, as well as that under the form of equities is to be taxed by both contracting countries, in the proportions agreed by those countries.

(c) The taxation of the income obtained from exercising on its own of a liberal profession (architect, medical doctor, lawyer, accountant, engineer, professional artist, professional athlete, etc) is to be made in his/her country of origin—when their beneficiary has a head office in order to exercise the liberal profession, or in the country in which the beneficiary of the income in residence—when he/she does not have a head office in the foreign country.

(d) The income from wages and fees, as well as that obtained under the form of shares, attendance fees or other similar fees by the members of the boards of trustees or the boards of statutory auditors is to be taxed in their country of origin. In reciprocity conditions, the employees of the embassies and of the diplomatic missions, as well as the correspondents of foreign press agencies are exempted from such a taxation.

(e) The assets owned abroad under the form of real estates are to be taxed by the country in which those are located. If the assets are movable goods, part of the assets of a stable head office or a stable base of operations, which serve to exercising a liberal profession, they are to be taxed in the country in which the stable head office or the stable base of operations. The ships, the aircrafts, the railroads or road vehicles exploited in the international traffic, as well as the movable goods used for these exploitations, are to be taxed in the country of residence of the exploitation company's management.

2.3.3 The UN Model Double Taxation Convention

The UN Model Double Taxation Convention was drafted in 1979 to assist developing countries to deal with double taxation, and it was also revised several times thereafter. The mandates of UN Model Convention are to keep under review and update as necessary the UN Model Double Taxation Convention between Developed and Developing Countries and the Manual for the Negotiation of Bilateral Tax Treaties between Developed and Developing Countries; provide a framework for dialog with a view to enhancing and promoting cooperation among national tax authorities and assess how new and emerging issues could affect this cooperation; and make recommendations on capacity-building and technical assistance. The particular aim of the UN Model is to facilitate entering of bilateral tax treaties by developing countries, which would contribute to attaining their development goals. The similarities between the models of the UN and OECD reflect the importance of achieving consistency, while the important areas of divergence reflect different memberships and priorities of the two organizations.

The UN Model generally preserves a greater share of tax revenue to the source state, the country where investment or other activity takes place, while the OECD Model preserves a greater share to the residence state, the country of the investor, trader, etc. The UN Model thus normally allows developing countries more taxing rights on income generated by foreign investments in these countries.

The 2011 update of UN Model takes into account recent development in the area of international tax policies of both developing and developed countries, seeks further consistency with the OECD Model, where in line with the priorities of developing countries, and further clarifies and improves the operation of provisions aimed to prevent double taxation over income from cross-border investments.

The main updates of the UN Model are: (a) it provides for mandatory binding arbitration (for countries wishing so) when a dispute cannot be resolved under the usual mutual agreement procedure, (b) it confirms and clarifies the importance of exchange of information under the UN Model; (c) it provides the rules under which states may assist each other in tax collection; (d) it addresses possible tax evasion related to taxing capital gains; and (e) it deals with income from independent personal services in line with the OECD Model.

The UN Model Tax Convention, as well as the OECD Model Tax Convention has had a profound influence on international treaty practice. They form the basis for most of the treaties between countries, aiming at protecting taxpayers against double taxation, with a view to improving the flow of international trade and investment as well as the transfer of technology, while retaining appropriate taxing rights to governments.

3 Cross-Border Tax Evasion

3.1 Causes of tax evasion

As different countries may adopt different tax rates, the determination of residence of a corporation is significant for its tax planning. To reduce their tax burden, corporations all have incentives to find the cheapest way to pay for their tax, and this is especially true for transnational corporations, as they usually conduct their business in several countries.

Tax evasion is different from tax avoidance. Tax avoidance does not involve activities directly violating the law, while tax evasion is a crime in which an individual or entity intentionally underpays, or avoids paying, taxes. Tax evasion may be conducted through concealing or lowing one's income or inflating deductions or expenses. Tax evasion hurts a state's tax sovereignty and economic interests, and it disturbs fair market competition among different countries. States improve their legislation and enforcement of taxation law to reduce the possibility of tax avoidance, but impose administrative and criminal liabilities on those engaged in tax evasion.

3.2 Measures against tax evasion

There are various measures to prevent people or corporations from tax evasion.

As regard to the tax evasion of natural person, one measure is to use migration policies to restrict a national change residence for the purpose of cross-border tax avoidance. That is, the states prohibit those persons from leaving their borders if the taxes have not been paid, even they have migrated to other countries. Or a state can require a national to remain as its tax resident in certain years after his/her migration. This is what the UK migration and tax law does. It is said that there is an unofficial rule of UK Treasury that in some circumstances a natural person emigrating or moving to another state would still keep his identity as a UK tax resident in three years after his/her migration.①

In respect of corporations, corporations may avoid or evade taxes through corporate migration, reorganization, transfer pricing, and transferring its business to tax haven or establishing a subsidiary in tax haven. Measures restricting tax evasions include measures restricting corporations alienation of business and assets, reorganization, transfer price and use of tax haven.

Many corporations have tried to avoid taxes by transferring their main business and assets to a foreign state. In order to regulate this, it is stipulated that no corporation could migrate to tax havens, nor establish its subsidiaries in tax havens, nor transfer part or all of its business to tax havens. Alienating business of a resident corporation to non-resident corporations, selling subsidiaries of the resident corporation to non-resident corporations shall also be approved by the UK Treasury.

Firstly, it is regulated by the US Internal Revenue Code that in respect of alienation of properties having foreign corporations taking part in, all capital gains from restructuring,

---

① 参见盛建明编著：《国际经济法》（英文版），对外经济贸易大学出版社 2017 年版，第 422 页。

reorganization and liquidation shall be taxed unless the Internal Revenue Service determines that such an activity is not for the purpose of tax avoidance.[①]

Secondly, as it is easier for a transnational corporation to engage in tax avoidance and tax evasion, most states adopt the principle of arm's length transaction to regulate transfer pricing among associated enterprises, and to prevent associated enterprises from transferring profits by manipulating contract prices and thus allocating profits among associated enterprises.

A third method is for a state to sign bilateral tax treaties with other states. Some states, like the US, would refer to conclude tax treaties with other countries to prevent the corporation's treaty shopping for most preferable tax treatment. Thus, by signing the treaty, a resident of one treaty party cannot choose to establish an entity in the territory of another treaty party for the purpose of enjoying tax preference. Tax treaties can prevent avoidance and evasion of taxes on various forms of income flows between the treaty partners by providing for the allocation of profits between related parties on an arm's length basis, generally preserving the application of domestic law rules that are designed to address transfer pricing and other international avoidance practices, providing for exchanges of information between the respective taxation authorities, and facilitating investment, trade, movement of technology and movement of personnel between jurisdictions—for example, by reducing rates of withholding tax.

A fourth option is to impose tax on capital gains upon expatriation. When property of a resident corporation is transferred to a non-resident associated corporation, such property is deemed as having been sold out at a fair market price, and the income based on such a fair market price is taxable. The purpose of such rule is to prevent tax avoidance in respect of property transfer among associated enterprises. The US has provided that when taxpayers are no longer resident corporations, they shall pay tax for such constructed gains.[②]

Tax avoidance is common among TNCs, and it usually involves two or more countries. Governments lose substantial corporate tax revenue because of aggressive international tax planning that has the effect of artificially shifting profits to locations where they are subject to non-taxation or reduced taxation. Thus, base erosion and profit shifting are a pressing issue not only for industrialized countries but also for emerging

① 参见盛建明编著：《国际经济法》（英文版），对外经济贸易大学出版社 2017 年版，第 423 页。
② 参见盛建明编著：《国际经济法》（英文版），对外经济贸易大学出版社 2017 年版，第 425 页。

economies and developing countries.

3.3 Bilateral, regional and multilateral efforts to deter tax avoidance

Double taxation agreements are not new to the international tax scene. The first bilateral treaty was between Prussia and Austria-Hungary in 1899 and the International Financial Conference in 1920 in Brussels is generally recognized as the first manifestation of multinational interest in the field of international double taxation. Nevertheless, the present network of over 200 bilateral double taxation agreements is largely the result of negotiations which have taken place since World War II. Although there are wide variations among the treaties currently in force, the tenor of these agreements is that the country of the taxpayer's residence is given the exclusive or primary right to tax income while the source country has little or no right to tax such income.

On the regional level, there are several treaties successfully adopted to combat tax avoidance and evasion. For example, in 1972, Sweden, Finland, Norway, Denmark and Iceland signed the Convention on Mutual Administrative Assistance in Tax Matters. The US, UK, France and Canada also reached an agreement for the prevention of cross-border tax evasion. In 1975, the EC adopted a resolution on the tax matters to deal with tax evasion and avoidance for its member countries.

The OECD tries to establish multilateral cooperation against tax avoidance and evasion in international community. In November 2016, over 100 jurisdictions concluded negotiations on the Multilateral Convention to Implement Tax Treaty Related Measures to Prevent Base Erosion and Profit Shifting (MLI) that will swiftly implement a series of tax treaty measures to update international tax rules and lessen the opportunity for tax avoidance by multinational enterprises. The MLI already covers 94 jurisdictions and entered into force on 1 July 2018. Signatories include jurisdictions from all continents and all levels of development and other jurisdictions are also actively working towards signature.

For example, the MLI suggests states to enter into covered tax agreements to eliminate double taxation and adopt options provided. In case of option A, provisions of a covered tax agreement that would otherwise exempt income derived or capital owned by a resident of a contracting jurisdiction from tax in that contracting jurisdiction for the purpose of eliminating double taxation shall not apply where the other contracting jurisdiction applies the provisions of the covered tax agreement to exempt such income or capital from tax or to limit the rate at which such income or capital may be taxed. In the latter case, the first-mentioned contracting jurisdiction shall allow as a deduction from the tax on the income or capital of that resident an amount equal to the tax paid in that other contracting jurisdiction.

In case of option B, provisions of a covered tax agreement that would otherwise exempt income derived by a resident of a contracting jurisdiction from tax in that contracting jurisdiction for the purpose of eliminating double taxation because such income is treated as a dividend by that contracting jurisdiction shall not apply where such income gives rise to a deduction for the purpose of determining the taxable profits of a resident of the other contracting jurisdiction under the laws of that other contracting jurisdiction.

In case of option C, where a resident of a contracting jurisdiction derives income or owns capital which may be taxed in the other contracting jurisdiction in accordance with the provisions of a covered tax agreement (except to the extent that these provisions allow taxation by that other contracting jurisdiction solely because the income is also income derived by a resident of that other contracting jurisdiction), the first-mentioned contracting jurisdiction shall allow (a) as a deduction from the tax on the income of that resident, an amount equal to the income tax paid in that other contracting jurisdiction; (b) as a deduction from the tax on the capital of that resident, an amount equal to the capital tax paid in that other contracting jurisdiction.①

The MLI also provides solutions of avoiding tax evasion for different types of income.

For dividends, provisions of a covered tax agreement that exempt dividends paid by a company which is a resident of a contracting jurisdiction from tax or that limit the rate at which such dividends may be taxed, provided that the beneficial owner or the recipient is a company which is a resident of the other contracting jurisdiction and which owns, holds or controls more than a certain amount of the capital, shares, stock, voting power, voting rights or similar ownership interests of the company paying the dividends, shall apply only if the ownership conditions described in those provisions are met throughout a 365-day period that includes the day of the payment of the dividends (for the purpose of computing that period, no account shall be taken of changes of ownership that would directly result from a corporate reorganization, such as a merger or divisive reorganization, of the company that holds the shares or that pays the dividends).②

---

① See MLI, Article 5.

② See MLI, Article 8.

For capital gains, provisions of a covered tax agreement providing that gains derived by a resident of a contracting jurisdiction from the alienation of shares or other rights of participation in an entity may be taxed in the other contracting jurisdiction, provided that these shares or rights derived more than a certain part of their value from immovable property (real property) situated in that other contracting jurisdiction [or provided that more than a certain part of the property of the entity consists of such immovable property (real property)]: (a) shall apply if the relevant value threshold is met at any time during the 365 days preceding the alienation; and (b) shall apply to shares or comparable interests, such as interests in a partnership or trust (to the extent that such shares or interests are not already covered) in addition to any shares or rights already covered by the provisions.①

To avoid the abuse of permanent establishments situated in a third jurisdiction, where an enterprise of a contracting jurisdiction (Country A) to a covered tax agreement derives income from the other contracting jurisdiction (Country B) and Country A treats such income as attributable to a permanent establishment of the enterprise situated in a third jurisdiction; and the profits attributable to that permanent establishment are exempt from tax in Country A, the benefits of the covered tax agreement shall not apply to any item of income on which the tax in the third jurisdiction is less than 60% of the tax that would be imposed in Country A on that item of income if that permanent establishment were situated in Country A. In such a case, any income to which the provisions of this paragraph apply shall remain taxable according to the domestic law of Country B, notwithstanding any other provisions of the covered tax agreement.②

The MLI offers concrete solutions for governments to close the gaps existing in international tax rules by transposing results from the OECD/G20 Base Erosion and Profit Shifting Project into bilateral tax treaties worldwide. The MLI modifies the application of thousands of bilateral tax treaties concluded to eliminate double taxation. It also implements agreed minimum standards to counter treaty abuse and to improve dispute resolution mechanisms while providing flexibility to accommodate specific tax treaty policies.

① See MLI, Article 9.

② See MLI, Article 10.

Chapter Review

1. What does tax jurisdiction mean?
2. What is the meaning of resident jurisdiction? What are the criteria used to determine a taxpayer's resident?
3. What is the meaning of source jurisdiction?
4. Can you explain the difference between resident jurisdiction and source jurisdiction?
5. Name some countries that adopt resident jurisdiction and source jurisdiction respectively.
6. What does international double taxation mean?
7. In what circumstance that international double taxation happens?
8. State briefly the negative effects of double taxation.
9. How can we avoid international double taxation?
10. Summarize the main provisions of OECD Model Double Taxation Convention.
11. Why is OECD Model Double Taxation Convention significant?
12. How is UN Model Double Taxation Convention different from the OECD Model Double Taxation Convention?
13. What is tax avoidance and what is tax evasion? Can you name the difference between them?
14. Why is tax avoidance and evasion harmful to states?
15. What are the measures taken by states to combat tax avoidance or evasion?
16. What is the multilateral convention drafted by the OECD to tackle the tax avoidance?
17. What are the regional treaties signed by states to deal with tax avoidance or evasion?

Key Terms

double taxation	双重征税
Model Convention for the Avoidance of Double Taxation with Respect to Taxes on Income and on Capital (OECD Model Double Taxation Convention)	《经济合作与发展组织关于对所得和财产避免双重征税的协定范本》
tax allowance	免税额
tax avoidance	逃税
tax evasion	避税

tax haven	避税天堂
tax holiday	免税期
tax jurisdiction	税收管辖权
transfer price	价格转移

Further Readings

1. Dagan, Tsilly, *International Tax Policy: Between Competition and Cooperation*, Cambridge University Press, 2017.

2. Herzfeld, Mindy, *International Taxation in a Nutshell*, 12th ed., West Academic Publishing, 2019.

3. Jogarajan, Sunita, *Double Taxation and the League of Nations*, Cambridge University Press, 2018.

4. Wells, Bret, *International Taxation*, 5th ed., Foundation Press, 2022.

Part VI International Rules on Dispute Settlement

Study Guide

The law on international economic and trade dispute settlement mechanism is an integral part of IEL. In this Part three issues are studied, which are different methods of solving international economic and trade disputes, the specific dispute settlement mechanism adopted in dealing with investor-state investment disputes and the dispute settlement mechanism in solving disputes arising from the covered agreements of the WTO.

The students are supposed to learn the merits and demerits of each type of dispute settlement methods, and understand how investor-state dispute settlement (ISDS) and WTO dispute settlement mechanism work. The subject matter and personal coverage of ICSID, the selection of arbitrators and annulment of arbitral awards are learnt in this Part, as well as the conciliation, the panel process, the appellant process, and the enforcement of the reports in WTO's dispute settlement mechanism.

In a rule-based international society, peaceful settlement of disputes is necessarily a part of it. The past two decades have seen a significant increase in the political reach and influence of international law, and a central element in this process has been an intensified adjudication of international relations and a steep growth in international judicialization through a steadily growing population of international courts. International economic and trade dispute settlement mechanism has been developed robustly to interpret international law and shape state's behavior. The adjudication of international law is especially active in realm of trade and investment, illustrated by the judicial decisions made by Appellate Body in the WTO and tribunals trailing the investor-state investment disputes.

1 Methods of Solving International Economic and Trade Disputes

Disputes are inextricably linked to international relations. Increasingly these disputes are no longer just primarily between states but also between states and other parties like international organizations and other non-state actors, and between these actors mutually. The peaceful resolution of international disputes constitutes a continuous, uninterrupted process based on international law, in which states participate as equal entities in rights. Forced to prevent the occurrence of any international situation or dispute, states have the duty to resort only to peaceful means of settlement for disputes between them, however, they have the right to freely decide and choose, on the basis of their joint agreement, those peaceful means that are considered convenient, timely and appropriate for a peaceful settlement.

In this context the Charter of the United Nations (UN Charter) plays a major role, in particular, regarding disputes between states. Article 2(3) of the UN Charter states that all member states have to settle their international disputes by peaceful means in such a manner that international peace and security, and justice, are not endangered. This view was confirmed in 1982 in a resolution (Res. 37/10) of the UN General Assembly, the so-called Manila Declaration on the Peaceful Settlement of International Disputes (Manila Declaration).

The section hereunder first introduces the normal methods of dispute settlement in the realm of international public law, then discusses the specific mechanisms that solve the investment disputes and trade disputes, and the pros and cons of each mechanism.

1.1 Local remedies

Investment disputes between a private investor and the host state, traditionally, was confined to local remedies, diplomatic protection or state to state arbitration. In case of disputes, the first choice for the foreign traders and investors is to bring a claim against its contracting parties or government of host state through its domestic courts, which is preferred by the host state as the local courts would enjoy the jurisdiction and local law would apply. However, most foreigners do not trust the domestic courts in the host states. Sometimes, the courts may deny the jurisdiction over the matter if the dispute involves a sovereign actor, or even if it accepts the jurisdiction, the impartiality of the dispute settlement cannot be guaranteed. The timing factor is also a problem. The procedure of local remedies sometimes is prolonged and time-consuming, and it could take several years to have the final binding decisions, and investor might have been bankrupt before the decision is made. Thus, the local remedies are not preferred by the investors and traders in settling their disputes, especially in a less developed judicial system.

1.2 Diplomatic protection

Diplomatic protection is a very old method of dispute settlement, which has been embodied in customary international law for a very long time. In case of a dispute involving a sovereign actor, traders and investors might probably ask its home state for diplomatic protection first. Diplomatic protection was once strong to solve the disputes in the era of colonialism. The imperial system could protect the investors against the weak host state through coercion and threat of war.

There are definite rules on the basis of which diplomatic intervention to protect the interests of the foreign investor could be made. They are the genesis of what some states regard as customary international law. Where diplomatic intercession fails, the same rules become the basis on which litigation could be brought against the recalcitrant state before an international tribunal or the International Court of Justice. There have been very few cases that have been brought before the International Court of Justice or its predecessor.

The system of diplomatic protection itself is prone to be influenced by specific interests reigning in the bilateral state-state relationship. First, diplomatic protection is a right of a state *vis-à-vis* another state to ensure the interest of its nationals will not be damaged without cause for the rules of international law. There is, however, no corresponding duty of the home states towards its own nationals to grant diplomatic protection. Instead, states remain free to exercise this right in a discretionary way. Hence, it is up to the home state to decide whether to afford diplomatic protection and to what extent to offer such protection, which means it is normally difficult for small or less influential companies to initiate such procedure. Even for big ones, once the diplomatic protection is initiated, the investor or the trader cannot decide how it goes or controls the procedure.

1.3 Negotiation, conciliation and mediation

As the UN Charter does not prescribe in which way or by what means disputes need to be resolved, the parties are free to choose their dispute settlement mechanism. In the framework of international peace and security, Article 33 of the UN Charter provides a number of alternatives to choose from in resolving disputes such as negotiation, enquiry, mediation, conciliation, arbitration, and judicial settlement. Notwithstanding the free choice of means, the Manila Declaration underlines the legal obligation of parties to find a peaceful solution to their dispute and refrain from action that might aggravate the situation.

Traditionally, states settle their disputes through negotiation, conciliation, and mediation. Occasionally, they go to the International Court of Justice for a judicial settlement. As many disputes among states are political rather than commercial, it is not urgently needed to have more judicial methods of dispute settlement.

Negotiation and conciliation could be held between two sovereign actors, and it could also be held between a private person and a state. They are believed to be the most friendly method of dispute settlement, so they are included in multilateral, regional and bilateral treaties. For example, before a member of the WTO requests the establishment of a panel, it has to consult with the other party for at least 60 days, which is a way of negotiation.

Many regional and bilateral treaties, following the lead of Chinese treaties, now require that there be a period of negotiations after a dispute has arisen before recourse can be brought to arbitration. There may be cultural predispositions towards negotiated settlement, which host states prefer. Investors may prefer it too, as the continuation of a harmonious relationship may be a more desirable objective than a termination in the context of hostility. This requirement thus ensures that negotiations are attempted. There must be a good faith attempt to secure a settlement. The western IIAs also encourage the claimant and the respondent to resolve the dispute through consultation, negotiation, good offices, conciliation, or mediation initially.

Mediation is clearly stipulated in the UN Charter as an important method of peaceful settlement of international dispute. It is further regulated by a new convention adopted by the United Nations, namely, United Nations Convention on International Settlement Agreements Resulting from Mediation (2018), which is also called the Singapore Convention on Mediation. Compared with other dispute settlement methods which have more adversarial features, mediation reflects the importance of harmony and traditional values cherished by the Eastern culture. The Convention is an instrument for the facilitation of international trade and the promotion of mediation as an alternative and effective method of resolving trade disputes. Being a binding international instrument, it is expected to bring certainty and stability to the international framework on mediation, thereby contributing to the sustainable development goals.

Article 1 provides that the Convention applies to international settlement agreements resulting from mediation, concluded in writing by parties to resolve a commercial dispute. Settlement agreements concluded by a consumer for personal, family or household purposes, or relating to family, inheritance or employment law, and a settlement agreement that is enforceable as a judgment or as an arbitral award are excluded from the Convention.

Further, Article 3 addresses the key obligations of the Parties to the Convention with respect to both enforcement of settlement agreements and the right of a disputing party to invoke a settlement agreement covered by the Convention. Each Party to the Convention may determine the procedural mechanisms that may be followed where the Convention does not prescribe any requirement. Article 4 covers the formalities for relying on a settlement agreement, namely, the disputing party shall supply to the competent authority the settlement agreement signed by them and evidence that the settlement agreement results from mediation. The competent authority may require any necessary document in order to verify that the requirements of the Convention are complied with.

The Convention defines in Article 5 the grounds upon which a court may refuse to grant relief at the request of the disputing party against whom it is invoked. These grounds can be grouped into three main categories, namely in relation to the disputing parties, the settlement agreement and the mediation procedure. Article 5 includes two additional grounds upon which the court may, on its own motion, refuse to grant relief. Those grounds relate to public policy and the fact that the subject matter of the dispute cannot be settled by mediation. With the aim to provide for the application of the most favorable framework for settlement agreements, Article 7 foresees the application of the more favorable law or treaty.

Article 8 includes reservations. A first reservation permits a Party to the Convention to exclude from the application of the Convention settlement agreements to which it is a party, or to which any governmental agencies or any person acting on behalf of a governmental agency is a party, to the extent specified in the declaration. A second reservation permits a Party to the Convention to declare that it will apply the Convention only to the extent that the disputing parties have agreed to its application.

On 7 August 2019, China signed the Singapore Mediation Convention and became a party of it. Singapore Mediation Convention further perfected the mediation mechanism for resolving international commercial disputes. Numerous countries signed the Convention, manifesting the consensus in the international community on the significance of multilateralism.

2 Specific Methods of Solving Investment Disputes

Globalization of international economy requires more effective and legitimate methods of dispute settlement, especially in the realm of international trade and investment. With efforts of states, international organizations, and private entities, new mechanisms have been adopted to serve the needs. Among them, investor-state arbitration has evolved as a modern device to solve investment disputes between investor and host state. Such arbitration derived from commercial arbitration and was first based on an investment agreement signed between an investor and the host state, and later footed on the investment treaty ratified by an investor's home state and host state. The former is called contract-based arbitration and latter is termed treaty-based investor-state dispute settlement.

2.1 Contract-based arbitration between investor and state

Before the emergence of the investment treaty system in 1959, there was an earlier system of investment protection which the multinational corporations had virtually devised by themselves for the protection of their investments. This system worked entirely on the basis of contractual structures of protection that were negotiated with the host state at the time of the entry of the investment. Virtually every foreign investment entry is accomplished through a contract, except where entry is made through a merger or acquisition. The contract is negotiated with the host state or its agency at the time of entry. In a contract-based arbitration, the consent is specific to disputes arising from the contract. It is usually expressed in the arbitration clause.

The contract-based arbitration mechanism usually contains two special provisions which are absent in the bilateral investment treaties. One is a stabilization clause seeking to freeze the law when the investor makes investment in the host state to ensure that later changes to the law do not apply to their concession. This clause guarantees the profitability of investment, but restricts host state's regulatory power of changing investment and social policies.① The other provision contained in the concession is the choice-of-law clause which would seek to exclude the application of the domestic laws of the host state and subject the contract to some nebulous external standard such as "general principles of law" or "standards that prevail within the industry". The objective of the latter technique is to ensure the application of a system which could not be unilaterally altered by the home state as its own laws could have been.②

The contract-based arbitration mechanism protects the transnational corporations with

① See M. Sornarajah, *The International Law on Foreign Investment*, 3rd ed., Cambridge University Press, 2010, p. 281.

② See M. Sornarajah, *The International Law on Foreign Investment*, 3rd ed., Cambridge University Press, 2010, p. 284.

strong bargain power to the greatest extent. But such mechanism is not without limits. For those small investors that are not able to negotiate a beneficial concession for themselves, treaty-based ISDS will ensure more continuous and consistent investment protection for them.

2.2 State-state arbitration

IIAs usually provide for both investor-state and state-state arbitration. Standard state-state arbitration clauses permit any contracting party to seize a tribunal to settle any dispute with another contracting party as to the application or interpretation of the respective IIA. Such broad wording opens various possibilities for conflict with investor-state arbitration, e.g., if the investor's home state introduces a parallel diplomatic protection claim or if the investor's host state and respondent in the investor-state arbitration resort to state-state arbitration in order to settle a matter of interpretation that is pertinent in the investor-state dispute. Beyond the issue of parallel proceedings, questions arise as to the effect of a state-state award, particularly pertaining to the interpretation of the IIA, in subsequent investor-state arbitrations where the interpretation of the same IIA clause is relevant for resolving the investor-state dispute.

2.3 Emergency of ISDS and its significance

The emergency of ISDS produces a private right of action for individuals and corporations investing abroad against a sovereign state's breach of a treaty. Such introduction of a private right of action fundamentally breaks with the traditional enforcement mechanism of international investment law. Investors under modern investment treaties are no longer mediated through an interstate prism. Instead of depending upon their home state's power and willingness to espouse their claim, they have an independent right of action to initiate investor-state arbitration and are able to seek redress in their own name against violations by the host state of the applicable investment treaty. The available remedies, in this context, are generally those that are also available on the interstate level under the law on state responsibility. The most common and readily enforceable remedy consisting in a claim for damages, is also available to the investors.

The treaty-based ISDS generates more profound influence on investment protection than contract-based arbitration. In treaty-based arbitration, the consent of the state is said to be given to all present and potential investors who satisfy nationality criteria and whose investment is protected by the treaty in advance of the dispute. This has introduced four changes to the settlement of investment disputes.

First, the ISDS entrusts the investors with the direct right of action to seek damages for a violation of an investment treaty, and the exercise of the right is completely decided by the investors. Second, the host state would have limited influence on the arbitral process. The procedure has been pre-determined and it is usually held in a third country, the members of tribunal are selected by the investors and host state, but the investor as the initiator of such proceeding enjoys the first mover advantage. Third, the arbitral award is subject to limited review. The arbitral award once issued is final and binding unless the host state initiates the annulment process. There is no appeal process for it and the reasons for annulment are limited and restricted. And lastly, the awards are provided with a recognition and enforcement mechanism by New York Convention.

The investors can initiate ad hoc arbitration or institutional arbitration. The establishment of ICSID is a landmark to the development of ISDS mechanism, which provides institutional support for such mechanism. In 1965, on the initiative of World Bank, the Convention on the Settlement of Investment Disputes between States and Nationals of Other States (Washington Convention) was signed and then came into effect in 1966, in accordance with which the ICSID was established for the settlement of controversies and resolution of disputes between the contracting states and the nationals of contracting states.

Unlike other arbitral tribunals, the ICSID is a specialist organization tasked with the settlement of investment disputes and operates on the basis of an international convention. Its juridical status is as an intergovernmental institution, whereas other arbitral tribunals are either private bodies, creatures of single sovereigns or of the intermediate parties to a dispute as in the case of ad hoc tribunals. Based on Article 25 of Washington Convention, ICSID has jurisdiction over disputes between investors and the host countries, both of which consent in writing to submit to ICSID. In February 1990, China signed the Washington Convention and it was ratified in February 1993. Up to 2019, there have been 163 signatory and contracting states.

Since its establishment, ICSID has become the most popular institution hosting dispute settlement for investors and host states. Today, most of the ISDS provisions in FTA Investment Chapters allow an investor of either party to submit a claim to arbitration under either the ICSID or UNCITRAL rules. UNCITRAL is a set of rules providing the investors with ad hoc arbitration. Overall, about 60% of investor-state disputes are brought to the ICSID for decisions. The ICSID rendered over 400 decisions on the investment disputes.

2.4 Constraint to the ISDS and MFN clauses

ISDS has become an indispensable part of IIAs. But most states would like to constrain investors' right of action by inclusion of provisions of waiting period, "fork in the road" and exhaustion of local remedies.

Access to investor-state arbitration under international investment agreements often requires the fulfillment of certain preconditions. Most BITs, for example, require initial negotiations between investor and host state prior to submitting the dispute to arbitration. Other treaties require the expiration of waiting periods prior to arbitration, sometimes as long as 18 months, or the exhaustion of local remedies. While these restrictions may serve to facilitate the amicable settlement of disputes and to allow the host state's judicial system to redress wrongful conduct, local remedies and waiting periods can also impede the enforcement of rights granted under an IIA and delay efficient dispute settlement. So the investors have endeavored to avoid such pre-arbitration conditions. One effective tool is through the MFN clause in an IIA.

To date, arbitral jurisprudence has rather consistently accepted that investors may circumvent such admissibility-related requirements such as waiting period by relying on more favorable provisions for investor-state dispute settlement under third-country BITs. The dispute *Maffezini v. Spain* was such a case that allowed investors to circumvent a comparatively long waiting period in the BIT that it referred to.[①] It was also the first ICSID award to apply the MFN clause to circumvent pre-arbitration restrictions by allowing the investor to rely on a shorter waiting period from a third-party BIT. In this dispute, the Tribunal faced with the question of whether an Argentine investor in Spain was bound by an 18-month waiting period before initiating investor-state arbitration under the Spanish-Argentine Bilateral Investment Treaty (basic treaty) or whether it could rely, based on the BIT's MFN clause, on more favorable access conditions under the Spanish-Chilean Bilateral Investment Treaty (targeted treaty), which required only a six-month waiting period. The Tribunal resorted to the first principle in its interpretation of Article 4.2 of the Spanish-Argentine BIT which reads: in all matters subject to this Agreement, this treatment shall not be less favorable than that extended by each Party to the investments made in its territory by investors of a third country.

It is believed by many tribunals if a third-party treaty contains provisions for the settlement of disputes that are more favorable to the protection of the investor's rights and

① See Emilio Agustín Maffezini *v.* Kingdom of Spain, ICSID Case No. ARB/97/7.

interests than those in the basic treaty, such provisions may be extended to the beneficiary of the most-favored-nation clause as they are fully compatible with the ejusdem generis principle.

The fork in the road provision in a treaty seeks to confine the foreign investor to one remedy by precluding resort to others if he is shown to have made a prior election. That is, if an investor has chosen local remedies, it cannot resort to the ISDS after it suspends its domestic proceeding, vice versa. Provisions on waiver or a defense relating to waiver have a similar effect of seeking to confine the foreign investor to his earlier choice. In a sense, where one of the procedures resorted to has already been completed, the situation is akin to the consideration of a *res judicata* plea, as one tribunal has to decide to what extent it is bound by an earlier decision of a court or tribunal belonging to a different system. The principles used to dispose of a defense based on waiver are very similar to those used in considering *res judicata*.

Exhaustion of local remedies, literally, requires the investors to exhaust all types of remedies provided by the host state before it submits its dispute to the ISDS. Some treaties expressly exclude the need for exhaustion of local remedies. Some prescribe a time during which local remedies are to be attempted. In the latter case, there must be a good faith effort to pursue the remedies. Both folk in the road and exhaustion of local remedies requirements burden the investors in seeking redress. These limitations have usually resulted in recourse to MFN clauses by investors. In some instances, tribunals have held that the MFN clauses could be used.

In *Siemens v. Argentina*,① this case built further on the *Maffezini* decision and bolstered the application of MFN clauses by allowing the investor to incorporate benefits from third-country BITs without being bound by the latter treaty's restrictive provisions. It thus allowed the investor to cherry-pick more favorable provisions from third-country BITs without being bound to any less favorable conditions contained in those treaties.

The claimant initiated investor-state arbitration before an 18-month waiting period required by the German-Argentine BIT had elapsed. In order to overcome this requirement, the investor invoked the treaty's MFN clause in order to benefit from the six-month waiting period in the Argentine-Chilean BIT. Argentina argued that if the claimant could rely on the shorter waiting period in the Argentine-Chilean BIT, it also should be bound by that treaty's fork in the road provision which requires Chilean investors to make a final and

---

① See Siemens A.G. *v.* The Argentine Republic, ICSID Case No. ARB/02/8.

binding choice between domestic proceedings or international arbitration.

The Tribunal rejected all of Argentina's arguments and went beyond the *Maffezini* decision, and held that MFN treatment had the effect of selectively importing benefits without concurrently incorporating the limitations of the third-party BIT.

2.5 Appointment of arbitrators

Where an investor submits a dispute for settlement under the UNCITRAL Arbitration Rules, Article 5 provides that should the parties to the dispute fail to agree on one arbitrator, then the tribunal is to comprise three arbitrators. Arbitration under ICSID is not limited to either one or three arbitrators as under Article 37.2(a) tribunal can comprise one or any uneven number of arbitrators. However, Article 37.2(b) requires a tribunal to consist of three arbitrators when the parties fail to agree on the number of arbitrators.

UNCITRAL and ICSID also provide different processes for the appointment of arbitrators. Under Article 7.1 of the UNCITRAL Arbitration Rules, each party is required to appoint an arbitrator and for these two arbitrators to agree on the third arbitrator. In contrast, Article 37.2(b) of the ICSID Convention requires each disputing party to appoint an arbitrator and for the disputing parties to agree on the appointment of the third and presiding arbitrator.

Under ICSID, if either party to the dispute fails to appoint an arbitrator, the ICSID Chairman, defined as the President of the World Bank, appoints those arbitrators not yet appointed from the panel of arbitrators.

2.6 Review of the decisions

It has been traditionally recognized that the principle of finality is one of the most significant characteristics of international investment arbitration, which provides the quickest and the most economical way for the parties to settle disputes.

Thus, the ICSID Convention provides that an award shall be binding on the parties and shall not be subject to any appeal or to any other remedy except those provided for in this Convention. In addition, it also provides that each contracting state shall recognize an award rendered pursuant to this Convention as binding and enforce the pecuniary obligations imposed by that award within its territories as if it were a final judgment of a court in that state.[①]

---

① See ICSID, Articles 53–54.

Section 5 in Chapter IV of the Washington Convention provides ICSID's mechanism of supervision, including the interpretation, revision and annulment of the awards. Article 50 stipulates that if the parties have any dispute over the meaning or the scope of an award, either of the party can request interpretation of the award. Actually, the interpretation of the award is at the discretion of the arbitral tribunal, so Article 50 only has a limited effect on the supervision of the arbitral tribunal. Article 51 formulates that if one fact which is decisive to an award is discovered but such fact was unknown to the tribunal and either of the party, then that party may request revision of the award. Such revision mechanism is seldom used in reality.

Article 52 provides that either of the party may request annulment of the award if: (a) the arbitral tribunal was not properly constituted; (b) the tribunal obviously exceeded its powers; (c) any member of the tribunal was corrupted; (d) there was a serious departure from a fundamental rule of procedure; or (e) the award did not state the reasons on which it is based. Procedural defects such as improper composition of tribunal and manifest procedural error could effectively bar the decision. According to this Article, even if either of the parties can prove that the arbitral tribunal erred in findings of fact or application of law, it cannot request annulment of the award, because these are not enumerated as grounds for annulment. This leads to the weak supervision of the arbitration process.

Overall, the interpretation, revision and annulment are far from adequate to provide a coherent system of redressing wrongful decisions made by the tribunals.

2.7 Other procedural issues

Among the deficiencies of ISDS, the frivolous claims brought by the investors reduce the legitimacy of the ISDS mechanism. The ISDS provisions in several FTAs seek to reduce the possibility that investors may raise frivolous claims. For example, the US-Singapore Free Trade Agreement and US-Chile Free Trade Agreement state that a tribunal shall address and decide as a preliminary question any objection by the respondent that, as a matter of law, a claim submitted is not a claim for which an award in favor of the claimant may be made. These ISDS provisions also allow a tribunal in these instances to award costs and attorney fees against the party who submits such suits.

There are a number of different approaches addressing the transparency and openness of tribunals under the ISDS provisions in FTA Investment Chapters. Whether an ISDS process is open and transparent is decided by different benchmarks which include whether the tribunal hearings are open to the public, whether the documents submitted in the disputes and decisions are accessible by the public, and whether the NGOs can submit their experts opinion to the tribunal. One approach is to give clear instructions via FTA terms. Like in USMCA, it is required that the tribunal shall conduct hearings open to the public and shall determine, in consultation with the disputing parties, the appropriate logistical arrangements. And the respondent shall, "after receiving the following documents, promptly transmit them to the non-disputing Annex Party and make them available to the public: the notice of intent; the notice of arbitration; pleadings, memorials and briefs submitted to the tribunal by a disputing party and any written submissions submitted; minutes or transcripts of hearings of the tribunal and orders, awards and decisions of the tribunal."①

The other approach is not to address these issues of transparency and openness in the ISDS provisions, and instead, to rely on the procedures, where they exist, in the applicable arbitration rules, if they adopt ICSID or UNCITRAL rules. This is the approach taken in numerous FTAs, such as Republic of Korea-Singapore FTA, India-Singapore Comprehensive Economic Cooperation Agreement, Japan-Singapore Economic Partnership Agreement and the Thailand-Australia FTA.

With respect to the publication of tribunal awards, both UNCITRAL and ICSID require the consent of the parties. However, under ICSID Rule 48(4), the center will publish excerpts of the legal reasoning of the tribunal. Some FTAs allow either party to the dispute to publish the award. Further, neither ICSID nor UNCITRAL allows for non-parties to the dispute to attend hearings.

2.8 Reforms of ISDS by investment court system

The ISDS has long been criticized for its inconsistent awards, over-protection toward the investors, and lack of transparency of the proceedings. Reforms have been taken by many capital exporting countries to enhance their control over the ISDS proceedings and improve the legal certainty and transparency of the ISDS procedure.

The EU has made strong determination to amend the defects of the ISDS. Evidenced by the CETA, the EU Commission showed a clear break from the current ISDS system and committed to establish a multilateral investment court with other parties. In November 2015, the idea of investment court system was first raised in a concept paper titled "EU Commission Proposal for Investment Protection and Resolution of Investment Disputes".

---

① USMCA, Article 14.D.8.

The idea was subsequently embodied in the negotiation of EU-US Transatlantic Trade and Investment Partnership (TTIP). And both the Canada-EU Comprehensive Economic and Trade Agreement (CETA) and EU-Vietnam Free Trade Agreement finalized such mechanism with comprehensive and detailed rules. The investment court system is a two-tiered mechanism for investor-state dispute settlement, combining elements of traditional investor-state arbitration (ISA) with judicial features.[①] The investment court system proposed by EU differs from ISDS in three main aspects.

Firstly, the tribunal members adjudicating a specific dispute are selected randomly by the investment court instead of disputing parties, and qualifications of tribunal members are explicitly required. That is, the investors have no right to appoint the adjudicators and lose its first mover advantage. According to Article 8.27(2) of CETA, it is stipulated that the 15 members of the Tribunal shall be appointed by the CETA Joint Committee for a renewable five-year term. Among them, five of the Members shall be nationals of a member state of the EU, five shall be nationals of Canada, and the other five shall be third-country nationals. Qualifications for appointment resemble those of other international courts and tribunals by requiring specific knowledge in the field. In particular, Article 8.27(4) of CETA requires the tribunal members to possess qualifications required in their respective countries for appointment to judicial office, or be jurists of recognized competence and they shall have demonstrated expertise in the field. Individual cases shall be adjudicated by divisions of three members of the Tribunal, and they shall be appointed by the President of the Tribunal on a random and unpredictable way. The stability of adjudicators in the investment court will also benefit the consistence of the investment awards, and high qualification requirement ensures the proficiency of the panel award.

Secondly, an appellant mechanism has been established by the investment court proposed by the EU, which provides a stable review system to the investment dispute settlement. Awards rendered by the Tribunal (of first instance) can be appealed to the Appeal Tribunal within 90 days of their issuance. The proposed appeal system enlarges the annulment grounds of the ICSID Convention with the power to review errors of law and manifest errors in the appreciation of facts. Based on these grounds, the Appeal

---

① See August Reinisch, *Will the EU's Proposal Concerning an Investment Court System for CETA and TTIP Lead to Enforceable Awards?—The Limits of Modifying the ICSID Convention and the Nature of Investment Arbitration*, 19 Journal of International Economic Law 761, 761 (2016).

Tribunal may uphold, modify, or reverse the Tribunal's award.[①] Although similar appellant mechanism has been proposed by the US in several IIAs, no review system has been adopted by the US so far.

Thirdly, the investment court mechanism improves the transparency and participation of the proceedings, and clarifies the applicable law and concerns that shall be taken into account. For example, the tribunal process is open to the third party. That is, a non-disputing party, for example, the home state of the investor, can participate in the dispute. Amicus curiae briefs from NGOs will also be allowed in the proceeding. The applicable law of investment disputes adjudicated by the investment court shall be the treaty itself. But adjudicators in the investment court can take into account the environmental and human rights conventions adopted by the host state and home state.

The investment court system proposed by the EU has provided a more permanent, neutral investor-state dispute settlement forum for the investment dispute settlement. As a newly born scheme, it is too early to comment on its influence over investment dispute settlement. But it has to be admitted that such mechanism does address many defects of existing ISDS mechanism.

3 Dispute Settlement Mechanism in WTO

When trade disputes arise, what methods of dispute settlement shall be chosen depends on the nature of dispute. For private disputes between a buyer and a seller in international trade, they are mainly solved by domestic litigation and international commercial arbitration based on their choice of forum in the contract, which is nothing different from contractual disputes. While for disputes arising from breach of WTO covered agreements, they can be solved through the dispute settlement mechanism provided by the WTO. It was only in 1995 when the WTO's Dispute Settlement Understanding (DSU) became effective. But since its birth, it has become the most successful and active trade dispute settlement mechanism that was ever created and implemented. It is the central pillar of the multilateral trading system, and the WTO's unique contribution to the stability of the global economy. Without a means of settling disputes, the rules-based system would be less effective because the rules could not be enforced. The WTO's procedure

① See CETA, Article 8.28.

underscores the rule of law, and it makes the trading system more secure and predictable. The system is based on clearly-defined rules, with timetables for completing a case. Till the end of 2019, 596 disputes have been brought to the WTO and over 350 rulings have been issued.

A procedure for settling disputes existed under the old GATT, but it had no fixed timetables, rulings were easier to be blocked due to the consensus principle, and many cases dragged on for a long time inconclusively. The Uruguay Round agreement introduced a more structured process with more clearly defined stages in the procedure. It introduced greater discipline for the length of time a case should take to be settled, with flexible deadlines set in various stages of the procedure. The agreement emphasizes that prompt settlement is essential if the WTO is to function effectively. It sets out in considerable detail the procedures and the timetable to be followed in resolving disputes. If a case runs its full course to a first ruling, it should not normally take more than about one year—15 months if the case is appealed. The agreed time limits are flexible, and if the case is considered urgent, it is accelerated as much as possible.

The Uruguay Round agreement also made it impossible for the country losing a case to block the adoption of the ruling. Under the previous GATT procedure, rulings could only be adopted by consensus, meaning that a single objection could block the ruling. Now, rulings are automatically adopted unless there is a consensus to reject a ruling—any country wanting to block a ruling has to persuade all other WTO members (including its adversary in the case) to share its view. The wisdom of this change has rendered the decisions of WTO dispute settlement automatically effective like a binding judgment made by a domestic court.

3.1 Approaches of trade dispute settlement provided by the WTO

A dispute arises when a member government believes another member government is violating an agreement or a commitment that it has made in the WTO. A third group of countries can declare that they have an interest in the case and participate in the dispute as a third party.

To be more specific, provided by Article 23.1 of GATT, if any contracting party should consider that any benefit accruing to it directly or indirectly under this Agreement is being nullified or impaired or that the attainment of any objective of the Agreement is being impeded as the result of (a) the failure of another contracting party to carry out its obligations under this Agreement, or (b) the application by another contracting party of any measure, whether or not it conflicts with the provisions of this Agreement, or (c) the existence of any other situation, the contracting party may, with a view to the satisfactory adjustment of the matter, make written representations or proposals to the other contracting party or parties which it considers to be concerned. Any contracting party thus approached shall give sympathetic consideration to the representations or proposals made to it.

The dispute settlement process covers the WTO agreements, GATT 1994, other agreements on goods, services, and the DSU itself. The DSU provides for more than one method to settle disputes between WTO members, which include consultations or negotiation, adjudication by panels and the Appellate Body, arbitration, and good offices, conciliation and mediation. Articles 22 and 24 provide for consultation between Members with respect to any matter affecting the operation of an agreement. If no satisfactory solution is reached, a Member may request that a consultation should be held jointly by the Members with any other member.

The most frequently used dispute settlement mechanism in WTO is the adjudication processes by panels and the Appellate Body. Such dispute settlement process entails four major steps: (a) consultations between the claimants and defendants; (b) panel proceedings; (c) appellate review proceedings; and (d) implementation and enforcement. The dispute settlement system of the WTO is a central element in providing security and predictability for the multilateral trading system.①

3.2 How is a dispute settled

Settling disputes is the responsibility of the Dispute Settlement Body (the General Council in another guise), which consists of all WTO members. The Dispute Settlement Body has the sole authority to establish panels of experts to consider the case, and to accept or reject the panels' findings or the results of an appeal. It monitors the implementation of the rulings and recommendations, and has the power to authorize retaliation when a country does not comply with a ruling.

If a member wishes to initiate the panel process, it shall prove that any benefit accruing to it under a particular agreement is being nullified or impaired, or the attainment of any objective of the agreement is being impeded. If the nullification or impairment of a benefit is caused by a member failing to carry out its obligations under the agreement,

① See DSU, Article 3.2.

such situations are commonly called violation cases, otherwise, the disputes are non-violation cases, which do not conflict with the agreement, and yet cause the nullification or impairment of benefits.

The first step to settle a dispute under the WTO is to host a consultation by the claimant and the country he/she has argument with, which is up to 60 days. Before taking any other actions the countries in dispute have to talk to each other to see if they can settle their differences by themselves. If that fails or the required consultation period passes, they can ask the WTO Director-General to mediate or try to help in any other way.

After the consultation, the panel procedure can be invoked, which is up to 45 days for a panel to be appointed, plus six months for the panel to conclude a decision on the dispute.

The panel process includes four stages. The first stage is the formation of panel. The member requesting the DSB for the formation of a panel must make such request in writing and give the required information. The request shall include an indication as to whether or not a consultation is held, the specific measures which are at issue, and a brief summary of the legal basis of the complaint which should present the problems clearly.

Normally, a panel consists of three members. Nominations to the panel are proposed initially by the Secretariat of the WTO, and the parties to the dispute accept them except if they have compelling reasons not to. In cases where no agreement is reached within 20 days of the date of establishing the panel, either party may request the director-general to make the nominations. Panel members are expected to function in their individual capacities and not as representatives of governments or of any organization.

The panel will hold written and oral presentations, and the deliberations in the panel and the documents submitted to it have to be kept confidential. The panel will also decide whether to solicit or accept an amicus brief from certain expert group, with respect to a factual issue. The panel has to issue the final report to the parties to the dispute within six months of the date of the final agreement on the composition of the panel. In cases of urgency, including those concerning perishable goods, the deadline is shortened to three months.

A minimum of two days is to pass between the circulation of the panel report to members and the consideration of the report by the DSB. Members who have objections to the report have to give written reasons for their objection which have to be circulated at least ten days prior to the commencement of the DSB meeting. If a party has not notified the DSB about its decision to go for an appeal, the DSB has to adopt the report within 60 days of the date of circulation of the report to members, except if it decides by consensus not to adopt the report. Because the panel's report can only be rejected by consensus in the Dispute Settlement Body, its conclusions are difficult to overturn.

The parties to the dispute have the right to appeal against the panel report. Actually, either side can appeal a panel's ruling. Sometimes both sides do so. Appeals have to be based on points of law such as legal interpretation—they cannot reexamine existing evidence or examine new issues. Each appeal is heard by three members of a permanent seven-member Appellate Body set up by the Dispute Settlement Body and broadly representing the range of WTO membership. Members of the Appellate Body have four-year terms. They have to be individuals with recognized standing in the field of law and international trade, not affiliated with any government.

The appeal can uphold, modify or reverse the panel's legal findings and conclusions. Normally appeals should not last more than 60 days, with an absolute maximum of 90 days. The report of the Appellate body will be adopted by the DSB within 30 days of its circulation to the members, except if the DSB decides by consensus not to adopt it. Although the DSU establishes time limits for rendering of panel and Appellate Body reports, in practice those limits are commonly exceeded.

Table VI-1 Proposed Periods for the Dispute Settlement Procedure[①]

60 days Consultations, mediation, etc
45 days Panel set up and panelists appointed
6 months Final panel report to parties
3 weeks Final panel report to WTO members
60 days Dispute Settlement Body adopts report (if no appeal)
Total = 1 year (without appeal)

① Source: https://www.wto.org/english/thewto_e/whatis_e/tif_e/disp1_e.htm.

Continuation

60–90 days Appeals report
30 days Dispute Settlement Body adopts appeals report
Total = 1 year and 3 months (with appeal)

One of the key questions in dispute settlement is how to interpret the covered agreements of the WTO. The interpretation of WTO covered agreements is pursuant to Vienna Convention on the Law of Treaties. According to Article 31 of Vienna Convention on the Law of Treaties, a treaty shall be interpreted in good faith in accordance with the ordinary meaning to be given to the terms of the treaty in their context and in the light of its objects and purposes. Treaty terms, the context, and objects and purpose are three components that the Appellate Body mainly take into account.

Regarding the burden of proof, in *US–Wool Shirts and Blouses*, the Appellate Body explained that it is a generally accepted cannon of evidence in civil law, common law and, in fact, most jurisdictions, that the burden of proof rests upon the party, whether complaining or defending, who asserts the affirmative of a particular claim or defense. If that party adduces evidence sufficient to raise a presumption that what is claimed is true, the burden then shifts to the other party, who will fail unless it adduces sufficient evidence to rebut the presumption.

Where a panel or the Appellate Body has concluded that a measure is inconsistent with an agreement, it has the obligation to recommend that the member concerned brings the measure into conformity with the agreement. Once the panel and, if requested, Appellate Body review, have been completed, the DSB (a committee of the entire WTO membership) approves the reports unless there is a consensus not to provide approval, which has not happened in the almost 18 years since the DSU system has been in operation.

If the recommendations or rulings have not been implemented within reasonable period of time, the complaining member may ask for negotiation with the former in order to arrive at an agreement on compensation. If no agreement is reached in 20 days, the complaining member may request the DSB for authorization to suspend some concessions or other obligations. Thus, the report can be enforced with the suspension of trade benefits, although the type and magnitude of such suspensions are subject to arbitration.

As a consequence, in case of a violation of WTO norms, a WTO member cannot react directly by violating other WTO norms but shall have recourse to the DSU mechanism. According to Article 22 of the DSU, if the losing party of a WTO dispute fails to bring its measure into compliance with the covered agreements of the WTO, or does not comply with the recommendations within a reasonable period of time, the winning party can request authorization from the DSB to suspend the application to the member concerned of concession or other obligations under covered agreements. Such authorization of cross-retaliation has greatly enhanced the binding force of WTO's dispute settlement.

The timetable in practice usually prolongs. The following dispute between Venezuela and the US shows how long a dispute could be finally resolved and enforced in reality.

On 23 January 1995, Venezuela complained to the Dispute Settlement Body that the United States was applying rules that discriminated against gasoline imports, and formally requested consultations with the United States. Just over a year later (on 29 January 1996) the dispute panel completed its final report. (By then, Brazil had joined the case, lodging its own complaint in April 1996. The same panel considered both complaints.) The United States appealed. The Appellate Body completed its report, and the Dispute Settlement Body adopted the report on 20 May 1996, one year and four months after the complaint was first lodged.

The United States and Venezuela then took six and a half months to agree on what the United States should do. The agreed period for implementing the solution was 15 months from the date the appeal was concluded (from 20 May 1996 to 20 August 1997).

The case arose because the United States applied stricter rules on the chemical characteristics of imported gasoline than it did for domestically-refined gasoline. Venezuela (and later Brazil) said this was unfair because US gasoline did not have to meet the same standards—it violated the national treatment principle and could not be justified under exceptions to normal WTO rules for health and environmental conservation measures. The dispute panel agreed with Venezuela and Brazil. The appeal report upheld the panel's conclusions (making some changes to the panel's legal interpretation). The United States agreed with Venezuela that it would amend its regulations within 15 months and on 26 August 1997, it reported to the Dispute Settlement Body that a new regulation had been signed on 19 August.

Since China's entry into the WTO, it has gradually become a frequent user of the dispute settlement mechanism. China has been involved in 65 disputes, among which 21 was brought by China. China has also participated in the disputes as a third party in 185 cases. The following case shows how China challenges unfair trade remedies from the US.

Case VI-1

US–Anti-dumping and Countervailing Duties[①]

This dispute concerns countervailing and anti-dumping duties simultaneously imposed by the United States on four products originating in China following concurrent countervailing duty and anti-dumping investigations. The United States began applying its countervailing duty legislation to imports from China in 2007, after the United States Department of Commerce (USDOC) determined that China's economy, albeit still not a market economy, had undergone sufficient economic reform as to enable the USDOC to identify and countervail subsidies granted by the Chinese government. In the four anti-dumping investigations, the USDOC treated China as a non-market economy (NME) and determined normal value using prices in a surrogate country rather than Chinese domestic prices.

China appealed certain Panel findings regarding the USDOC's determinations on public body, specificity, benefit benchmarks, and double remedies.

Appellate Body's Findings

The Appellate Body reversed the Panel's finding that the term "public body" in Article 1.1(a)(1) of the SCM Agreement means any entity controlled by a government. The Appellate Body found, instead, that a public body is an entity that possesses, exercises, or is vested with, governmental authority. The Appellate Body completed the analysis of China's claims and found that the USDOC had acted inconsistently with the obligations of the United States under Articles 1.1(a)(1), 10, and 32.1 of the SCM Agreement in finding, on the basis of government ownership, that certain Chinese state-owned enterprises that supplied steel, rubber, and petrochemical inputs to investigated companies constituted public bodies. The Appellate Body also found that the USDOC had not acted inconsistently with the same obligations in determining, on the basis of evidence relating *inter alia* to the Chinese government's role in the

① Source: WTO Appellate Body Report, United States–Definitive Anti-Dumping and Countervailing Duties on Certain Products from China, WT/DS379/AB/R, adopted on 25 March 2011.

banking sector, that certain state-owned commercial banks that provided loans to investigated companies constituted public bodies.

The Appellate Body upheld the Panel's finding that China did not establish that the USDOC acted inconsistently with the obligations of the United States under Article 2.1(a) of the SCM Agreement by determining in the OTR investigation that SOCB lending was specific to the tyre industry. With regard to the USDOC's regional specificity determination in the LWS investigation, the Appellate Body also upheld the Panel's interpretation of the term "subsidy" in Article 2.2 of the SCM Agreement and rejected China's allegations concerning a statement by the Panel about a "distinct regime" in the context of the LWS investigation, which the Appellate Body considered to be obiter in nature.

The Appellate Body upheld the Panel's interpretation of Article 14(d) of the SCM Agreement as allowing an investigating authority to reject in-country private prices if these were distorted due to the government's predominant role in the market and found that the Panel properly concluded that, given the evidence of the Chinese government's predominant role as a supplier of hot-rolled steel, and having considered evidence of other factors, the USDOC could determine that private prices in China were distorted and could not be used as benchmarks for calculating the amount of the benefit.

The Appellate Body upheld the Panel's interpretation of Article 14(b) of the SCM Agreement and found that the Panel did not err in finding that the USDOC's decision not to rely on interest rates in China as benchmarks for SOCB loans denominated in renminbi (RMB) was not inconsistent with the obligations of the United States under Article 14(b). The Appellate Body reversed the Panel's finding that the proxy benchmark actually used by the USDOC to calculate the benefit from RMB denominated SOCB loans was not inconsistent with the obligations of the United States under Article 14(b), on the ground that, in evaluating this claim, the Panel adopted a standard of review that was too deferential and thus failed to comply with its duty under Article 11 of the DSU to make an objective assessment of the matter. Absent from sufficient factual findings by the Panel or undisputed facts on the Panel record, the Appellate Body was unable to complete the legal analysis of China's claim under Article 14(b) of the SCM Agreement regarding the proxy benchmark used by the USDOC.

Finally, the Appellate Body reversed the Panel's finding that double remedies, that is, the offsetting of the same subsidization twice through the concurrent imposition of anti-dumping duties based on an NME methodology and countervailing duties, were not prohibited under the SCM Agreement. The Appellate Body found that double remedies were inconsistent with the requirement in Article 19.3 of the SCM Agreement that countervailing duties be levied in the appropriate amounts in each case. The Appellate Body completed the legal analysis and found that, by declining to address China's claims concerning double remedies in the four countervailing duty investigations at issue, the USDOC had failed to fulfill its obligation to determine the appropriate amount of countervailing duties within the meaning of Article 19.3 of the SCM Agreement and that, therefore, the United States acted inconsistently with its obligations under Article 19.3 and, consequently, with its obligations under Articles 10 and 32.1 of the SCM Agreement.

Discussions:

1. Could USDOC conclude that certain Chinese state-owned enterprises that supplied steel, rubber, and petrochemical inputs to investigated companies constituted public bodies on the basis of government ownership?

2. Did the USDOC fail to fulfill its obligation by rejecting in-country private prices when finding government's predominant role as a supplier of hot-rolled steel in the market?

3. Are double remedies consistent with the requirement in Article 19.3 of the SCM Agreement?

Chapter Review

1. What are the general methods of dispute settlement provided by UN Charter?
2. What kinds of dispute settlement methods are preferred by the host state? Please explain.
3. How does diplomatic protection work? What is the demerit of such method?
4. State briefly the main contents of United Nations Convention on International Settlement Agreements Resulting from Mediation (2018).
5. What kind of remedies are provided by international investment law to redress investment dispute?

6. State briefly the development of ICSID and its significance.
7. What kind of right is created by ISDS, and why does it break with the traditional international law?
8. What do ad hoc arbitration and institutional arbitration mean?
9. Why treaty-based ISDS is more far-reaching than the contract-based arbitration?
10. What does stabilization clause in a contract-based arbitration mean?
11. How are the three members of a tribunal selected in ISDS?
12. How does an investor avoid the pre-arbitration conditions?
13. Do you think the traditional ISDS over-protect the investors?
14. What are the unique features of International Arbitration Court proposed by EU?
15. Compare the Maffezini case with the Siemens case.
16. How do you describe the significance of WTO dispute settlement?
17. How is WTO dispute settlement mechanism different from the GATT dispute settlement mechanism?
18. What does reverse consensus mean? How does it work?
19. What are the different kinds of dispute settlement methods provided by DSU?
20. What is a panel composed of?
21. On what issues that the Appellate Body can review?
22. What is the time limit for the panel process, and what is the time limit for appellant process?
23. Do members need to consult first before they establish a panel?
24. What is the rule of burden of proof in the dispute settlement of the WTO?
25. What is the rule of treaty interpretation adopted by the Appellate Body?

Key Terms

amicus curiae briefs	法庭之友意见书
Canada-European Union Comprehensive Economic and Trade Agreement (CETA)	《加拿大—欧盟综合经济与贸易协定》
choice-of-law clause	法律适用条款
conciliation	调解
consultation	磋商
contract-based ISDS	基于合同的国际投资仲裁
diplomatic protection	外交保护

fork in the road	岔路口条款，禁止掉头条款
international investment court	国际投资法庭
mediation	居中调停
state-state arbitration	国家间仲裁
Transatlantic Trade and Investment Partnership (TTIP)	《跨大西洋贸易与投资伙伴关系协定》
treaty-based ISDS	基于条约的国际投资仲裁
United Nations Commission on International Trade Law (UNCITRAL)	联合国国际贸易法委员会
United Nations Convention on International Settlement Agreements Resulting from Mediation	《联合国关于调解所产生的国际和解协议公约》

Further Readings

1. Bown, Chad P. & Joost Pauwelyn, *The Law, Economics and Politics of Retaliation in WTO Dispute Settlement*, Cambridge University Press, 2014.

2. Júnior, Alberto do Amaral, Luciana Maria de Oliveira Sá Pires & Cristiane Lucena Carneiro, *The WTO Dispute Settlement Mechanism: A Developing Country Perspective*, Springer, 2019.

3. Lim, C. L., Jean Ho & Martins Paparinskis, *International Investment Law and Arbitration*, 2nd ed., Cambridge University Press, 2021.

4. Reinisch, August, *Will the EU's Proposal Concerning an Investment Court System for CETA and TTIP Lead to Enforceable Awards?—The Limits of Modifying the ICSID Convention and the Nature of Investment Arbitration*, Journal of International Economic Law , Vol. 19: 761, 2016.

5. World Trade Organization, *A Handbook on the WTO Dispute Settlement System*, 2nd ed., Cambridge University Press, 2017.